# International Review of Strategic Management

VOLUME 3      1992

# MEMBERS OF THE EDITORIAL BOARD

# International Review of Strategic Management

## VOLUME 3     1992

*Edited by*

**D. E. Hussey**

*Harbridge Consulting Group Ltd*

JOHN WILEY & SONS

CHICHESTER · NEW YORK · BRISBANE · TORONTO · SINGAPORE

International Review of Strategic Management ISSN 1047–7918

Published annually by John Wiley & Sons

Volume 3 — 1992 £55/$110 (Institutions)

Personal subscription at reduced rate
available for prepayment direct to the publisher.
For details telephone 0243 770 397 or write to
The Journals Subscriptions Department,
John Wiley and Sons Ltd,
Baffins Lane, Chichester, West Sussex PO19 1UD, England.

Future volumes will be invoiced to subscribers prior to
publication, and subscriptions may be cancelled at any time.

**Library of Congress Cataloging-in-Publication Data**

is available 90–641036

**British Library Cataloguing in Publication Data**

International review of strategic management—vol 3 (1992)—
658

ISBN 0-471-93463-1

Typeset in 11/12pt Palatino by APS Ltd, Salisbury, Wilts.
Printed and bound in Great Britain by Biddles Ltd, Guildford and King's Lynn

# CONTENTS

## PART THREE: OTHER TOPICS

# ABOUT THE CONTRIBUTORS

DON COMBS serves as Vice-President for Institutional Advancement of the Medical College of Hampton Roads. He holds faculty appointments in the Department of Psychiatry and Behavioral Sciences of the Eastern Virginia Medical School and in the Department of Community Health Professions at Old Dominion University, Norfolk, Virginia. Prior to joining the medical college, Dr Combs served as an administrator of various health planning and management agencies.

LORETTA CORNELIUS is Assistant Professor of Urban Studies and Public Administration at Old Dominion University, Norfolk, Virginia. Dr Cornelius has served as the deputy director of the United States Office of Personnel Management. She has worked as an organizational consultant for numerous organizations.

DOROTHY G. DOLOGITE is a Professor of Computer Information Systems at City University of New York, Bernard M. Baruch College. Her research efforts focus on the human factors issues of user-developed knowledge-based systems. She has written nine books and many articles related to computer information systems as well as knowledge-based systems development, training and implementation. She has over 15 years of direct computer industry experience, including positions with computer hardware manufacturing and software development firms. Her current work in this area, *Knowledge-Based Systems: An Introduction to Expert Systems*, is being published by Macmillan during 1992.

KATHLEEN DONOGHUE is a graduate research assistant in the Department of Urban Studies and Public Administration at Old Dominion University, Norfolk, Virginia. She has worked previously in executive positions in the fields of human resources and regional government planning.

KASRA FERDOWS is Professor of Technology Management at INSEAD (Fontainbleau) and Professor of Business Administration at Georgetown University (Washington DC). His research focus has been on the manufacturing strategies of large companies in the USA, Europe and Japan. His writings have appeared in numerous journals, and in *Managing International Manufacturing* (North Holland, 1989), of which he is editor. He has been a visiting faculty member at Harvard and Stanford Business Schools. He holds an MS in mechanical engineering, an MBA and a PhD in industrial engineering. He is on the boards of several scientific societies and journals and is the Director of the INSEAD Manufacturing Programme. He has also served as a consultant to a number of large multinational companies.

KAY M. FISCHER studied business economics and political science at the University of Hamburg. In 1988 he was a consultant to the planning team of Pharmavit Ltd. He is now marketing manager of the company.

DAVID HUSSEY has had many years of experience in corporate planning, as a practitioner in industry from 1964 to 1975 and as a consultant since 1976. Prior to moving into corporate planning, he was engaged in industrial development work in a developing country. He is managing director of the European operations of a well-known US consultancy, and is the author of several books on the subject of strategic management, including *Corporate Planning: Theory and Practice* (Pergamon, 1974), which won the John Player management author of the year award. He was one of the founders of the Society for Strategic Planning, and has been associated with the official journal of the society, *Long-Range Planning*, since its foundation. He is a member of the editorial board of *Strategic Directions*, and is a director of the Japanese Society of Strategic Management. He is editor of the *Journal of Strategic Change*, launched during 1992.

JOHN McGEE is at Templeton College, Oxford. He has written widely on strategic management. His publications include *Strategic Management Research* (Wiley, 1986), which he coedited with Howard Thomas.

PATRICK McNAMEE is Professor of International Business at the University of Ulster. He has written widely on strategic management, including *Tools and Techniques for Strategic Management* (Pergamon, 1985). His most recent book is a standard text for the Chartered Institute of Management Accountants. He has taught in the USA and Scandinavia in addition to the UK, where he also undertakes consultancy. He edits the Pergamon series of books on strategic management. He is a member of the editorial board of the *International Review of Strategic Management*.

ROBERT J. MOCKLER is a Professor of Business at St John's University's Graduate School of Business, where he teaches strategic planning and knowledge-based (KBS) development. He founded their Centre for Artificial Intelligence Systems. Over the past 20 years he has written 29 books and many articles in areas related to strategic corporate planning, management decision-making, and computer systems' use for management decision-making. He has worked extensively for corporations, for his own companies, and as an independent consultant. In addition to his current work in strategic management and multinational planning, he is working on KBS development for a variety of management decision areas, Two of his books on the subject were published by Prentice Hall in 1989. Further reviews of his KBS work and of the KBS resulting from them, as well as of his other work in strategic management, are being published by MacMillan Publishing during 1992 and Simon and Schuster Educational Group in 1993.

GEN-ICHI NAKAMURA has 20 years of business experience and 15 years of academic experience. He has been developing an extensive consultancy practice in Asia, Europe and the USA. He is principal researcher/consultant of Gen-Ichi Nakamura Associates, Professor at the Nishi Tokyo University, and co-founder of the Japan Strategic Management Society. He is also the author of a number of books, primarily on strategic management and related subjects. His recent works are *Management of Kao Corporation, NEC: Super 21 Management* and *Handbook of Corporate Philosophy and Long-term Vision*. All three are in Japanese.

WOLFGANG PINDUR holds the positions Professor of Urban Studies and Public Administration, and Director of the Bureau of Research, in the Graduate School of Business and Public Administration at Old Dominion University, Norfolk, Virginia. Dr Pindur is the author of over 125 articles, books and technical reports, and has conducted training and research for many government and private organizations.

IMRE SOMODY has a masters degree in business economics from the East Berlin University and a doctorate from the Budapest University of Economics. He is managing director of Pharmavit Ltd.

RUTH STANAT is the founder and president of Strategic Intelligence Systems International. She is a former strategic planning and marketing executive with several Fortune 100 international firms. Prior to the founding of SIS, she was the senior planning manager for the Information Services Group, a Division of the Mars Corporation. Here she developed a strategic intelligence database within the corporation which integrated internal and external information. She has BA, MA and MBA degrees. She is a frequent international lecturer on the topics of strategic intelligence. Her book *The Intelligent Corporation* was published by Amacom, New York in 1990.

KARL ERIK SVEIBY is publisher of *Ledarskap*, the biggest management magazine in Scandinavia, and the executive chairman of Ekonomi & Teknik Förlag, a major Scandinavian publishing company specializing in business and technical information. He is a BA in business administration and a researcher at the University of Stockholm, and is a world leader in his research field. He has been a manager both in industry and in knowledge-intensive industries for well over a decade. He is currently a consultant to and board member of several 'knowhow' companies. His books about managing knowledge-intensive organizations are translated into most European languages and have been best-sellers in the Scandinavian countries since 1986.

ATSUHIKO TAKEUCHI is a Professor of Economic Geography and Regional Planning and a member of the board of directors at Nippon Institute of Technology, Japan. He holds a PhD in geography. His research activities and consulting work focus on regional industrial systems, locational strategy, and regional diagnostics. He has published many books on these subjects, one important recent book being *Technological Innovation and Industrial Regions* (Taimedo, Tokyo). He has also contributed to several books published in the English language.

HOWARD THOMAS is the James F. Towey Professor of Strategic Management and Policy, and the Director of the Office of Global and Strategic Management at the University of Illinois. He has held permanent and visiting appointments at universities in the UK, Australia, and a number of other North American universities. He has written numerous books and articles, and is on the editorial boards of seven journals. He was awarded the designation of University Senior Scholar in 1986 and Outstanding Educator, Executive MBA Program 1986, 1988 and 1989. He received the Excellence-in-Teaching Award from the Commerce Alumni Association in 1990. He became Acting Dean at the University of Illinois at Urbana-Champaign in 1991.

# INTRODUCTION

This is the third volume of the *International Review of Strategic Management* and continues to follow the objective of the series, which is to produce an annual critical review of developments and best practice in strategic management. Over the years this will accumulate to a significant reference source. Because of the intended reference nature of the series, in future there will be five-year cumulative indexes to the whole series.

It has been the practice to begin each volume with a state of the art review of strategic management. As chapters are contributed by different authors, the treatment of each is very different. In this edition the lead chapter is by Professor Nakamura, a member of the editorial board and a strong supporter of this series. He writes about the development of strategic management in the Asia/Pacific region. His chapter follows that of Professor Igor Ansoff in volume 2 and my own chapter in volume 1.

Each volume in the *Review* has included a number of contributions grouped around a theme, as well as a variety of articles on other topics. This provides the opportunity of dealing with a topic in some depth, while still leaving space to cover other issues. In volume 1 the theme was competitor analysis. Volume 2, which consisted of two books, followed the themes of implementation of strategy, and issues for the 1990s. This volume clusters a number of contributions around the theme of strategic analysis and strategy formulation. Some of these articles continue the narrower competitor analysis theme, and to gain full value from the accumulated wisdom offered by the authors those interested in a particular topic may find more information in the cumulative contents lists and indexes.

My own chapter attempts to provide a glossary of analytical techniques. The main purpose of this has been to describe the technique and lead the reader to a selection of publications where more information can be found. It is thus intended as a research tool, rather than an encyclopaedia. Before I am deluged with letters about my sins of omission and commission, may I say that I regard this glossary as a challenge to readers? Please tell me of any techniques that you think I should have included, ideally with a brief description on the lines of those I have used and giving full details of the published works to which readers should be referred. The collection, with acknowledgements to the contributors, would be published in a future volume.

John McGee and Howard Thomas contribute a chapter on research into strategic groups. Those readers interested in this concept may care to refer back to the research of Patrick McNamee and Marie McHugh which appeared in volume 1.

We are privileged to carry a chapter by Patrick McNamee, another editorial board member. His work is always notable, but in this volume we are able to include his inaugural lecture as Professor of International Business at the University of Ulster.

All strategic analysis depends on information, and for this reason I was pleased to obtain the contribution by Ruth Stanat, who combines understanding of the strategy formulation process with intimate knowledge of information sources and the ways of setting up information systems within organizations. This is not a new theme for the *Review*, as we first dealt with it in the first volume, but as with all the topics in strategic management there is a lot to cover.

A completely different aspect to the use of computers in strategic management is provided by Robert Mockler and Dorothy Dologite, who write on a subject which did not even exist when I first became involved in planning. This is the use of expert systems to support management decision-making. I am particularly pleased to include this chapter as it represents my fourth attempt to find someone to write on the subject.

The last two chapters in this part are more specific and deal with strategy formulation. That by Professor Kasra Ferdows offers a model, based on his original research, for thinking about international manufacturing strategy. In Karl Sveiby's chapter attention is focused on businesses that have no factories. To my knowledge very little has been written about strategy formulation in the knowhow industries, and Karl's chapter, drawn heavily from his extensive experience, makes a welcome addition to the literature.

In Part three of this volume there are four important chapters. Professor Pindur and his colleagues have provided an excellent article on the strategic issues of the population trends. This continues the theme of issues for the 1990s, which began in volume 2, and the chapter makes an interesting complement to that provided by Amin Rajan in volume 2 on European population trends. Ralph Lewis provides a chapter on stategic management and organizational development, which is very welcome as much of strategic management is about the management of change. Finally, we have two case studies. Professor Takeuchi provides a view of the strategic development of the Japanese steel industry. With the chapter by Kay Fischer and Imre Somody we share the experience of setting up a joint venture in Hungary, a very topical issue for the 1990s.

In the introduction to the first volume I set out some simple models that I was following when thinking about contributions to this series. As not all readers will have seen the first volume, the description is repeated here.

The scope of strategic management is wide, and over time all facets will be considered. We can look at strategic management from several viewpoints.

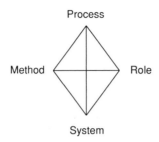

**Figure 1**    Concepts of strategic management

Figure 1 shows one way in which we might begin to conceptualize the subject.
The main value of the diagram is to emphasize the interdependence of the four
headings. 'Process' covers topics such as the way strategy is formulated, the
climate of the organization, and the integration of the different elements of
planning. Closely allied to Process is 'System', which covers topics such as how
planning is organized, how information flows are designed to assist planning, and
how the control system is established. 'Role' covers the part played by various
people within the process, such as the corporate planner, line managers,
functional managers, and, of course, the chief executive himself and the board to
which he reports. Role is closely allied to Process, since what managers do in the
context of planning is to a large degree affected by the culture of the
organization. 'Method' covers all the techniques that may be used in the process
of strategy formulation, and the principles of strategic decision-making on which
they are based.

The diagram is bounded by an interface with the world at large, and aspects of
this business environment may become important enough to cover in this series.

This model covers many of the topics that will be included in this review series
as it evolves, but the model is not quite complete. Figure 2 adds three further
areas of complexity.

A first addition is national differences. We may from time to time wish to
explore how planning is practised in particular countries, and how differences of
politics and culture may affect the way strategic management is applied.

Organizational differences provide us with a second fertile field for exploration. In this context the word organization is used to mean entity, and we would
expect to find that a global, large business had to approach strategic management
in a different way to a medium-sized, local firm. Firms which operate in only one
industry face a less complex planning situation than those which are in many
industries. A further difference is between businesses, government organizations
and non-profit-making activities, such as a charity or church.

Our final area of difference is functional. The role that different functions play
in the process of planning has been identified in the first model. Here we are
concerned with the detail of planning, which will be different for, say, a human

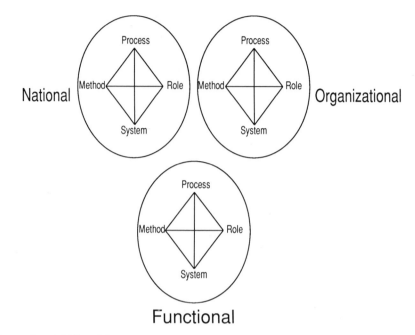

Functional

**Figure 2**   Additional issues

resource department than it would be for a manufacturing unit. Functional level planning is only a part of the strategic management process, but the requirements of functional plans are seen as within the scope of this review series.

State of the art reviews bridge all the classifications.

This scheme is used in the cumulative contents list.

Once again, my thanks are due to the editorial board, who have provided many ideas for themes and introductions to authors. It is the board which helps the series to be international, and I am fortunate in having a very active group of collaborators.

Part One

# STATE OF THE ART REVIEW

# 1

# DEVELOPMENT OF STRATEGIC MANAGEMENT IN THE ASIA/PACIFIC REGION

**G.-I. Nakamura**

*Principal, Gen-Ichi Nakamura Associates*

## BASIC POINTS AND FEATURES OF THE REGION

### Two Basic Points

The major purpose of this chapter is first to overview the evolution and the present state of strategic management in the Asia/Pacific region and secondly to consider the future development of the discipline as we approach the twenty-first century.

Before beginning discussion, the author would like to draw the attention of the reader in western society to the following two basic points, with additional reference to several features peculiar to this part of the world.

Regarding the first point, when talking about the "Asia/Pacific region" in this chapter, the author will be considering Japan, four ANIEs (Hong Kong, Korea, Singapore, and Taiwan) and four ASEAN countries (Indonesia, Malaysia, the Philippines, and Thailand) (Brunei and Singapore are excluded from the discussion).

As to the second point, in order to indicate more precisely the specific level of technological development, Figure 1.1 shows the present position of these nine countries/economies. Having reached a high level of development, Japan has a high amount of high-tech with some dependence on medium-tech. The four

International Review of Strategic Management.
Edited by D. E. Hussey. © 1992 John Wiley & Sons Ltd

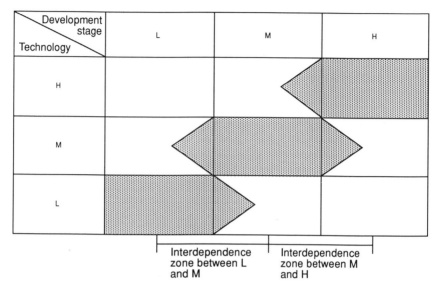

**Figure 1.1**  Matrix of development stages of countries/companies and technologies

ASEAN countries, at a low level of development, are forced to limit themselves mostly to low-tech with some access to medium-tech. The four ANIEs, frequently referred to as the four dragons/tigers by westerners, are situated between the above two extremes, with a wider coverage of medium-tech and some access to both high and low technologies. As well as an imbalance between Japan, the ANIEs and the ASEAN countries, the reader will see a growing interdependence, as shown by the interdependence zones between L and M and M and H. Although unplanned, the resultant imbalance of and interdependence between the different levels of technology in this region has been working so effectively so far that some specialists argue that these nine countries/economies, together with mainland China, will play a leading role in the economic development of the world towards the twenty-first century.

The above two points suggest that, since the development level of strategic management in any country is relatively proportional to its own level of economic/technological development, it will be more relevant for the purpose of the chapter to concentrate the discussion on Japan in the next two sections and then to extend this to the other eight countries/economies in the final section.

## Features of the Region

In addition to these two basic points, the reader is invited to consider the following features peculiar to this part of the world:

- Highly "contextual" society
- Division society
- Fit and misfit of TQC
- High population density
- Chinese dominance/leadership

A brief explanation may be in order..

First, the Asia/Pacfic region, by and large, may be characterized as a highly "contextual" society, with a relatively low level of logical thinking among the population in general as well as a greater dependence on family and/or human relationships among society at large. This has resulted in significantly different approaches to business, including strategic management, from those developed in western business society. To be specific, it will become more essential for companies in this region to change their existing organizational mentality in order to develop a logical way of strategic thinking and become effectively integrated within their organizations.

Secondly, with the exception of Japan, this region has in common the division of society into a small number of the elite (governing class) at one extreme and a large number of people (governed class) at the other, leaving less or no room for the development of a middle class in between. Typically, the elite of these countries/economies enjoy a higher level of education at prestigious American and European business schools and get MBA degrees. It is not surprising, therefore, to see within a number of organizations/companies a division between a handful of highly educated top managers skilled at logical ways of strategic thinking and a majority of people more accustomed to do exactly what they are told to by the former. This makes it relatively difficult to apply a principle such as "Doers should be planners" in these countries/economies.

Thirdly, it may be worthwhile to spend some time discussing the relationship between the above two features and TQC (total quality control). With the original concept developed by Dr Demming and incorporated into Japanese practice, TQC has been successfully implemented in both a number of Japanese companies and some non-Japanese counterparts in the region. Successful experience in those countries/economies in the last two decades shows that TQC is concerned with "continuous and corporate-wide willingness and skilfulness in search of a better quality for tomorrow".

From a strategic viewpoint, however, TQC is characterized by an extrapolative and logically incremental approach through continuous, planned interactions between corporate associates, having a better fit with operational activities. It should be pointed out that these characteristics have contributed significantly to the planned resultant change in organizational mentality by encouraging a "clear and explicit" process of discussion in operational activities. It should also be pointed out, however, that the across-the-board approach of TQC plays a negative role in the development of creative modes of thinking in strategic activities, as has been frequently experienced by the author in his consultation/ education practice in this particular region.

Regarding its application to business practice in the other eight Asian countries/economies, TQC has faced reluctance or relatively stronger resistance from an organizational mentality less accustomed to this interactive or bottom-up approach. As an example, some Philippine companies have been using the term "corporate-wide productivity development" (acronymed as CWPD) in order to avoid the rejection expected when the word "TQC" is used.

Fourthly, Japan and the four ANIEs share the common denominator of a high level of population density. It is not surprising, therefore, to see a high level of survival consciousness or "hungry spirit" in these countries/economies leading to aggressive export activities by Japanese, Korean and Taiwanese companies in particular.

Fifthly and lastly, seven South East Asian countries/economies of the above nine excluding Japan and Korea have the common factor of Chinese dominance or leadership as far as economic/business activities are concerned. It is of interest that typical Chinese companies are characterized above all by family management as well as by trading capital, in keen contrast to their typical Japanese counterparts, which incline more to the separation of capital and management as well as to manufacturing capital. The author's personal impression is that these characteristics have made a negative contribution to the development of strategic management as well as of the economy/technology in these seven countries/ economies.

# EVOLUTION OF STRATEGIC MANAGEMENT FROM THE EARLY SIXTIES TO THE MID-EIGHTIES IN JAPAN

## Extrapolative Long-Range Planning in the Sixties

The origin of strategic management in Japan dates back to the early sixties, when an increased number of big companies began to adopt the concept and the technique of extrapolative long-range planning imported from the United States. Although they had practised annual profit planning or annual budgeting since the mid-fifties, they gradually began to realize that annual profit planning would not be sufficient for them to deal with a newly arriving era of high growth economy. To be specific, they were increasingly challenged by a series of major long-term decisions both on huge amounts of investment in production facilities to be financed by sizeable bank loans and on the regular recruitment of a large number of new university graduates.

Despite the fact that long-range planning faced some major difficulties including a lack of commitment at top management level, it continued, at least to all appearances to penetrate into big Japanese companies so that its adoption rate had reached about 80 % at the end of the sixties. Looking back, it had a relatively good fit with a continuous change of environment and an extrapolative growth of the economy up until the late sixties.

Regarding the typical attitude to long-range planning during the decade of the sixties, corporate staff took the leadership in gathering necessary information from operating managers in order to develop long-range plans at divisional/ departmental level and aggregating them into coherent long-range plans at corporate level, frequently in the form of a five-year projection profit and loss statement with a balance sheet at the end of the target year attached. The underlying philosophy shared implicitly during that period was that "an aggregate of division/department optimum leads to corporate optimum".

It was no wonder, therefore, that top management participation was passive, with little or no involvement of operating managers in the planning process. This resulted in several corporate planning syndromes which western predecessors had encountered in the past—"one-man staff show" syndrome, "delegation/ abdication" syndrome, "separation" syndrome, "paralysis by analysis" syndrome and "death-in-the-drawer" syndrome, to name just a few. In this sense, Japanese students were loyal to their western teachers.

The above situation is summarized in the second column of Figure 1.2.

## Non-Planning Period During the Early Seventies

With the opening of the seventies, the whole Japanese corporate environment picture began to show a dramatic change. A new economy policy developed by the Nixon Administration in August 1971 triggered a shift of the dollar–yen exchange relationship from the fixed to the fluctuating system. The oil embargo in 1973 shook the base of the Japanese economy and industry, with its high dependence on imported oil, by quadrupling the price. A high growth economy was enforced to decelerate the pace. About a dozen major industries suddenly found themselves at a plateau/maturity stage or even at one of decline. As Peter F. Drucker rightly put it in 1968, "the age of discontinuity" had arrived in Japan. A large number of big Japanese companies who had indulged in extrapolative long-range planning were forced to abandon their long-cherished practices of the good old days. As a result, the adoption rate of long-range planning nose-dived to a level of about 20 %. The typical sentiment of these companies was that "it is meaningless or even dangerous to develop long-range planning in this uncertain climate". Thus, there was a break of several years in the practice of strategic management during the early seventies which is referred to as the "non-planning period" by the author.

| | | 1960s | Mid-70s – Mid-80s | Late 80s – 1990s |
|---|---|---|---|---|
| 1 | Approach | Extrapolative Extended | Extrapolative + entrepreneurial | Entrepreneurial +philosophy/vision driven +geared for creation of values |
| 2 | Optimum orientation | Division/ department optimum | Division/department optimum + corporate optimum | Corporate/group optimum |
| 3 | Major growth strategies developed | Market penetration strategy along business dimension | Several growth strategies only along business dimension | Growth strategies along logistics/ technology/ business dimensions |
| 4 | Supporting strategies | | Spin-out strategy L&M strategy Evacuation strategy | Spin-out strategy Alliance/M&A strategy Divestment strategy |
| 5 | Planning emphasis | Quantitative Emphasis on profit projected into the future | Quantitative + qualitative Emphasis on environmental forecasting | Qualitative Emphasis on objective setting/corporate posture Participative + interactive |
| 6 | Planning view | Planning as profit projected into the future | Planning as essential for copying with environmental change | Planning as essential for developing organizational capability which will guarantee corporate survival in the future environment |
| 7 | Initiative | Middle-up Bottom-up | Top-down | Interactive Top-down + middle-up Middle-down + bottom-up |
| 8 | Roles of top/ operating managers and corporate staff | Leadership by staff Participation by top managers Non-participation by operating managers | Involvement by top managers Support by corporate staff Participation by operating managers | Commitment by top managers Leadership by operating managers Active support by corporate staff |

**Figure 1.2** Evolution of corporate strategy/planning in Japan. Nakamura (1984)

## Strategic Planning from the Mid-Seventies to the Mid-Eighties

A handful of distinguished Japanese companies, however, gradually began to learn a precious lesson from their own non-dependence on planning during the above non-planning period. It was represented by a new sentiment, "Not in spite of, but because of the unpredictable future, we must pierce through the fog by developing a plan with a long time-horizon". However, this did not mean a simple return to the traditional approach of extrapolative long-range planning which had worked in the age of continuity. With some recourse to the portfolio management approach imported from the United States in the mid-seventies, a slowly increasing number of distinguished Japanese companies began to change their planning mode by 180 degrees to strategic or entrepreneurial planning.

In the peculiar situation of the late seventies, as an aftermath of what the Japanese called "dollar shock" (1971) and "oil shock" (1973), portfolio management was frequently used in association with L&M (learning and meaning) strategy in order to get rid of the burden imposed by overinvestment in the good old days of the sixties. Thus, evacuation strategy, which had been unpopular or abnormal in Japanese companies, became the normal practice after the mid-seventies.

An interest in portfolio management was followed by a search for other US-imported approaches such as contingency planning, PPBS, and ZBB (zero base budgeting). It is interesting to note that the portfolio management approach has since been relatively well accepted by several major Japanese companies as simply a part of strategic management in the ensuing decade, while an interest in other approaches has, by and large, disappeared like a grass-fire.

Since strategic planning for future survival is, by definition, concerned with the design of a corporate picture in the future environment, top managers in big Japanese companies were forced to change their basic attitude from a relatively low level of commitment to a higher one. As their Western predecessors had previously experienced, an embryonic stage of strategic planning in Japan in the late seventies was characterized by a preoccupation with the formulation of a strategic plan at corporate level with less or no attention paid to its implementation.

One remarkable feature in the corporate environment in the late seventies was the opening of the second chapter of US–Japan trade friction in some major industries including home appliances, steel and bearings.

It may be worthwhile noting here that the first chapter of US–Japan trade friction started in the textile industry in the late sixties and resolved itself in the late seventies, partly through the so-called "voluntary" restraint of exports from Japan to the US followed by the investment of some Japanese textile manufacturers in production sites there.

As increased Japanese exports began to replace American products resulting in an increased level of US unemployment after the mid-seventies, Japanese exporters were accused of "exporting unemployment". Thus, a recurrence of US–Japan trade friction led an increased number of major Japanese manufacturers to invest in the United States. This response, however, did not help resolve the friction between the two economic giants. As early as the late seventies, a couple of years after the so-called "voluntary" export regulation of Japanese color TV sets to the US became effective on July 1, 1977, the resultant overinvestment of Japanese color TV manufacturers began to give birth to further concern about "Japanese industry dominance".

The period from the seventies to the eighties began to see more discontinuous change in the corporate environment in terms of a higher appreciation of the Japanese yen against the US dollar, the development of high-tech at an accelerated speed, and industrial restructuring in some major industries. Japanese executives began to realize the meaning of the term "turbulent environment" coined by Igor Ansoff in 1974. In order to direct their strategy more specifically, they made increasing use of the three essential dimensions—logistics, technology and business—of growth strategy. As a result, they became more committed to many segments/boxes of the corporate strategy cube as represented by Figure 8.4, page 182, volume 1, 1990 of the *International Review of Strategic Management*. The enlarged scope of their commitment to the corporate strategy cube in turn impelled them to rely more on several types of supporting strategies such as alliance, M&A, spin-out and divestment in terms of resource reallocation.

In keen contrast to these developments in the strategy arena, experience with the newly introduced strategic management in preceding years began to reveal a substantial lack or even non-existence of implementation, leading to a "pie-in-the-sky" syndrome. As a result, there was a growing recognition of the need for positive interaction on three dimensions of strategic management, S1 (strategy), S2 (planning system) and S3 (organization structure), by way of greater involvement of corporate associates. In summary, the mid-eighties began to see a gradual rise of strategic management in the real sense of the word as summarized in the third column of Figure 1.2.

# EVOLUTION OF STRATEGIC MANAGEMENT FROM THE MID-EIGHTIES TOWARDS THE TWENTY-FIRST CENTURY IN JAPAN

## Arrival of a Relatively Affluent Society

The so-called "post G5 environment" after the Plaza Agreement of G5 on the higher valuation of the Japanese yen against the US dollar reached on September

22, 1985 has been characterized by a series of contingent events such as an unexpected boom in major industries lasting for only a couple of years, record high stock prices nose-diving within several months as an aftermath of the destructed "bubble economy", the dramatic rise and fall of interest rates and the Gulf War. The highly discontinuous and turbulent changes of the "post G5 environment" have had an unprecedented impact on strategic management in Japanese companies, particularly in the following two respects.

Firstly, the new basic trend of higher appreciation of the Japanese yen brought about two types of concerns, direct and indirect.

Direct concern about the decreasing competitiveness of local production and procurement in the late eighties triggered a wave of overseas investment in North America as well as in ANIEs/ASEAN countries/economies which was followed by another wave of investment in EC countries vis-à-vis EC 1992.

Indirect concern referred to the "hollowing out" of existing local factories expected to arise from the above-mentioned shift of production and procurement sites from Japan to foreign countries/economies. Since the basic attitude of typical Japanese companies is not to adopt "fire-and-hire" policies, like their western counterparts, in the face of factory closures and business evacuation, a majority of them tried to rely primarily on diversification/new business development strategies in order to create a sizeable number of "internal jobs" for workers who might be asked to leave their existing factories and businesses as targets for hollowing-out. This resulted in a rush of entries into new businesses to which they had no previous exposure.

As ordinary Japanese companies, by and large, were forced to develop these two types of underprepared strategies on a rush basis, following a trend, their low level of responsiveness—integrated flexibility of system (S2) and openness of structure (S3)—allied with a high level of aggressiveness (S1) has begun to reveal many failures, leading to the rise of a "retreat to present local business" syndrome and to an increased need for "re"development of the corporate strategy cube within the context of a corporate standpoint towards the twenty-first century discussed below.

Secondly, the "post G5 environment" encouraged the shift of Japanese society to a "relatively" affluent society as defined by J. K. Galbraith. The reason for emphasizing the word "relatively" comes from the author's recognition of the difference in affluence between advanced western countries and Japan in terms of the substantial delay in Japanese membership of the affluence club, the Japanese lack of affluence on a cumulative basis including an underdeveloped social infrastructure and Japanese corporate wealth at the expense of the individual's quality of life.

## Rise of Philosphy/Vision-Driven Management

The increasingly common recognition of the above points, therefore, has recently provoked a series of discussions not only at political/social levels, but also at industry/company ones on the pressing necessity to shift to an affluent society oriented towards individual dignity and individual quality of life. These include discussion at company level on the urgent need to develop a corporate standpoint towards the twenty-first century based on a clearly and explicitly defined corporate philosophy so that Japanese companies can position themselves effectively regarding respect for individual dignity and quality of life within the context of an emerging affluent society moving towards the twenty-first century.

This trend has been summarized in the fourth column of Figure 1.2 together with other new emphases on strategy/planning management during this period.

On the strategic management front, an increasing number of major Japanese companies, irrespective of industry, have been led to develop or "re"develop a corporate philosophy based on the founder's/neo-founder's world view as well as on individual top managers' ones within a clearly and explicitly defined framework as shown in Figure 1.3.

Seiko Epson Corporation (hereafter Epson), a distinguished electronics manufacturer under the umbrella of Seiko Group, is a pioneer in the development of an explicitly defined corporate philosophy, with President Tsuneya Nakamura's individual philosphy as a base. Epson published first and revised versions of a compact eight-page brochure titled *Management Philosophy* in both English and Japanese in 1989 and 1991, respectively. Figure 1.4 is taken from the first page of the brochure of the English version. The reader may be interested to know that their management philosophy, which appears on the first page of both versions, has been translated into six other languages, including German, French, Spanish, Italian and Chinese, at the end of both versions.

Corporate philosophy at top management level as discussed above is projected into the space-time of the long-term future to construct a long-term vision. Since the twenty-first century is drawing closer, the tendency is to construct a corporate standpoint towards the twenty-first century projected from a corporate philosophy as logically and specifically shown in Figure 1.5. This emphasizes the importance of logical correspondence between corporate philosophy and long-term vision both at corporate (S1 + S2 + S3) level and at three Ss (S1, S2 and S3) level in a coherent framework of strategic management system.

For the reader's information, corporate management view at top management level (S1 + S2 + S3) in Figure 1.3 and corporate attitude towards the twenty-first century (S1 + S2 + S3) in Figure 1.5 are primarily made up of two essential elements, philosophy/vision-driven management and entrepreneurial management by creation (MBC). Figure 1.6 describes the creation of specific values through MBC broken down from corporate standpoint (S1 + S2 + S3) into three different types of sub standpoints (S1, S2, and S3).

In order to guarantee effective utilization of corporate philosophy with its projection of corporate vision into the twenty-first century, it is essential for

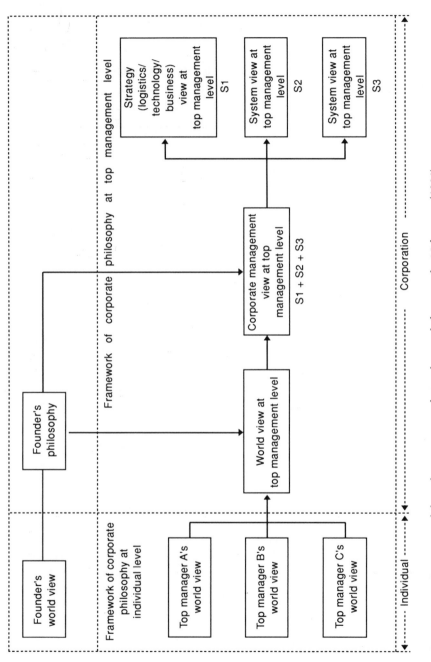

**Figure 1.3** Corporate philosophy—its interrelationship and framework. Nakamura (1990)

## MANAGEMENT PHILOSOPHY

We shall strive to be a "good company" trusted in every part of the world, by placing the CUSTOMER FIRST, respecting the INDIVIDUAL and displaying COLLECTIVE STRENGTH.

A "good company" is one that:
1. Secures fair and reasonable profit.
2. Has employees who are constantly creative and meet challenges with confidence and pride.
3. Can meet the future expectations of both its employees and society.

A company that pursues these goals will enjoy continual growth and development.

**Figure 1.4**   Seiko Epson's management philosophy. Reproduced by permission of Seiko Epson Corporation

Japanese companies to integrate corporate philosophy families with existing planning ones as shown in Figure 1.7.

By way of a tentative conclusion, the author's argument, although not yet matured, is that Japanese companies will face a series of real challenges to strategic management in the last decade of this century in terms of their shift from pragmatism-driven to philosphy-driven management. A shift which must be well understood, accepted, supported and trusted by their stake-holders in a global society.

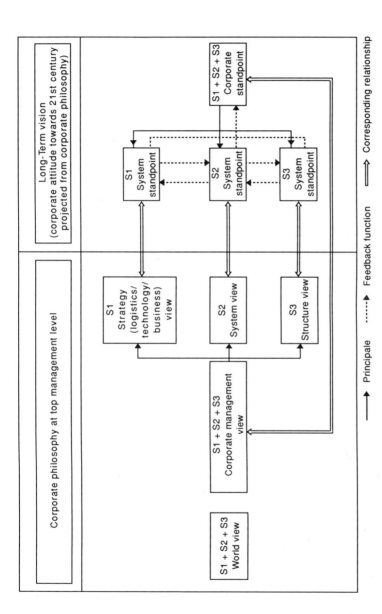

**Figure 1.5** Corresponding relationship of framework between corporate philosophy and long-term vision (corporate standpoint regarding the twenty-first century projected from corporate philosophy). Nakamura (1990)

| Standpoint of strategic management | New values created through MBC |
|---|---|
| S1 + S2 + S3 Corporate standpoint | Creation of different relevant values offered to different stakeholders |
| Partial standpoint: S1 —— strategy posture | Creation of economic values offered to customers |
| Partial standpoint: S2 —— system posture | Creation of added values offered to interest groups (inclusive of the organization itself) |
| Partial standpoint: S3 —— structure posture | Creation of mental/spiritual values offered to individual associates Creation of organizational values offered to the organization itself Creation of societal values offered to stakeholders (inclusive of the public at large) |

**Figure 1.6**    Creation of values through management by creation (MBC). Nakamura (1991)

## FUTURE PROSPECTIVES FOR STRATEGIC MANAGEMENT IN ASIA/PACIFIC REGION

This last section will relate the above discussion, which focused on the evolution of strategic management in Japan, to discussion on future prospects for the discipline in other countries/economies in Asia/Pacific Region.

Researches by specialists in Asian economy/technology development at macro level recognize a ten to fifteen year gap between Japan and ANIEs as well as between ANIEs and ASEAN countries. The author's professional observations on, and experiences with, the practice of strategic management in this particular region in the last fifteen years share similar or relatively longer length gaps with the above recognition at macro level.

Thus, according to the author's personal assessment based on Figure 1.2, the present stages of strategic management evolution in ANIEs and ASEAN countries are, by and large, relatively close to the mid-seventies–mid-eighties stage for the former and the 1960s stage for the latter, with some variations derived from different features of the different countries/economies discussed in the first section. Following the same line of discussion, the author may safely predict that, by the end of this century, strategic management in these two economies, will, by and large, shift to the transitionary phase from the mid-seventies to mid-eighties stage to the late eighties to nineties stage for ANIEs and to the transitionary phase from the 1960s stage to the mid-seventies to mid-eighties stage of Figure 1.2, with some of the above-described variations.

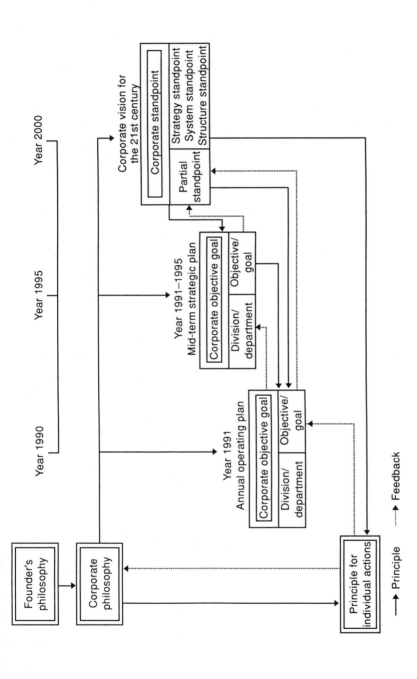

**Figure 1.7** Interrelationship between corporate philosophy/planning families. Nakamura (1990)

Focusing on some issues for major non-Japanese companies in the Asia/Pacific region, the challenge for major Korean companies will be the development of a specific strategic management approach tailored to their own needs and conditions, while the challenge for major companies in Chinese-dominant countries/economies will be the development of non-family management so that they can include more capable associates on the one hand and attract more non-family capital on the other.

Effective development and practice of strategic management within a relevant context, particularly in terms of making the above-described shift and overcoming the above-discussed issues in the final decade of this century, will be the key for these eight countries/economies in the ASIA/Pacific region, together with Japan and mainland China, to becoming a real driving force in the economic development of the world towards the twenty-first century.

Part Two

# STRATEGY ANALYSIS AND FORMULATION

# 2

# COMPETITIVENESS AND INDUSTRIAL DEVELOPMENT IN AN INTERNATIONAL ERA

**Patrick McNamee**

*Professor of International Business, The University of Ulster*

## INTRODUCTION

The strategy document issued by the Industrial Development Board for Northern Ireland (IDB) shows clearly the emphasis that government now places upon fostering companies which can be described as "competitive". Indeed, the chief executive of IDB in his foreword to the Forward Strategy document has written:

> IDB believes that competitiveness analysis should form part of every company's planning discipline and will be advocating its adoption by industry in Northern Ireland.
>
> *Industrial Development Board of Northern Ireland* (1991)

However, the task of translating such an excellent *aspiration* into *an operating reality* is one that has, for most countries, proved at best rather difficult and at worst impossible. This chapter is concerned with examining some contributions to the debate on competitiveness and then reflecting upon directions in which regions might travel in pursuit of enhancing their competitiveness.

International Review of Strategic Management.
Edited by D. E. Hussey. © 1992 John Wiley & Sons Ltd

# COMPETITIVE COMPANIES

As a first step, consider the following alphabetically ordered list of winning companies from the island of Ireland:

| Company | Industrial sector |
| --- | --- |
| BKS | Aerial mapping |
| Cement Roadstone Holdings | Building materials |
| Desmond and Sons | Clothing |
| Fyffes Plc | Fruit importing and distribution |
| Glen Electric | Electrical appliances |
| Guinness Peat Aviation | Aircraft leasing |
| Jefferson Smurfitt | Paper and board packaging |
| Waterford Co Operative Plc | Agribusiness |
| Leckpatrick | Dairy products |
| Masstock | Agricultural systems |
| Norbrook Laboratories | Animal health |
| Mivan | Construction |
| O'Kane Chickens | Chickens |
| Powerscreen International | Quarrying equipment |

These are winning companies in the sense that each of them now has an *enduring* record of:

• Profitability
• Growth
• Net economic contribution

There is, however, another dimension to their success which seems to endow them with an enhanced cachet of competitiveness. These companies are competitive not so much in relation to other companies in their *region* but, more crucially, they are competitive in relation to their *international rivals*. In other words, when their performance is being analysed their achievements are not captured adequately by their financial results, or say their sales growth, excellent though they are, but rather by their performance in foreign markets relative to foreign rivals, i.e. they have developed robust strategic positions in the global business arena. Thus, the competitive locus of these companies is measured using global rather than regional coordinates, a sure sign of competitiveness. These are the true axes for the measurement of competitiveness.

There is another aspect to this list of winners that appears worthy of study. Industrial development or the regional promotion of competitiveness is also concerned with the issue of selecting winners. Not just selecting, but selecting, promoting and investing in those companies which are likely to be tomorrow's winners. This is not easy. For example, around 20 years ago many of the companies which were making the regional headlines in terms of success are included in the following list. The list shows that much has changed in this period:

| Company | Sector |
| --- | --- |
| Albion | Clothing |
| Belfast Ropework | Ropes |
| Bernard Hughes | Bread |
| British Enkalon | Textiles |
| P. J. Carroll | Tobacco |
| Cement Roadstone Holdings | Building materials |
| Fitzwilton | Industrial group |
| Irish Distillers | Distilling |
| Jefferson Smurfitt | Print and packaging |
| Sunbeam Wolsey | Clothing |
| Waterford Glass | Glass |
| Youghal Carpets | Carpets |

There is some, but not a lot of, correspondence between the two lists.

The purpose of this chapter is to make some suggestions about how to select companies today which will have sustainable competitive advantage tomorrow. This will be done by progressing from the above historic orientation to a consideration of some alternative theoretical scaffolds which might be considered as serious contenders as suitable structures for boosting regional international competitiveness.

# RECEIVED VIEWS ON INTERNATIONAL COMPETITIVENESS

First, some of the most prevalent received views on the topic of international competitiveness and industrial development will be considered.

The most widely followed theories in this area tend to be built around a few core principles which, because of their great age and illustrious pedigrees, seem to be widely accepted. The main core principles are:

- The principle of comparative advantage and the gains from trade
- The principle of superior competitiveness through lower unit costs and hence prices

- The principle that the best industrial sectors are those that are growing most rapidly
- The principle that industrial development should be sectoral

Each of these "core principles" is now considered in more detail before an alternative set of theoretical perspectives is presented.

## First: The Principle of Comparative Advantage and the Gains from Trade

This theory was formulated in 1817 by David Ricardo in response to Adam Smith's book *The Wealth of Nations* which was published in 1776, so the source of the theory is around 225 years old. In spite of its age, however, it still commands widespread support and indeed it is difficult to think of any course in international economics which does not devote considerable time to it.

In a nutshell, the theory asserts that most countries have some natural advantage or advantages in one or more of the factors of production. Consequently a country should specialize in producing those products in which it enjoys factor of production advantages, and then trade them with foreign countries in exchange for products in which *they* have natural advantages. In other words, a country will have the highest level of economic welfare if it specializes in those products and services in which it is most productive and then trades with foreign countries for its other requirements. If this model is followed then, it is claimed, all parties, both the domestic economy and the foreign economies, will benefit.

This would seem to suggest that Ireland, for example, with its principal natural advantage in grass-based products such as dairy and beef products, ought to specialize in these and then trade them for other goods in which we have no natural advantage—for example electrical equipment.

Adherence to this theory seems to lead to two major policy directives:

*First:* Industrial development or competitiveness should be promoted on a sectoral basis
*Second:* Priority should be given to those sectors in which the region or country enjoys a natural advantage

The great attribute of this theory is that it is logical. It is simple and it seems to make sense. Indeed, it is only commonsense. However, its great shortcomings are that:

- It diverges from reality
- It is not a complete theory of why international trade takes place and, finally,
- If followed strictly it condemns countries with poor factor endowments

always to be poor and asserts that countries with rich factor endowments will always be rich

Each of these criticisms is now considered.

If the list of winning companies of today is reconsidered, it appears that although we have *representation* of sectors in which Ireland would appear to have natural advantages, the majority of the companies are from sectors which, far from enjoying competitive advantage, appear to suffer from natural disadvantage. And indeed, on reflection, many of these winning companies are in sectors that have never been mentioned as ones likely to yield globally competitive companies.

| Industrial sector |
| --- |
| Aerial mapping |
| Building materials |
| Clothing |
| Fruit importing and distribution |
| Electrical appliances |
| Aircraft leasing |
| Paper and board packaging |
| Agribusiness |
| Dairy products |
| Agricultural systems |
| Animal health |
| Construction |
| Chickens |
| Quarrying equipment |

If the net is spread somewhat wider and the question is asked "How well is the comparative advantage view supported by empirical verification from other countries?", then the evidence becomes overwhelming.

Thus, Korea, which had virtually no capital after the Korean War, achieved substantial exports in such capital-intensive industries as steel, shipbuilding and automobiles, while America, which was well endowed with capital, scientists and skilled labour, has seen its export market share of industries such as machine tools, semiconductors and electronic products continuously eroded. Indeed, Wassily Leontief showed in 1954 that the capital-rich United States specialized in exporting goods which were labour-intensive. This was called by economists the Leontief paradox. Leontief paradoxes abound:

Why is Italy a world leader in shoe manufacture?
Why is Sweden a world leader in trucks?

Why is Germany a world leader in printing presses?
Why is Britain a world leader in aircraft?

It would appear that this type of evidence should at least cause us to question the *universal validity* of the theory of comparative advantage.

## Second: The Principle of Superior Competitiveness Through Lower Unit Costs and Hence Prices

The attraction of this principle appears to be that it is very simple, easy to measure, and consequently when problems are refracted through this particular optic remedies are simple, straightforward and clear. It is so straightforward—everyone can understand the frank lesson: lower costs lead to lower prices and hence greater competitiveness. It is easy to measure—official government statistics provide national output figures by industry classification and from these figures national unit costs can be computed easily. These figures have always, since most managers can remember, pointed the one way: reduce unit costs, which is often taken to mean wages.

There does appear to be, however, at least the evidence of casual observation, which refutes the view that lower wages, and lower prices are prerequisites to competitiveness. The first piece of evidence is the price and cost structures of leading internationally competitive countries and the second is some empirical research into the nature of competitiveness recently carried out in the University of Ulster.

### The price and cost structures of leading European countries

The table shows the average hourly wage rates in the textile and electrical machinery industries in five European countries, Denmark, Germany, Norway, Sweden and the UK. The UK has been set at 100.

| Average hourly wages (UK = 100) | | |
|---|---|---|
|         | Textiles | Electrical machinery |
| Denmark | 224 | 205 |
| Germany | 176 | 154 |
| Norway  | 163 | 167 |
| Sweden  | 166 | 149 |
| UK      | 100 | 100 |

*Source:* OECD.

The average hourly wage rate in the UK can be seen to be considerably lower than any of the other countries shown. (The issue of productivity will be considered later.) Suffice it to say that low wages do not necessarily equal high productivity.

Similar conclusions can be drawn when prices are considered. The table shows that for fridges and gas cookers the UK is by no means a high-price region.

| Price of consumer goods (UK = 100) | | |
|---|---|---|
| | Fridges | Cookers |
| Denmark | 523 | 206 |
| Germany | 256 | 85 |
| Norway | 260 | 99 |
| Sweden | 378 | 101 |
| UK | 100 | 100 |

*Source:* OECD

So competitiveness does not appear to be about prices.

A second piece of evidence to support this view is taken from a major empirical study of competitiveness in the Northern Ireland clothing industry which the University of Ulster carried out in 1989. In the study the consequences of following alternative generic pricing and quality strategies were analysed. The study showed that price was not the crucial determinant of competitiveness. Rather, customers made their purchases on the basis of a vector of buying influences. Indeed, the study showed that those companies which charged a higher price than their direct competitors seemed to be the most profitable and competitive. The studies led to the conclusion that in this industry (a similar conclusion was reached in a replicated study into the meat industry) in Northern Ireland there seemed to exist a phenomenon that has since been called the semi-U-shaped curve.

### The semi-U-shaped curve for the clothing industry

In this study 77 out of the 101 clothing companies operating in Northern Ireland were questioned and the semi-U-shaped curve, as shown in Figure 2.1, resulted. This curve clearly shows that the highest returns, i.e. the most competitive companies, are those that charge high relative prices. In other words, their successful competitive position is due to consumer purchases made on the basis of non-price factors.

Once again these, admittedly selective, data should at least cause us to question this principle.

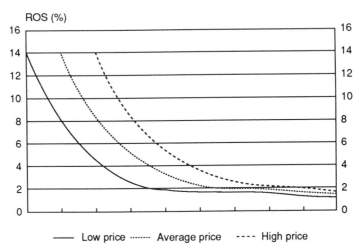

**Figure 2.1**   The semi-U-shaped curve

## Third: The Principle that the Best Industrial Sectors are Those that are Growing Most Rapidly

There is often an assumption that those markets which have the highest growth rates are the most attractive and are therefore the ones in industrial development to which agencies ought to direct their greatest efforts. This may or may not be correct. It all depends upon the competitive terrain that prevails within the sector.

For example, although many extremely fast-growing markets, such as personal computers, have appeared to be rather attractive, they have, in reality, experienced such high levels of competition and technical change that the majority of competitors have not, in the long run (over say 10 years), been profitable. Indeed, the attrition rate for PC companies has been so high that most competitive victories have often been Pyrrhic and, with the benefit of hindsight, were merely flickers before extinction.

In contrast to the mirage of glamour which may be associated with such fast-growing markets, there are many examples of mature industries which have had a much more pedestrian growth rate and image but which have provided the incumbent players with higher and more enduring levels of profitability. For example, Table 2.1 shows the average return on sales and the average return on assets by industry for the world's largest companies for 1989.

## Fourth: The Principle that Industrial Development Should be Sectoral

This will be dealt with more comprehensively below in the Section "The detail of the alternative".

**Table 2.1** The average return on sales and the average return on assets by industrial sector for the world's largest companies

| Industry sector | Return on sales (%) | Return on assets (%) |
|---|---|---|
| Aerospace | 3 | 3 |
| Beverages | 6 | 6 |
| Building materials | 6 | 5 |
| Chemicals | 6 | 5 |
| Computers | 3 | 3 |
| Electronics | 4 | 3 |
| Food | 3 | 5 |
| Forest products | 5 | 5 |
| Metal products | 5 | 5 |
| Minerals and crude oil | 9 | 5 |
| Pharmaceuticals | 10 | 9 |
| Publishing | 7 | 7 |
| Rubber and plantations | 2 | 2 |
| Transportation equipment | 2 | 1 |

*Source: Fortune (1990).*

In conclusion, although the theory of comparative advantage is the principal contribution which traditional economics makes to understanding international competitiveness, today it receives scant recognition by business people. To quote Michael Porter of the Harvard Business School:

> It is not surprising that most managers exposed to the theory find that it assumes away what they find to be most important and provides little guidance for appropriate company strategy.
>
> *Porter (1980, p. 13)*

# AN ALTERNATIVE PERSPECTIVE

Having been somewhat critical of the "traditional offerings" in this area, the question must now be asked

"What is the alternative to economics?"

It is suggested that the alternative ought to lie in the discipline of strategic planning, and in that respect it is useful to trace the historical development of this discipline.

# A BRIEF SKETCH OF THE EVOLUTION OF STRATEGIC PLANNING

It could be argued that a primary starting point for the practice of strategic planning lies in the discipline of industrial economics. This discipline has, as a central tenet, the relationship between structure, conduct and performance. This tenet holds that all industries have particular structures which cause their constituent firms to engage in certain types of conduct which ultimately leads to particular levels of individual firm performance. This relationship is shown in Figure 2.2.

This model is therefore known as the S–C–P model. Driving this model is the underlying economist's view that competition should be "fair", should be "free" and, assuming that there are sufficient safeguards to ensure such free and fair competition, then the industry as a whole will tend towards equilibrium.

In contrast to this view, the strategist's central tenet could be described as Conduct, Structure and Performance. This view maintains that firms can engage in particular types of conduct (strategies) to influence the structure of their industry and the performance of their firm. This is shown in Figure 2.3.

Furthermore, driving the strategy model is the underlying assumption that, far from seeking equilibrium, the firm is striving the competitive advantage over competitors. In summary, the goal of the strategic planner could be described as "proactively building sustainable and profitable competitive advantage". How this can be achieved in the context of industrial development will now be explored.

Industrial economics
and performance

Industrial economics

Structure
↓
Conduct
↓
Performance

Fair competition
leading to equilibrium                              **Figure 2.2**   The S–C–P model

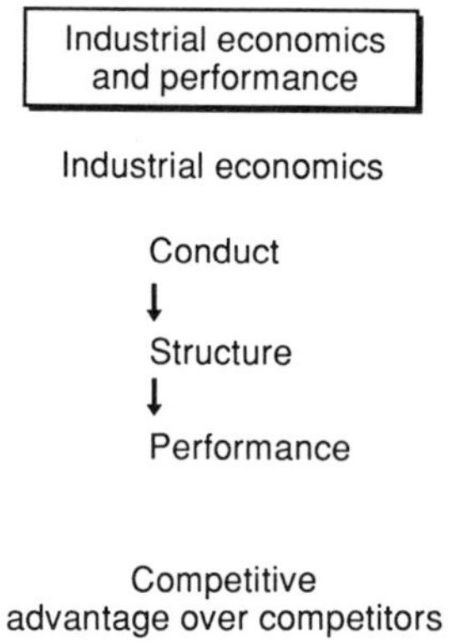

Industrial economics
and performance

Industrial economics

Conduct

$\downarrow$

Structure

$\downarrow$

Performance

**Figure 2.3**   The C–S–P model

Competitive
advantage over competitors

# THE CONTEXT OF THE ALTERNATIVE PERSPECTIVE

The alternative perspective to the traditional economics view must be placed in an appropriate context. The context adopted here is Michael Porter's diamond of competitive advantage. In this model Porter has suggested that nations achieve international success in particular industries because of four broad attributes that shape their competitive posture. These attributes are:

(1)   *Factor conditions*, i.e. the nation's command of factors of production
(2)   *Demand conditions*, i.e. the level of home demand for the industry's output
(3)   *Related and supporting industries*, the presence of absence in the nation of supplier and related industries. This is similar to the Japanese idea of the enterprise group
(4)   *Firm strategy, structure and rivalry*, i.e. how the firms are managed and the strategies they pursue

It is the last item in the list, firm strategy, structure and rivalry, that lies most within a region's control and, for that reason, this alternative perspective will concentrate exclusively on this aspect of the model.

Consequently, this perspective will consider the issue of national competitiveness largely at the level of the firm.

# THE DETAIL OF THE ALTERNATIVE

In Figure 2.4 there are two companies A and B in the same industrial sector. Which company ought to be supported: company A or company B?

In the figure the area of each circle is constructed so that it is proportional to annual sales. It can be seen immediately that:

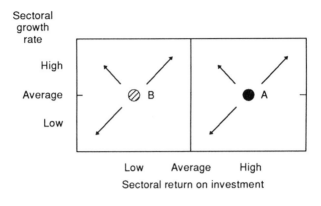

Figure 2.4    Which company should be supported: A or B?

A has larger sales
A is earning above-average returns for its industrial sector

However, it is not clear which will be the long-term winning company. Superficially A appears to be superior: it has larger sales and a higher return on investment (ROI). However, its best days may be over and rather than continuing to grow through following the upper trajectory it may follow the lower trajectory and its performance decline. Similar arguments could be advanced about B.

This is the dilemma. When historical and forecasted sectoral data are used there is no means of making a judgement about the likelihood of future success. All that is known is that A has been a superior performer in the past. What is needed is a benchmark for making a judgement about the future. Is such a benchmark available?

It is by no means certain that there is, but it is instructive to reflect on another discipline which continuously uses such benchmarks to forecast winners and losers and see if a similar methodology can be employed. The discipline is that of medicine.

What is the medical profession's approach to forecasting future health? In other words, how are practitioners able to make reasonably correct forecasts of the future health of individuals?

These judgements or forecasts tend to be made on the basis of two major influences:

Historical data about the individual—the longitudinal health record or history
Cross-sectional data

Most people are familiar with longitudinal data—they are a person's own unique health history.

However, contributing to most medical diagnoses or predictions are cross-sectional data. Cross-sectional data are not unique to any individual. Rather, they are data drawn from a very large pool of cases without reference to any particular individual. They are, for example, data on the recorded physiological characteristics of all individuals suffering from a particular disease without reference to any single person by name. This cross-sectional database enables the medical profession and, of course, insurance actuaries to forecast fairly accurately the future health potential of individuals on the basis of a limited number of certain fundamental health-determining characteristics. Indeed, over time, the medical profession has distilled from this large pool of recorded cross-sectional data a limited number of guidelines that could be called "the fundamental rules for health".

These general fundamental rules enable fairly accurate judgements to be made about any individual's health prospects without an individual diagnosis. These rules apply universally and are fairly accurate. They assert that the health of any individual is largely determined by factors such as the following:

Inherited factors, i.e. parental health record and physique
Behaviour factors, i.e. diet and lifestyle
Environmental factors, i.e. physical environment and working environment.
Personal factors, i.e. age, education and affluence

In other words, a doctor furnished with this type of information can normally make a fairly good judgement about the likely health prospects for any person. This judgement will not be correct in every case, but will be correct in general and in the aggregate.

Indeed, when the technique of diagnosis and prescription is considered more deeply, it appears to proceed by aligning the personal data of the individual with the cross-sectional data for many individuals who are in similarly structured circumstances.

Expressing this slightly differently, when this type of cross-sectional data is available it is possible to forecast, with a fair degree of certainty, what any person's "level of health" ought to be. Or, expressing it slightly differently once again, everyone has a "par level of health", as shown in Figure 2.5 where this reflects a cross-sectional expectation.

Over time it would be expected that an individual would fluctuate around his or her particular level of health. But each person will, over time, return to par. Those individuals who are above par will, over time, sink to par, while those who are below par will rise to it as shown in Figure 2.6.

What is being suggested is that an analogous approach ought to be applied to the process of selecting winning companies. In other words, if longitudinal

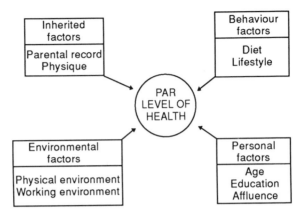

**Figure 2.5** Factors determining our par level of health

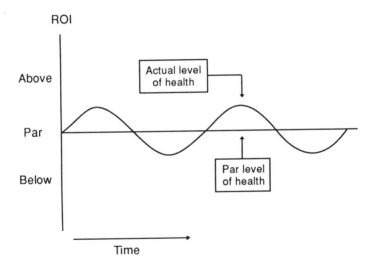

**Figure 2.6** How health returns to par

history of an individual company is aligned with general cross-sectional data of many companies it ought to provide guidance on how to pick winners.

Consider now how a cross-sectional perspective could be applied to company A in Figure 2.4 where a sectoral view was taken.

As was seen previously, A enjoys an above-average sectoral return on investment. But this approach does help forecast future performance.

Now, consider A's sectoral position again, this time in more detail. Figure 2.7 shows its position in terms of a frequency distribution of return on investment within its industrial sector.

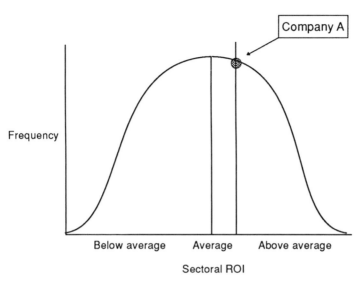

Company A

Frequency

Below average        Average        Above average

Sectoral ROI

**Figure 2.7**   Frequency distribution of ROIs of sectoral firm

Traditionally, sectoral analyses are used to make judgements about the performance of firms first in relation to their sector and second in relation to other firms in the sector. For example, if we take Dun and Bradstreet or ICC data reports we will see phrases such as: "The average return on investment for the clothing industry last year was $X\%$".

From this we can then deduce whether or not a clothing company is performing well. If its return on investment is above average it is performing well, while if it is below average it is not. Nothing could be simpler.

However, if company A is now examined from a cross-sectional perspective a different view may be formed. First, however, there must be some guidance on just what is a cross-sectional perspective for a firm?

Consider the following three hypothetical clothing companies which may be characteristic of the clothing industry in a region of the United Kingdom.

The firm on the right-hand side of Figure 2.8 is a large integrated unit which has a major presence in this region only. It manufactures a very wide variety of product lines which it sells to a variety of buyers including retailers, agents, wholesalers in a variety of markets in a variety of countries. It has invested heavily in design, research and development, distribution and marketing. Its direct competitors are similarly structured.

The firm on the left-hand side of Figure 2.8 is an integrated multinational which has a relatively large production unit only in the region. It has a limited range of products which it distributes throughout Europe. It has no regional design, research and development, marketing or sales departments. Its direct competitors are similarly structured.

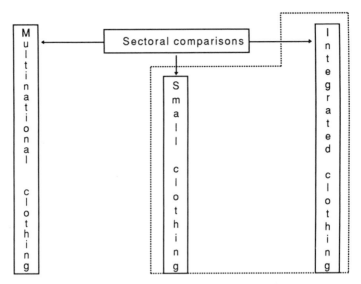

**Figure 2.8**   Sectoral comparisons in the clothing industry

Finally, the firm in the centre of the figure is a small locally owned single-product manufacturing unit which sells all of its output to a large multiple. It manufactures to specification; it has just one customer, no design or research and development facilities and no foreign markets.

In fact, it could be argued that for these three companies the only real connection is the tenuous one of industry label, i.e. the word clothing.

However, in Figure 2.9 there are three companies which although they are in

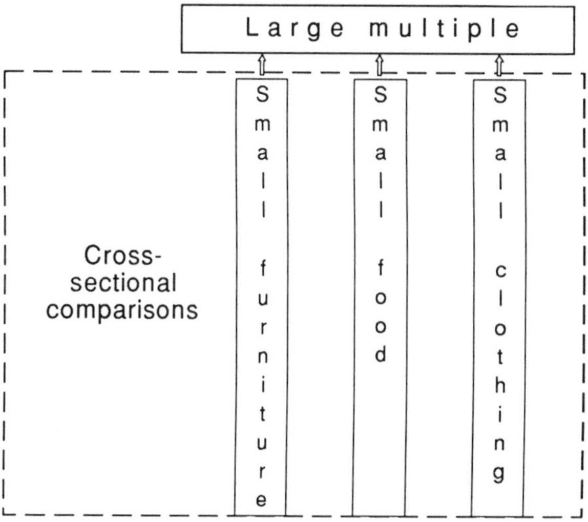

```
                    ┌──────────────────────────────┐
                    │    L a r g e   m u l t i p l e │
                    └──────────────────────────────┘
```

**Figure 2.9**   Similarly structured firms in different industries

different industries—clothing, food processing and furniture—are none the less similarly structured.

They are all small local companies which supply all of their output to a single large multiple. The thrust of this argument is that when their performances are being assessed, they should be assessed not just in relation to other companies in the same industrial sector, but also in relation to their strategic peers, where a strategic peer is a similarly structured company, irrespective of its industry sector. To do this, data which are cross-sectional as well as sectoral are needed.

As shown in Figure 2.10, firms in the same industry could be called sectoral

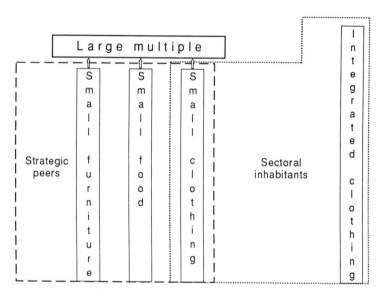

**Figure 2.10** Sectoral inhabitants and strategic peers

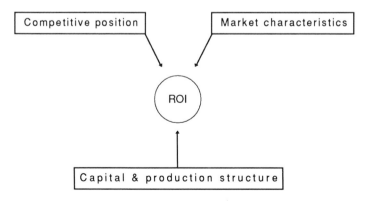

**Figure 2.11** Determinants of par ROI

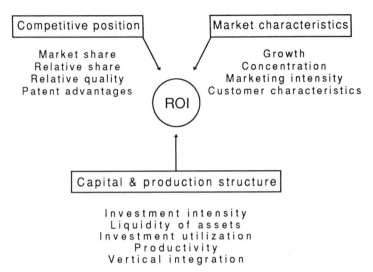

Figure 2.12   Determinants of par ROI

inhabitants, while firms which are similarly structured can be called strategic peers.

What ought these cross-sectional data to be? There is already in existence one major cross-sectional database—the Strategic Planning Institute's (SPI) (1981) database—and this gives us some indications about the type of data that we ought to use in this kind of exercise.

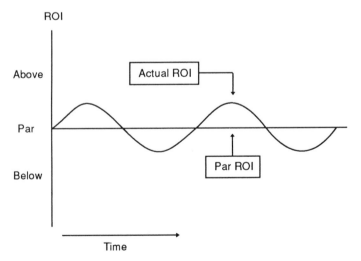

Figure 2.13   How ROI returns to par

The research of SPI shows that, just as there are fundamental determinants of personal health, there are also fundamental determinants of strategic health. Indeed, the medical analogy can be taken even further and it can be asserted that every business has a par level of strategic health or more precisely a par return on investment, determined by a relatively small number of strategic health-determining factors as shown in Figures 2.11 and 2.12.

Furthermore, over time all businesses will fluctuate about their par return on investment as shown in Figure 2.13.

Thus businesses which are above their par will, over time, revert to par, while those which are below par will rise to par. In other words, every business has a homoeostatic inclination towards its par. We can take the par-determining factors for any business and compute what its par return on investment is.

## COMPANY A's PERFORMANCE RELATIVE TO ITS CROSS-SECTIONAL PEERS

Now consider company A's performance relative to its cross-sectional peers by examining, in Figure 2.14, the frequency distribution of the ROIs of A's strategic peers.

A is indeed performing at a lower level than similarly structured companies. In other words, the sheer competitive structure of the company indicates that it could do much better. It is performing below its par. Companies which are

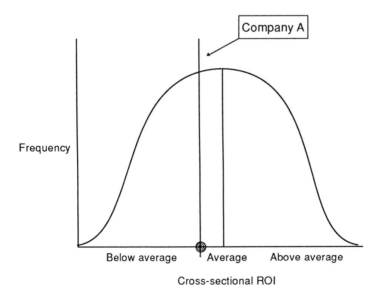

**Figure 2.14** Frequency distribution of the ROIs of A's strategic peers

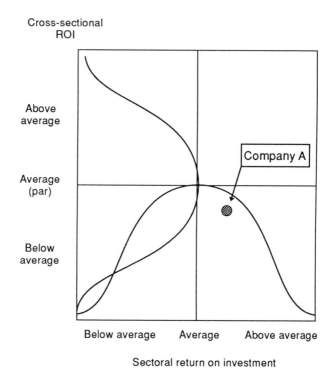

**Figure 2.15**   Company A from sectoral and cross-sectional perspectives

performing below par will, over time, adjust their strategies and their structures and move towards par, while companies which are performing above par will, over time, adjust their strategies and their structures and move back towards par. We would expect company A's return on investment to improve.

Now combine the cross-sectional and the sectoral data as shown in Figure 2.15 and see what picture emerges. (Note that the cross-sectional frequency distribution has been flipped.)

Here there is a situation where company A is performing above average for its industry sector yet below par for its strategic peers. It is likely to move towards par and so it will increase its return on investment.

Should company A be supported?
It ought to be—its best days are yet to arrive.

## The Conclusion: Strong Support

Figure 2.16 shows how this company would be expected to develop.

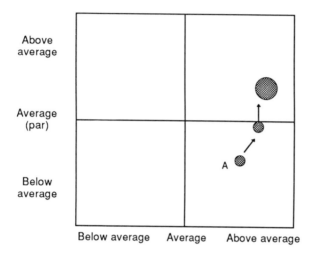

Cross-sectional
ROI

Figure 2.16    The likely performance of company A

## COMPANY B's EXPECTED FUTURE PERFORMANCE

Should the second company, company B, be supported? This company is performing below its sectoral average and also below its cross-sectional par. A movement towards par would be expected. As this happens it will also increase its sectoral return on investment. The problem for this company is that it needs advice. Strategic advice. It could do much better.

### The Conclusion: Support, Subject to Guidance

Figure 2.17 shows how this company would be expected to develop.

## COMPANY C's EXPECTED FUTURE PERFORMANCE

Should a company occupying company C's competitive position be supported? It appears to be an outstanding success. Indeed, it is. Its performance is above average in its sector and is also superior to its strategic peers; its performance is above par. But what about the future? This company is being managed superbly. It is unlikely that this will be sustainable for ever. It will, over time, return to par.

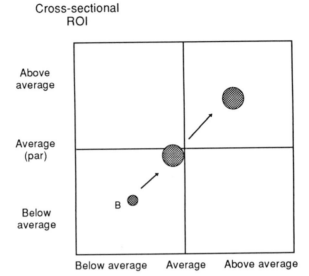

**Figure 2.17** The likely performance of company B

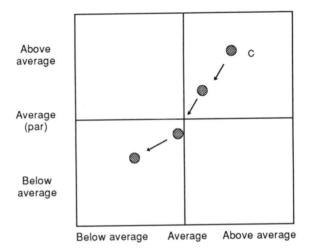

**Figure 2.18** The likely performance of company C

## The Conclusion: Maintain the Status Quo

Figure 2.18 shows how this company would be expected to develop.

## COMPANY D's EXPECTED FUTURE PERFORMANCE

Company D can be considered to be both a success and a failure. It is a failure in that it is not achieving the sectoral average return on investment; however, it is a success in that its return on investment is above its par value. This implies that this company is being managed better than similarly structured companies. However, the par ROI for such companies is really very low and one would expect that over time the low sectoral return which this company is earning will become even lower as it moves towards par.

## The Conclusion: No Support

Figure 2.19 shows how this company would be expected to develop.

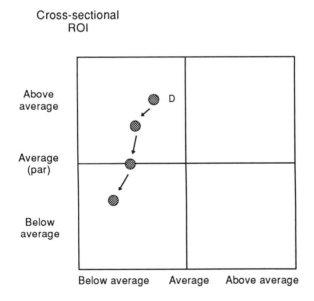

Figure 2.19   The likely performance of company D

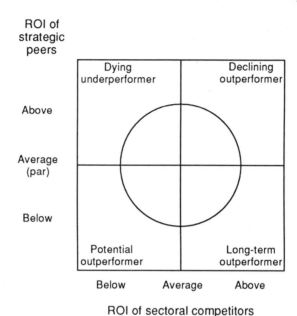

ROI of
strategic
peers

|                      | Dying<br>underperformer | Declining<br>outperformer |
|----------------------|-------------------------|---------------------------|
| Above                |                         |                           |
| Average<br>(par)     |                         |                           |
| Below                |                         |                           |
|                      | Potential<br>outperformer | Long-term<br>outperformer |

Below          Average          Above

ROI of sectoral competitors

**Figure 2.20**    The industrial development matrix

## THE INDUSTRIAL DEVELOPMENT MATRIX

Finally, all these messages can be included in a single matrix which can be called the industrial development matrix as shown in Figure 2.20. This matrix suggests policies for individual companies which are determined by the intersection of their strategic position as measured by both sectoral and cross-sectional data.

## NOTE

This chapter formed the inaugural lecture of Professor McNamee, delivered at the University of Ulster on March 12, 1991.

## REFERENCES

*Fortune Magazine* (1990) November.
Industrial Development Board of Northern Ireland (1991) *Competitiveness and Growth: How Forward Strategy Will Work*. IDB, Belfast, NI.
Porter, M. (1980) *Competitive Strategy: Techniques for Analysing Industries*. Free Press, New York.

Ricardo, D. (1817) *The Principles of Political Economy and Taxation*.
Smith, Adam (1776) *The Wealth of Nations*.
Strategic Planning Institute (1981) *Basic Principles of Business Strategy*. SPI, Cambridge, MASS.

# 3

# GLOSSARY OF MANAGEMENT TECHNIQUES

### D. E. Hussey

*Managing Director, Harbridge Consulting Group Ltd*

## PURPOSE

Anyone who sets out to offer a glossary is taking a great risk, and may well be accused of many sins of omission and commission. There are almost certainly techniques which I have overlooked, and it may be that some people would quarrel with some of the descriptions. I feel less concerned about the second possibility because the main purpose of this glossary is to show sources where more detailed descriptions can be obtained. Thus the glossary is not trying to fulfil the role of a handbook, but instead gives a brief description of the major techniques and leads the reader to more information. I make no claim that the references given are exhaustive, in that there may be many other books and articles which describe the techniques at least as effectively. I have not tried to track down the earliest references to each technique; my task has been to provide adequate references, where possible quoting those which I find helpful and which are still readily obtainable. There is no need to try to provide a complete bibliography under each heading when the purpose of the glossary is only to point the way. A few of the entries might be more accurately described as aids to thinking rather than "techniques". They are usually approaches which I have found useful, and are included for this reason.

In addition to other books and articles, I have set out to cite any significant descriptions of the techniques that have appeared in earlier pages of the *International Review of Strategic Management*.

Techniques do not make strategy: this is the role of managers. However, they

International Review of Strategic Management.
Edited by D. E. Hussey. © 1992 John Wiley & Sons Ltd

serve a useful purpose in presenting information in different ways so that new insights can be gained. There is no one right technique for all occasions and the analyst's first task is to select approaches that are relevant and potentially helpful. My experience is that it is usually better to use two or three different techniques to let the information fall in different patterns, rather than to rely on only one. The analogy I like to use is that of a child's kaleidoscope. It is a number of pieces of coloured material in a glass-sided box, but each time the user moves the toy the pieces shift and a new pattern can be revealed. In analysis, the situation is not changed by the techniques, but the shaking up of the information brings out different pictures. And as every analyst knows, the application of a technique often reveals a need for information that has hitherto not been used in the organization.

Techniques may also aid the presentation of complex issues, and may be seen as valuable communication devices, on top of the role of analysis. It often becomes possible to reduce many pages of narrative plan to one or two of the diagrams which result from the use of some of the techniques listed in this glossary. The ability to compress information, thus making it easier to reach a shared understanding on complicated situations, is to my mind one of the most important justifications for using many of the approaches listed.

There is no restriction on the development of new techniques. Matrix displays can give great insight, and I frequently find that using one approach sets me on the road to developing another that is original to the situation. The analyst should be willing to experiment.

It would be wrong to move on to the glossary without drawing attention to three more detailed "encyclopaedias", although the older of these may no longer be in print. Each of the books fulfils a different objective, and all make a useful addition to the strategist's reference library.

Argenti, J. (1969) *Management Techniques.* Allen and Unwin, London.
Karlöf, B. (1989) *Business Strategy: A Guide to Concepts and Models.* MacMillan, London.
Kempner, T. (Ed.) (1987) *The Penguin Management Handbook,* 4th edition. Penguin, London.

| Techniques listed | Classification |
| --- | --- |
| Breakeven analysis | Financial analysis |
| Business definition | Information manipulation |
| Competitor analysis | Information manipulation |
| Competitor profiling | Information manipulation |
| Core competencies | Information manipulation |
| Corporate modelling | Mathematical relationships |
| Critical skills analysis | Information manipulation |
| Critical success factors | Information manipulation |
| Decision trees | Quantitative relationships |

| Techniques listed | Classification |
|---|---|
| Delphi technique | Forecasting method |
| Discounted cash flow | Financial analysis |
| Discount rate of return | Financial analysis |
| Diversification matrix | Financial analysis |
| Du Pont chart | Financial analysis |
| Econometric model | Mathematical relationships |
| Environmental assessment: facing up to change | Information manipulation |
| Environmental assessment: Neubauer and Solomon | Information manipulation |
| Environmental turbulence matrices | Information manipulation |
| Equilibrium analysis | Information manipulation |
| Experience curve | Mathematical relationships |
| Gap analysis | Financial analysis |
| Generic strategy matrix | Information manipulation |
| Global strategy matrix | Information manipulation |
| Group competitive intensity map | Information manipulation |
| Historical analogy | Forecasting method |
| Industry analysis | Information manipulation |
| Industry mapping | Information manipulation |
| Key success factors | Information manipulation |
| Learning curves | Financial analysis |
| Life cycle concepts | Information manipulation |
| Net present value | Financial analysis |
| PIMS | Empirical relationships |
| Portfolio analysis | Information manipulation |
| Product/market matrix | Information manipulation |
| Profits graph | Financial analysis |
| Risk analysis | Financial analysis |
| Risk matrix | Information manipulation |
| ROI chart | Financial analysis |
| Scenario planning | Information manipulation |
| Segmentation, strategic | Information manipulation |
| Sensitivity analysis | Financial analysis |
| Strategic group mapping | Information manipulation |
| Strategy cube | Information manipulation |
| SWOT | Information manipulation |
| Synergy matrix | Information manipulation |
| Technology-based resource allocation | Information manipulation |
| Technology grid | Information manipulation |
| Trends projection | Forecasting method |
| Value-based strategy | Financial analysis |
| Value chains | Information manipulation |
| V matrix | Financial analysis |

# Breakeven Analysis

A very simple, very useful approach based on fixed and variable cost analysis which enables the impact of price and volume decisions on profit to be charted. In its basic form it enables the user to determine either the volume that has to be sold at a given price in order to break even or the price at which a given volume must be sold to achieve the same effect. It is also possible to use the same concept to examine price/volume relationships at various target levels of profit.

The approach is very useful for a simple business, or at simple levels in a complex business. A breakeven analysis for the consolidated operations of a global company would have little value. A breakeven analysis for a new product launch in one trading unit, or for the operation of a focused business within a particular country, would be a very useful approach. The technique facilitates the exploration of sensitivities, and hence the understanding of the business.

It is also known as a profits graph (although graphical presentation is not needed as calculation can be made by formula). Some prefer this alternative title, on the basis that businesses aim to make profits, not to break even.

## References

Anthony, R. N. and Reece, J. S. (1983) *Accounting: Text and Cases*, 7th edition. Irwin, Homewood, Illinois, Chapter 16.

Wilson, R. M. S. and McHugh, G. (1987) *Financial Analysis: A Managerial Introduction*. Cassell, London, Chapter 11.

## Business Definition

A form of three-dimensional strategic segmentation analysis, using the axes customer function, customer group, and alternative technologies. This enables the organization to plot its own business definition, compared to that of competitors, both to understand the current business and to plan future strategic moves. In essence, the concept is very little different from other multidimensional approaches to segmentation. Abell (1980) argues that "... even portfolio strategy cannot be discussed until very basic decisions are made about the definition of the activity and the competitive arena(s) in which strategy will be implemented. This issue has been lurking in the background in the academic literature up to now. It has, however, been of considerable concern to practitioners who have long recognised that contemporary planning methods can only be used once this more fundamental question of 'what business(es) are we in?' has been addressed".

## Reference

Abell, D. F. (1980) *Defining the Business: The Starting Point of Strategic Planning*. Prentice-Hall, Englewood Cliffs, New Jersey.

*See also*

Strategy cube

## Competitor Analysis

This is not itself a technique, but a process, which is aided by a number of techniques. Competitor analysis is an approach to the systematic collection and analysis of information about competitors. The aims are to assess competitor strategies, their likely response to your strategy, and to define approaches which build competitive advantage. In addition, good competitor analysis can aid the identification of alliance partners or acquisition candidates.

### References

Fuld, L. M. (1987) *Competitor Intelligence*. Wiley, New York.
Hussey, D. E. (1991) *Introducing Corporate Planning: Guide to Strategic Management*, 4th edition. Pergamon, Oxford, Chapter 5.
Porter, M. E. (1980) *Competitive Strategy*. Free Press, New York.
Porter, M. E. (1985) *Competitive Advantage*. Free Press, New York.
Stanat, R. (1990) *The Intelligent Corporation*. Amacom, New York.
(Note that this book deals with information rather than analysis)

*See also*

Business definition*
Competitor profiling
Group competitive intensity map
Industry analysis
Industry mapping
Portfolio analysis*
Strategic group mapping
Value chains

*Note competitor analysis is a subsidiary use of these two techniques.

## Competitor Profiling

This is an approach that aids the analysis of competitors through the focusing of all data on to a one-page profile for each competitor. This page is usually A3 size, and the identification of the key issues makes it easier to understand the competitor, to use the information that is available, and to identify gaps in that information. The approach needs the support of an information system.

Boxes on the profile can be viewed as notepads to record historical performance, market share trends, key facts, strengths and weaknesses, strategy and critical success factor ratings.

The approach can also be used to profile other actors on an industry map, such as customers. From the combination of industry map and profiles a series of possible strategic actions can be identified, and the point in the chain where the action might be initiated.

Although competitor profiling can be used as a stand-alone technique, it achieves its full potential when used in conjunction with industry mapping.

### References

Hussey, D. E. (1991) *Introducing Corporate Planning: Guide to Strategic Management*, 4th edition. Pergamon, Oxford, Chapter 5.

Steiner, G. A. (1979) *Strategic Planning: What Every Manager Must Know*. Free Press, New York, p. 139.

### See also

Group competitive intensity map
Industry analysis
Industry mapping
Strategic group mapping
Value chains

# Core Competencies

The concept of core competencies has been suggested as a more useful way of looking at an organization than the strategic business unit concept. Competencies are the skills, knowledge and technologies that an organization possesses on which its success depends. Those that are core are the ones that should be nurtured. Instead of developing strategy based on thinking only of dominating markets, it may be more useful to think in terms of core competencies, which will segment the organization in a totally different way.

The references quoted do not offer a technique for analysing competencies, but it should be possible to move from the concepts to a form of portfolio analysis which positions activities by core competencies.

### References

Ohmae, K. (1983) *The Mind of the Strategist*. Penguin, London, Chapter 14. (This book does not use the term core competencies, but offers some thoughts which are relevant to the concept)

Prahalad, C. K. and Doz, Y. L. (1987) *The Multinational Mission*. Free Press, New York, pp. 62–3 and 240–2.

Prahalad, C. K. and Hamel, G. (1990) The core competence of the corporation. *Harvard Business Review*, May/June.

## See also

Technology grid

# Corporate Modelling

Computer-based simulations of the total company or of a business activity within the company are useful in assessing the expected results of strategies. Manual quantification of options can be tedious. Models speed this up, make it possible to consider more options and sensitivities, and reduce the risk of mathematical error. In the 1960s, when many of the earlier models were developed, modelling was a major investment of time and money and, of course, used mainframe computers, making access difficult. With the availability of PCs, modelling is now within the reach of all. Useful models can be built on spreadsheet programmes, and can be highly sophisticated suites of models or a relatively simple way of looking at changes in the proforma final accounts.

## References

Chandler, J. and Cockle, P. (1982) *Techniques of Scenario Planning*. McGraw-Hill, London.
McNamee, P. B. (1985) *Tools and Techniques of Strategic Management*. Pergamon, Oxford.
McNamee, P. B. (1988) *Management Accounting: Strategic Planning and Marketing*. Heinemann Professional Publishing, Oxford.

## International Review of Strategic Management reference

McNamee, P. B. and McHugh, M. (1991) A hierarchical approach to modelling the strategic management process, 2.1.

# Critical Skills Analysis

*See* Critical success factors.

# Critical Success Factors

(Also known as Critical skills analysis or Key success factors.) An approach to strengths and weakness analysis which is also useful in competitor analysis and, if taken to lower levels of resolution, in the design of information systems. It seeks to identify the 5–10 things that have to be done well in order to be successful in a specific business. Lever Brothers and McBrides (own label contractors) are both in the detergent business, but they do not have the same critical success factors.

Among those critical to Lever brothers are product innovation, market segmentation and promotional skills, None of these matter to McBrides, who, among other things, have to be able to formulate substitutes for branded goods quickly, produce to low cost, and have flexible manufacturing capability.

Concentration on critical success factors is one way of honing the strengths and weakness analysis so that the important strategic issues are identified and dealt with. The approach also provides a standard against which it is possible to evaluate one's own business in relation to those of competitors.

The approach is long established and predates the references given by many years.

### References

Hussey, D. E. (1985) *Corporate Planning*. Gee and Co, London, Chapter 6.
Hussey, D. E. (1991) *Introducing Corporate Planning*, 4th edition. Pergamon, Oxford, Chapter 5.
Leidecker, J. K. and Bruno, A. V. (1984) Identifying and using critical success factors. *Long Range Planning*, February, 17.1.

### See also

SWOT
Equilibrium analysis

## Decision Trees

A useful approach which sets out diagrammatically a chain of optional decisions and chance events. Each chance event has several possible consequences, and each consequence may require that different strategic options be considered. The technique allows a complex array of risks and decisions to be charted, and this alone can aid understanding and bring clarity of thinking.

The technique goes further, by assessing financial consequences to each chance event, and calculating the outcomes of all the branches of the tree in financial terms. The combination of probabilities and outcomes along the various courses indicated by the decision allows an *expected monetary value* to be calculated for each possible final outcome. Quantification is usually in discounted cash flow terms, and the final figure aids the process of decision-making. As with all techniques, the worth of what comes out has considerable relation to the care with which the analysis is undertaken.

I have found this technique to be useful in brainstorming ideas, in communicating complex situations, as well as in analysis.

### References

Hussey, D. E. (1982) *Corporate Planning: Theory and Practice*, 2nd edition. Pergamon, Oxford, Chapter 23.
Mantell, L. H. and Sing, F. P. (1972) *Economics for Business Decisions*. McGraw-Hill Kogakusha, Tokyo, Chapter 16.
Moore, P. G. (1968) *Basic Operational Research*. Pitman, London, Chapter 8.
Pappas, J. L. and Brigham, E. F. (1979) *Managerial Economics*, 3rd edition. Holt-Saunders, Hindsdale, Illinois, Chapters 3 and 14.

### See also

Discounted cash flow
Risk analysis

## Delphi Technique

A technique which is used for developing scenarios of possible futures under conditions of discontinuity. A panel of experts is chosen and asked to complete a series of questionnaires about some future situation. In the second round they receive an analysis of others' views and are invited to defend or modify their own. It is a form of structured brainstorming of expert opinion. The technique, like all "futures" techniques, was more popular in the late 1960s and early 1970s than it is now, possibly because emphasis has changed from forecast dependent strategy to the management of strategy.

### References

Chambers, J. C., Satinedes, K. M. and Smith, D. D. (1971) How to choose the right forecasting technique. *Harvard Business Review*, July–August.
Wills, G. *et al.* (1972) *Technological Forecasting*. Penguin, London, Chapter 2.4.

## Discounted Cash Flow

A method of analysing capital expenditures which takes account of the time value of money by discounting future cash flows back to todays's value. The analysis is made on cash inflows and outflows, and provides a good basis for comparing options within a project. The time value of money is compared with the cost of money, usually a weighted figure that reflects the mix of debt and equity of the firm, the aim being to choose projects which offer a net gain over this figure.

The technique can be used in a way that takes account of inflation. It is also suitable for studying some elements of risk.

Although until recently used for project evaluation, the approach has for many years been advocated as a way of looking at all the strategies of the firm. Recently this concept has flowered in the value-based strategy concept.

Discounted cash flow demands a careful forward assessment of the project, and cannot be used unless a disciplined approach is taken. Results are affected by the conventions chosen, such as the treatment of residual value. Because of the discounting, this has more impact on the results if the project is evaluated over a short period, say five years, than it would if a long period were chosen, say 20 years. Against this, margins of error in the forecasts of costs and income are greater the longer the period chosen.

The technique measures the economic value of the project, and not its strategic desirability. It has been suggested that over-reliance on DCF can lead to bad long-term decisions, for example incremental changes to a factory to improve productivity give better returns than would the building of a state of the art facility, yet in the end the gap in competitive performance that opens up over the years means that the firm is eventually unable to command the resources to take the big move that eventually becomes necessary. This caution does not invalidate the worth of the technique.

Among the measures that result from DCF are:

*Discount rate of return*, which is the rate which would leave a zero net present value at the end of the project. A 15 % return would be better than 10 %, but neither would be attractive if the cost of capital were 16 %. This is sometimes known as the *internal rate of return*.

*Net present value*, which is the value *today* of the cumulative income/expenditure stream at the end of the project, using a given discount rate.

*Discounted payback* is the number of years to pay back initial outlay using discounted figures.

### References

Anthony, R. N. (1983) *Accounting: Text and Cases*, 7th edition. Irwin, Homewood, Illinois, Chapter 22.

Mantell, L. H. and Sing, F. P. (1972) *Economics for Business Decisions*. McGraw-Hill Kogakusha, Tokyo, Chapter 14.

Pappas, J. L. and Brigham, E. F. (1979) *Managerial Economics*, 3rd edition. Holt-Saunders, Hindsdale, Illinois, Chapter 13.

Van Horne, J. C. (1971) *Financial Management*, 3rd edition. Prentice-Hall, Englewood Cliffs, New Jersey, Chapter 12.

Wilson, R. M. S. and McHugh, G. (1987) *Financial Analysis: A Managerial Introduction*. Cassell, London, Chapters 13 and 14.

**See also**

Risk analysis
Value-based strategy

# Discount Rate of Return

*See* Discounted cash flow.

# Diversification Matrix

A matrix which seeks to stimulate new ideas and identify areas of synergy. One axis examines customers: same type, firm its own customer, similar type and new type. The other divides products into related and unrelated technology.

**Reference**

Ansoff, H. I. (1965) *Corporate Strategy*. McGraw-Hill, New York, Chapter 3.

**See also**

Product/market matrix

# Du Pont Chart

*See* ROI chart.

# Econometric Model

A system of interdependent regression models describing some aspect of economic activity. They provide a basis for testing economic options and for providing a quantified forecast. It is not a technique for amateurs, and specialist help is needed for effective model building.

**Reference**

Chambers, J. C., Satinedes, K. M. and Smith, D. D. (1971) How to choose the right forecasting technique. *Harvard Business Review*, July–August.

# Environmental Assessment

There are a number of similar approaches which use a structured checklist to help identify the trends in the environment and study the likely impact of these on the strategies of the business. Many have in common a scoring approach which takes into account impact and probability, thus enabling the most critical trends to be separated from the rest so that action can be taken. The most valuable element of these approaches is that the structured approach makes it less likely that things will be overlooked, while the scoring systems are of particular value in stimulating debate about the issues. In my view these approaches have more value in encouraging participative discussion than as a formal technique of analysis.

Some detailed approaches are proprietary to management consulting firms and have not been published. The references do not necessarily provide access to the most comprehensive of the approaches, but they are sufficient to illustrate the concepts.

### References

Argenti, J. (1980) *Practical Corporate Planning*. Allen & Unwin, London, Chapter 6.
Hargreaves, J. and Dauman, J. (1975) *Business Survival and Social Change*. Associated Business Programmes, London.
McNamee, P. B. (1988) *Management Accounting: Strategic Planning and Marketing*. Heinemann Professional Publishing, Oxford, Chapter 4.
Terry, P. T. (1977) Mechanisms for environmental scanning. *Long Range Planning*, June, 10.3.

### See also

Risk analysis
Risk matrix

## Environmental Assessment: Neubauer and Solomon

There are several techniques for looking at the impact of the environment, and the Neubauer and Solomon approach has some characteristics of some of the methods described in the previous entry in that it uses a concept of impact. Why it rates a separate listing is that it is a far more comprehensive approach, which hones down the vast array of influences from the environment to those with most impact and relates these to corporate strategies and missions. The technique studies trends, and also the expectations of different groups, or constituents, in the environment. It is not a technique to be learned on one reading, and needs considerable practice to gain proficiency. The whole approach has the merit of being oriented to making the strategies compatible with the business environment.

The method goes through a number of steps, beginning with the identification of the current strategies and mission of the business. Trends and constituents are identified, and an impact matrix created to establish the threats and opportunities.

The next step is to assess the effect of the issues identified on the strategies and mission of the business. In turn, this leads to a reassessment of corporate mission and strategies.

**Reference**

Neubauer, F-F. and Solomon, N. B. (1977) A managerial approach to environmental assessment. *Long Range Planning*, April, 10.2.

*See also*

Risk analysis
Risk matrix

# Environmental Turbulence Matrices

This approach presents a novel and useful way of looking at all aspects of strategic management against a grid which shows the level of environmental turbulence to which the organization is subject. The levels are 1 repetitive, 2 expanding (slow incremental), 3 changing (fast incremental), 4 discontinuous (but predictable), and 5 surpriseful (unpredictable). The position on the scale, which for most organizations will vary over time, affects not only how the organization should plan strategy, but the types of strategic response and the type of manager who would cope best. In designing this approach, Igor Ansoff, its originator, has provided a very useful diagnostic tool. It is not only of value to the analyst who is studying several businesses, but may also help the managers of single business entities think through the response needed as their businesses change position on the scale.

*International Review of Strategic Management reference*

Ansoff, H. I. (1991) Strategic management in a historical perspective, 2.1.

# Equilibrium Analysis

This is derived from the principles of force field analysis, and is a very simple way of looking at strengths and weaknesses in relation to a particular issue, such as market share. A horizontal line represents the issue under scrutiny, and the diagram sets out to identify those factors which keep it as low as it is and those which keep it as high. The technique attempts to weight the factors, and concentrates on designing responses to those factors which can be tackled and which are of most importance. It is an ideal technique to facilitate discussions and an alternative to the rather long "shopping lists" of strengths and weaknesses that some planning activities seem to generate. It is action oriented.

*Reference*

Hussey, D. E. (1991) *Introducing Corporate Planning: Guide to Strategic Management*, 4th edition. Pergamon, Oxford, Chapter 4.

*See also*

Critical success factors
SWOT

# Experience Curve

A concept which is based on industrial learning curve theories, extended from costs of production to the total costs of the whole firm. Empirically, it has been demonstrated that in most businesses the real costs per unit reduce every time cumulative output doubles. This is not the same as economies of scale (which relate to output over a given period), although this may play a part, and is related to the total cumulative experience of the organization.

If the experience curve is calculated it can be used to assess future costs based on volume increases. This leads to price and other related marketing strategies designed to gain volume to force costs down, often below the level at which most other firms can compete. In electronics, for example, the experience curve of larger companies has driven out many competitors who did not match their volume growth; calculators are a good example. The theory is less predictable in industries where there is frequent fundamental model change.

The experience curve is attributed to the Boston Consulting Group, although learning curve theory has been around since the 1940s.

*References*

Hedley, B. (1990) *Developing Strategies for Competitive Advantage*. In *Developing Strategies for Competitive Advantage* (P. B. McNamee, Ed.). Pergamon, Oxford (a selection from the journal *Long Range Planning*).
Hofer, C. W. and Schendel D. (1978) *Strategy Formulation: Analytical Concepts*. West Publishing, St Paul, Minnesota, pp. 132–135.
McNamee, P. B. (1985) *Tools and Techniques for Strategic Management*. Pergamon, Oxford, Chapter 3.

# Gap Analysis

A very simple technique with limited use. It measures the "gap" between company profit or growth targets and what is likely to be achieved if no new strategic initiatives are taken. The aim is to use this information to measure the size of the strategic task and to stimulate thoughts on new strategies.

The technique is mentioned in many books on strategic planning. It is so simple that the various authors can add little to it.

## References

Hussey, D. E. (1991) *Introducing Corporate Planning: Guide to Strategic Management*, 4th edition. Pergamon, Oxford, Chapter 4.
Kami, M. J. (1968) Gap analysis: key to super growth. *Long Range Planning*, June, 1.4.

# Generic Strategy Matrix

This is a thought-provoker rather than a complex method. It is a matrix based on the contention that all organizations have the choice of only three generic strategies: industry-wide differentiated, industry-wide cost leadership, or focus on a particular segment. The contention is not universally accepted.

## Reference

Porter, M. E. (1980) *Competitive Strategy*. Free Press, New York, Chapter 2.

# Global Strategy Matrix

More of an aid to thinking than a complex technique, this approach has been published in a number of variants. The two references given are thus not to identical matrices, although they are closely related. One variant has the need for globalization on one axis, moving from low to high. The other axis is need for local responsiveness, again moving from low to high. This matrix enables the globalization versus domestic requirements of various businesses to be compared. It may also be used to look at functions, or elements in the value chain, to establish the extent to which each of these should be integrated on a global basis. Questionnaires used in conjunction with the approach turn it into something a little stronger than an idea marshaller.

The alternative matrix studies the degree to which strategy is globalized against the globalization potential of the industry. In practice there is not a great deal of difference between the two matrices.

## References

Prahalad, C. K. and Doz, Y. L. (1987) *The Multinational Mission*. Free Press, New York, Chapter 2.
Yip, G. S. (1989) Global strategy in a world of nations. *Sloan Management Review*, Fall.

## Group Competitive Intensity Map

Derived from research by McNamee and McHugh, the technique builds on the work of Porter. The map displays in quantitive terms, using elipses on a matrix, the location of an industry's strategic groups, the competitive intensity they face, and the relative risks to which they are subject. The approach aids the study of competitive behaviour in industries where there are many competitors, where studying each individually would either be impossible or would yield results that cannot be interpreted.

*International Review of Strategic Management reference*

McNamee, P. and McHugh, M. (1990) The group competitive intensity map: A means of displaying competitive position, 1.

*See also*

Business definition
Competitor analysis
Competitor profiling
Industry analysis
Industry mapping
Portfolio analysis
Strategic group mapping
Value chains

## Historical Analogy

A form of forecast which analyses the history of something similar, or the same product, in another market (for example, what happened when product X was launched in the USA—now what is likely to happen when we launch in the UK?). It is used in a minor way when the results of a test market are translated to the total market. Most applications are in-depth studies of a previous or analogous situation.

*Reference*

Chambers, J. C., Satinedes, K. M. and Smith, D. D. (1971) How to choose the right forecasting technique. *Harvard Business Review*, July–August.

## Industry Analysis

An approach to analysing the structure of an industry. The basic model examines the balance of power between suppliers, buyers, and competitors in the industry.

These are three of the "five forces". The remaining two are substitutes and entry barriers. The principles of this approach were drawn together by Porter, although few of the components were new. Porter's contribution was offering a comprehensive basis for analysis out of a series of separate ideas. Industry analysis now underpins most modern thinking on strategic analysis.

### References

Hofer, C. W. and Schendel, D. (1978) *Strategy Formulation: Analytical Concepts.* West Publishing, St Paul, Minnesota, Chapter 5.
Hussey, D. E. (1991) *Introducing Corporate Planning: Guide to Strategic Management,* 4th edition. Pergamon, Oxford, Chapter 5.
McNamee, P. B. (1988) *Management Accounting: Strategic Planning and Marketing.* Heinemann Professional Publishing, Oxford, Chapter 4.
Porter, M. E. (1980) *Competitive Strategy.* Free Press, New York.

### See also

Business definition
Competitor analysis
Competitor profiling
Group competitive intensity map
Industry analysis
Industry mapping
Portfolio analysis
Strategic group mapping
Value chains

## Industry Mapping

This approach predated Porter's work by many years, but was refined as a result of his structural analysis of industry concept. It expands the "five forces" diagram to model all the key groups of "actors" in the chain, from suppliers through to final buyers, in a block diagram, and adds a further dimension of those who influence a buying decision but do not themselves purchase: general practitioners who prescribe drugs, architects who specify a lift, consultants who recommend a computer system, for example.

Key factual data are entered on this diagram in summary form, so that all the strategic elements of the industry are portrayed on one piece of A3 paper. Some industries are too complex to fit on one sheet, but these are the exception rather than the rule.

The approach is often used in conjunction with competitor profiling. The two techniques in combination provide a series of headings that may be used in a database to store information.

*Reference*

Hussey, D. E. (1991) *Introducing Corporate Planning: Guide to Strategic Management*, 4th edition. Pergamon, Oxford, Chapter 5.

*See also*

Business definition
Competitor analysis
Competitor profiling
Group competitive intensity map
Industry analysis
Portfolio analysis
Strategic group mapping
Value chains

# Key Success Factors

*See* Critical success factors.

# Learning Curves

*See* Experience curves.

# Life Cycle Concepts

The life cycle position of an industry or product has many implications for strategies and competitive behaviour. Empirically it has been observed that products, for example, pass through a number of stages, each of which may be associated with a different volume of sales and different levels of profits. One classification of stages is development, growth, shake-out, maturity, saturation, decline. Not only do competitors tend to behave differently at each stage of the life cycle, but there are also many implications for management in the profits/ cash needs of different positions and in strategies to extend the life cycle. Marketing strategy is also likely to be different at each stage of the life cycle. Not surprisingly, the concept also lies behind a number of approaches to portfolio analysis.

*References*

Barksdale, H. C. and Harris, C. E. (1982) Portfolio analysis and the product life cycle. *Long Range Planning*, December, 15.6.
Hofer, C. W. and Schendel, D. (1978) *Strategy Formulation: Analytical Concepts*. West Publishing, St Paul, Minnesota, Chapter 5.

Hussey, D. E. (1982) *Corporate Planning: Theory and Practice*, 2nd edition. Pergamon, Oxford, Chapter 6.

Kotler, P. (1988) *Marketing Management: Analysis, Planning, Implementation and Control*, 6th edition. Prentice-Hall, Englewood Cliffs, New Jersey, Chapter 12.

Yelle, L. E. (1983) Adding life cycles to learning curves. *Long Range Planning*, December, 16.6.

### See also

Portfolio analysis

## Net Present Value

*See* Discounted cash flow.

## PIMS

This stands for profit impact of market strategy. It is an assessment of strategy and performance based on data provided by subscribers which provides a sound empirical basis for deducing principles of strategy. It also provides a number of matrix analysis formats, through which a firm might contrast its own businesses with the findings from the data bank. The data allow relationships to be established between ROI and such factors as market share, vertical integration, capital intensity and quality.

### References

Buzzell, R. D. and Gale, B. T. (1987) *The PIMS Principles: Linking Strategy to Performance*. Free Press, New York.

Neubauer, F-F. *Portfolio Management*. Kluwer, Holland, Chapter E.

## Portfolio Analysis

A group of related methods of analysis of varying complexity which enable a variety of activities to be compared in strategic terms. The axes of the matrix may vary, but typically are some way of expressing market position compared with some way of expressing market prospects. There are some interesting variations, such as market prospects/corporate strengths. The approaches give a view of the relative strategic importance of a "portfolio" of strategic business areas, strategic business units or products, and can also be extended to consider the management skills needed to be successful in each position on the matrix. Too literal an acceptance of the findings has led many companies to take against portfolio analysis. However, careful usage can give considerable insight in complex situations, and can make it much easier to communicate the strategic shape of a multiactivity company. It makes sense to use the technique in conjunction with other analytical tools, and to be prepared to experiment with different types of portfolio analysis, including the devising of matrices which are useful in a particular situation. For example, the market share axis may be changed to contrast the technological position of the portfolio. Matrices may also be devised to study the portfolio on a geographical basis.

### References

Barksdale, H. C. and Harris, C. E. (1982) Portfolio analysis and the product life cycle. *Long Range Planning*, December, 15.6.
Clarke, C. J. and Brennan, K. (1990) Building synergy in the diversified business. In *Developing Strategies for Competitive Advantage* (P. McNamee, Ed.). Pergamon, Oxford.
Hedley, B. (1990) Strategy and the business portfolio. In *Developing Strategies for Competitive Advantage* (P. McNamee, Ed.). Pergamon, Oxford.
Hofer, C. W. and Schendel D. (1978) *Strategy Formulation: Analytical Concepts*. West Publishing, St Paul, Minnesota.
Hussey, D. E. (1991) *Introducing Corporate Planning: Guide to Strategic Management*, 4th edition. Pergamon, Oxford, Chapter 9.
Hussey, D. E. (1982) Portfolio analysis: Practical experience with the directional policy matrix. In *The Realities of Planning* (D. E. Hussey and B. Taylor, Eds). Pergamon, Oxford.
McNamee, P. B. (1985) *Tools and Techniques for Strategic Management*. Pergamon, Oxford, Chapter 3.
Neubauer, F-F. (1990) *Portfolio Management*. Kluwer, Holland.
Ohmae, K. (1983) *The Mind of the Strategist*. Penguin, London, Chapter 12.
Robinson, J., Hitchens, R. E. and Wade, D. P. (1982) The directional policy matrix: tool for strategic planning. In *The Realities of Planning* (D. E. Hussey and B. Taylor, Eds). Pergamon, Oxford.

### See also

Risk matrix
Technology grid

## Product/Market Matrix

This is a simple but very useful way of thinking through strategic options. One axis looks at markets, existing and new. Another looks at products, existing and new. The matrix thus consists only of four cells. One value of the approach is that the patterns of risks are likely to be different in each. The matrix is sometimes represented as a product/mission matrix.

Varients of this matrix include:

● Changing the axes to suppliers and technology, to analyse purchasing strategy

- Changing the axes to sources of finance/uses of finance, to study funding
- A more complex variant, which lists the four product market options on one axis and on the other shows possible strategic actions, such as licensing, joint venture, acquisition

### References

Ansoff, H. I. (1965) *Corporate Strategy*. McGraw-Hill, New York, Chapter 7.
Hussey, D. E. (1976) *Inflation and Business Policy*. Longman, London, Chapter 5.
Hussey, D. E. (1991) *Introducing Corporate Planning Guide to Strategic Management*, 4th edition. Pergamon, Oxford, Chapter 7.
Taylor, B. (1975) The crisis in supply markets: Developing a strategy for resources. In *Corporate Planning and Procurement* (D. H. Farmer and B. Taylor, Eds). Heinemann, London.

## Profits Graph

*See* Breakeven analysis.

## Risk Analysis

An approach using the Monte Carlo method to draw numerous possible values for all the factors in a capital project, with the chance of drawing any value being proportionate to its probability. This results in numerous combinations of factors, each of which is subjected to DCF analysis. The spread of outcomes gives an indication of the degree of risk to which the project is subject.

### References

Pappas, J. L. and Brigham, E. F. (1979) *Managerial Economics*, 3rd edition. Holt-Saunders, Hindsdale, Illinois, Chapter 13.
Van Horne, J. C. (1971) *Financial Management*, 3rd edition. Prentice-Hall, Englewood Cliffs, New Jersey, Chapter 12.

### See also

Discounted cash flow
Sensitivity analysis

## Risk Matrix

This approach was designed to be used in conjunction with a form of multifactor portfolio analysis which had competitive position and market prospects as the two axes. The technique keeps the market prospects axis and has degree of risk as the second axis. In concept this turns the portfolio chart into a 3-D cube, although in practice it is easier to colour or shade the circles by which SBUs are plotted to show different intensities of risk. The risk axis is reached through a worksheet which scores environmental factors for impact and probability.

The matrix allows three views to be taken:

- The degree of risk to which each area on the portfolio analysis is subject, relative to the other areas
- The particular trends which have most impact on the activity (from the worksheet)
- The particular trends which have the most impact on the company as a whole

### Reference

Hussey, D. E. (1991) *Introducing Corporate Planning: Guide to Strategic Management*, 4th edition. Pergamon, Oxford, Chapter 9.

### See also

Portfolio analysis
Environmental analysis

## ROI Chart

Sometimes called a Du Pont chart, this method allows presentation of income statement and balance sheet, in contribution analysis form, on one piece of paper. Complex information can be put into usable, easily communicated formats. The method concentrates on information that is important for strategic planning. It is a useful first step in strengths and weakness analysis, since it shows where contribution is coming from and where financial resources are being used.

### References

Anthony, R. N. and Reece, J. S. (1983) *Accounting: Text and Cases*, 7th edition. Irwin, Homewood, Illinois, Chapter 13.
Hussey, D. E. (1991) *Introducing Corporate Planning: Guide to Strategic Management*, 4th edition. Pergamon, Oxford, Chapter 4.

## Scenario Planning

This approach to planning accepts that the future is uncertain. Instead of producing one plan, with sensitivities, a number of plans are drawn prepared according to the various scenarios developed at the start. The pitfall to avoid is an overcomplex system driven by planners. The assumptions in the scenarios may drive the strategy without everyone understanding that this is happening.

### References

Chandler, J. and Cockle, P. (1982) *Techniques of Scenario Planning*. McGraw-Hill, London.
McNamee, P. (1985) *Tools and Techniques for Strategic Management*. Pergamon, Oxford, Chapter 7.
McNamee, P. (1988) *Management Accounting: Strategic Planning and Marketing*. Heinemann, London, pp. 91–93.

## Segmentation, Strategic

*See* Business definition.

## Sensitivity Analysis

This is a method for testing a plan for vulnerabilities. It may be applied to a strategic plan as a whole or to an evaluation of capital expenditure. Essentially, it is an assessment of financial results in response to a series of "what if..." questions, and may lead to different strategic decisions if the risks look too high.

Typically it deals with questions such as what if sales were to fall by 10%. Some care is necessary in definition, because sales value may fall because of a volume or a price drop and the impact on profit and cash flow will not be the same in both situations. Sloppy descriptions of sensitivities can lead to misunderstandings.

Sensitivity analysis can be made more useful if it is accompanied by an analysis of the causal factors that contribute to success or failure (for example, what happens if the competitors react with a price cut, or where we would be if the government changed). A table of impacts should be prepared, such as costs, capital costs, prices, sales volumes, tax, and the like, and the effect these changes would have on results. In the end several factors may have identical end results, so the mathematical calculations may be fewer than the events examined. This approach may help the development of strategies that avoid risk, where the more common, more passive style of sensitivity analysis ends at understanding where the project or plan is most sensitive.

### References

Mantell, L. H. and Sing, F. P. (1972) *Economics for Business Decisions*. McGraw-Hill Kogakusha, Tokyo, pp. 434–438.
Hussey, D. E. (1991) *Introducing Corporate Planning: Guide to Strategic Management*, 4th edition. Pergamon, Oxford, Chapter 14.

*See also*
Decision trees
Discounted cash flow
Risk analysis

# Strategic Group Mapping

A method of matrix display which groups competitors in an industry by their strategic dimensions, such as price policy, cost position, and specialization. Some 13 variables have been identified. For the matrix the analyst has to identify a few particularly important dimensions on which to construct the map. An example might be to use specialization (high to low) as one axis and vertical integration (high to low) as the other. This concept, and there is no reason why two or three matrices using different axes should not be employed, enables competitors to be grouped and positioned on the matrix by the common components of their strategy. This may be useful in any industry, but is particularly valuable in an industry with numerous competitors where little insight would be gained by studying each individually.

### Reference

Porter, M. E. (1980) *Competitive Strategy.* Free Press, New York, Chapter 7.

### See also

Group competitive intensity map
Industry mapping

# Strategy Cube

This approach to analysis has some similarities with the business definition concept. It argues that strategy can be looked at on three dimensions, technology, business and logistics. These are the three axes of the strategy cube. The position on each axis follows the subheadings familiar, partly familiar, and unfamiliar.

### International Review of Strategic Management reference

Nakamura, G-I. (1990) New dimensions of strategic management in the global context of the 1990s, 1.

# SWOT

Strengths, weaknesses, opportunities and threats, a simple approach which appears under several names: "WOTSUP" (the common initials have the same meaning; UP stands for underlying planning); SOFT (here fault is used instead of weakness); TOWS (same words, different order). If we wanted to be original I suppose we could call it TWOS analysis, which both stands for the same words and indicates that they cover the two dimensions of internal and external issues!

The value of the approach is that it summarizes the key issues from a complex corporate appraisal and can reduce these to one piece of paper. The pitfall is that for many it becomes a useless shopping list of weaknesses, few of which are strategic, accompanied by a few platitudes in place of real strengths. I am always suspicious when the only strengths listed are "a strong chief executive" and a "professional and loyal management team". This is not a fictional example! SWOT works best when it is tackled with the mindset of:

- Strengths and weaknesses *relative to market needs*
  and
- Compared to the competition

Simple techniques are often best for a situation, and SWOT can be recommended to those who are aware of the possible pitfalls.

### References

Hussey, D. E. (1991) *Introducing Corporate Planning: Guide to Strategic Management,* 4th edition. Pergamon, Oxford, Chapter 4.
Steiner, G. A. (1979) *Strategic Planning: What Every Manager Must Know*. Free Press, New York, Chapter 8.

### See also

Equilibrium analysis
Critical success factors

# Synergy Matrix

This is a matrix framework to facilitate the quantification of synergy in new strategic initiatives. The matrix analyses the effects on profit due to a pooling of competence, by functional areas. It is one of the first generation techniques of strategic analysis, but has some of the strands of thought that reappear in value chains and in the debate on shareholder value.

Reference

Ansoff, H. I. (1965) *Corporate Strategy*. McGraw-Hill, New York, Chapter 5.

## Technology-Based Resource Allocation

This is a matrix approach to deciding technology strategies. It is the third step in a methodology that consists of an audit, an understanding of the strategic implications of the technology portfolio, an implementation plan and a monitoring programme.

### *International Review of Strategic Management reference*

Henry, J. P. (1990) Making the technology–strategy connection, 1.

## Technology Grid

This is a way of analysing the portfolio by technology. One method uses a matrix showing technology position on one axis and relevance of the technology on the other. It was designed to give added insight to the positioning of SBUs on the more traditional competitive position/market attractiveness portfolio chart. A variant of this approach uses market growth and competitive strength as the two axes. In this case what would be plotted would be the key technologies. In common with portfolio analysis, positions would be indicated by circles drawn proportionate to their importance to the company.

### References

Clarke, C. J. and Brennan, K. (1990) Building synergy in the diversified business. In *Developing strategies for Competitive Advantage* (P. McNamee, Ed.). Pergamon, Oxford. Neubauer, F-F. *Portfolio Management*. Kluwer, Holland, Chapter D5.

### See also

Core competencies
Portfolio analysis

## Trends Projection

Most time-series analyses and projections are poor for long-term forecasting, although useful in the short term. Trend projection is good for longer-term forecasts, it designs and fits a mathematical equation to the data by, for example, measuring slope characteristics and using the results to project the curve.

*Reference*

Chambers, J. C., Satinedes, K. M. and Smith, D. D. (1971) How to choose the right forecasting technique. *Harvard Business Review*, July–August.

*See also*

Delphi technique
Econometric model
Historical analogy

# Value-Based Strategy

The debate about the need for strategy actions to add to shareholder value has led to the development of a mathematical technique that tries to ensure that all strategies are value adding, and that the business selects the options which add the most value. The method applies discounted flow analysis concepts to all the strategies of the entire organization.

The premises behind value-based planning are that the company's foremost obligation is to maximize returns to shareholders, and that the market value of shares is related to the expected cash-generating abilities of those shares.

There are several variations in the ways in which the concept may be applied, but all are based on forecast cash flow, discounted by the risk-adjusted cost of capital. Strategies are expected to deliver a discounted return in excess of the cost of capital.

*References*

Reimann, B. C. (1987) *Managing for Value*. Planning Forum, Oxford, Ohio.
Reimann, B. C. (1990) Creating value to keep the raiders at bay. In *Developing Strategies for Competitive Advantage* (P. McNamee, Ed.). Pergamon, Oxford.

*International Review of Strategic Management reference*

Day, G. and Fahey, L. (1991) Finding value in strategies, 2.1.

*See also*

Discounted cash flow

# Value Chains

A method for separating the activities the firm performs in order to identify the underlying areas of competitive advantage. All broad stages of the process from "inbound logistics" to after-sales service are identified. They are then broken down into more detailed chains of activity, so that the areas where the firm has advantages can be studied, Similar analysis is undertaken on competitors, leading to more effective competitive strategies and a fuller understanding of how each competitor is achieving differentiation.

## Reference

Porter, M. E. (1985) *Competitive Advantage*. Free Press, New York.

## See also

Competitor analysis
Competitor profiling
Group competitive intensity map
Industry analysis
Industry mapping
Strategic group mapping

# V Matrix

A graphical presentation which is based solely on financial data. Return on investment is plotted on one axis and weighted average cost of capital on the other. A diagonal line drawn from the zero points at the bottom left-hand corner of the matrix to the opposite corner at the top right-hand corner marks the position at which ROI and the cost of capital are equal. Anything positioned below this diagonal is likely to be inadequate; anything above it is adequate. An ROI of 4 % would be adequate if the cost of capital were only 2 %. However, an ROI of 14 % would be inadequate if the cost of capital were 16 %. The matrix allows the positions of all businesses in the portfolio to be plotted relative to each other.

ROI is defined as:

$$\frac{\text{Operating income } (1 - \text{the tax rate})}{\text{Assets}}$$

$K$ is the cost of capital, $V$ is value,

$$V = \frac{\text{ROI}}{K}$$

Although the matrix uses an undiscounted return on investment, it would probably be possible to adapt it to a discounted rate of return.

The main value of the matrix is that it focuses on more than ROI, which may be particularly useful in an organization with subsidiaries with local borrowing or minority shareholders.

### Reference

McNamee, P. B. (1985) *Tools and Techniques for Strategic Management*. Pergamon, Oxford, Chapter 5.

# 4

# STRATEGIC GROUPS AND INTRA-INDUSTRY COMPETITION

## John McGee

*Fellow in Corporate Strategy, Templeton College, Oxford*

## and Howard Thomas

*James F. Towey Professor of Strategic Management*
*University of Illinois at Urbana-Champaign*

## INTRODUCTION

The strategic groups concept (McGee and Thomas, 1986) directs attention to those groups of firms in an industry which may actively compete with each other by virtue of their investment in similar distinctive assets, strategic resources and core competences (Penrose, 1959; Prahalad and Hamel, 1990).

Hunt (1972) focused on strategic groups explaining heterogeneity of competition within the home appliance industry. Hunt had expected to observe that all firms would prefer one optimal strategy which would reflect the most effective way in which a firm could approach a market. This expectation had its roots in the field of industrial organization (IO) and is drawn from the view that all firms are similar except for size differences and all firms face the same environmental opportunities and threats. It follows from such a view that all firms should be

International Review of Strategic Management.
Edited by D. E. Hussey. © 1992 John Wiley & Sons Ltd

pursuing the same optimal strategy and that strategic choice becomes deterministic. The presence of groups of firms clustered around different strategies presents a different view (McGee and Thomas, 1986). Consistent with a contingency view of strategic management (Galbraith, 1973), managers are shown to be faced with alternative choices about how they will compete in markets. Alternative strategies have greater or lesser attraction for individual firms due to the variations in their resources and competences. The general manager is, therefore, faced with the task of trying to position the firm in the strategic group which best fits the firm's strengths.

Among themselves, group members compete directly because they share similar assets, strengths and competences. They target the same customers and can quickly copy the competitive moves of a rival. Competition between firms from different groups is less vigorous. However, membership in some groups is considered to be more desirable because of the attractiveness of that group's market or the absence of competitive rivalry. Ex ante it would, therefore, be expected that all firms would try to enter the most desirable group.

At the level of the individual firm, the asset stocks and organizational inertia resulting from the choices managers make create mobility barriers around groups of firms following similar strategies (Mascarenhas and Aaker, 1989). Group membership generally remains stable over time in many industries because these barriers foreclose easy movement to more desirable competitive positions. Although these barriers have often been compared to entry barriers (Bain, 1956; Caves and Porter, 1977), mobility barriers exist among competitors already in a marketplace with some degree of investment in a competitive posture. Investments in assets both tangible (plant and equipment) and intangible (name and reputation) and the uncertainty about a firm's ability to copy the successful formula of a competitor (Rumelt, 1984) contribute to the height of the mobility barriers which separate the groups. So, too, the establishment of standard operating procedures, bureaucracy and organizational culture may inhibit a firm's ability to change strategic groups. The mobility barriers may vary in height based on the extent to which firms outside a target group have to change their strategies in order to join the target group and the economic return which is expected to be gained by making the change. It is expected that the higher barriers surround the more profitable groups.

The variation in the desirability of different strategic groups in an industry (along with the associated mobility barriers) suggests that firms may follow a series of sequential steps in improving their competitive positions within an industry. Instead of attempting to enter an industry by initially entering the most desirable (and most protected) group, a firm may enter a group surrounded by lower mobility barriers. The firm then proceeds along a path through the industry, collecting assets, building competences and moving sequentially into more desirable groups (McGee and Thomas, 1990). Although firms at some point will often fail to progress further, the fact that such a progression exists suggests that strategic groupings may change over time either because firms may proactively change their strategy or because environmental discontinuities may disrupt the foundations on which the strategies of the various groups are built. However, the strategic group concept requires careful application and implementation. In succeeding sections we summarize the findings from current research studies and appraise the insights gained. We also evaluate the importance of the grouping concept and assess the directions in which it will be used in future analyses of competition and competitive strategy. We further provide examples drawn from the food processing and pharmaceutical industries which identify clearly the characteristics essential for an effective analysis of industry evolution, competition and dynamics.

# RESEARCH FINDINGS

In previous papers in the strategic management literature (McGee, 1985; McGee and Thomas, 1986, 1988; Thomas and Venkatraman, 1988) the authors have provided exhaustive reviews of the main studies in the field. Readers are therefore, referred to those sources, and to the more recent research of Cool and Schendel (1987, 1988), Fiegenbaum (1987), Fiegenbaum and Thomas (1990), Mascarenhas (1989) and McGee and Segal-Horn (1990).

Here we discuss the more important research patterns and research observations.

## Research Patterns

Certain clear patterns can be detected in existing research. First, many of the current studies could be described as "data driven" since they rely on analyses of dimensions drawn from well-known databases such as COMPUSTAT and Value Line. By defining groups in terms of "parts of strategies" using variables such as product lines (Hunt 1972), relative size (Porter 1973, 1979), product strategy (Oster, 1982) and financial strategy (Ryans and Wittink, 1985), there appears to be an *ad hoc* character attached to the development of those groups.

While these groups may be highly homogeneous in terms of the variables considered to develop them, they may not correspond to the competitive groups within the particular industry. For example, in the brewing industry studies (e.g. Schendel and Patton, 1978) the three groups are mainly defined around the geographical scope dimension and labelled as "national", "large regional", and "small regional". Such a classification could explain the intra-industry and intergroup differences in the average profitability levels (using the well-known "size effect" in industrial organization) but does not necessarily reflect the domain of a firm's competitive arena, which may be more important from a strategy perspective. This is because, in a given market area, it is conceivable that competing brands belong to "national" firms, "large regional" firms, and "small regional" firms who are all jockeying for a share of the market demand.

Therefore, the first important issue is to question whether the strategic groups identified in many research studies correspond to managers' conceptualizations of competitive groups in those industries. Clearly, in industries such as airlines (Ryans and Wittink, 1985), banking (Ramsler, 1982), brewing (Hatten and Schendel, 1977), and "white goods"/home appliances (Hunt, 1972), there appear to be well-established competitive classifications which can provide an additional test of the validity of empirically derived strategic groupings.

Second, research studies have concentrated upon industry settings such as manufacturing more than any other sector. Such studies include medical supply equipment (Howell and Frazier, 1983), paints (Dess and Davies, 1984), brewing (Hatten and Schendel, 1977; Hatten and Hatten, 1987), producer goods industries (Newman 1973, 1978), petroleum (Primeaux, 1985), and the home appliance industry (Hunt, 1972). Studies in the service sector including banking (Hayes *et al.*, 1983), insurance (Fiegenbaum, 1987), and airlines (Ryans and Wittink, 1985).

An analysis of strategic groups across different industry settings seems to indicate that the choice of industries appears to be based primarily on the extent to which the firms (within an industry) operate in one dominant business category. This enables researchers to discount problems of isolating data for a particular business from the overall portfolio of a diversified corporation. When primarily single-business industries (such as brewing or airlines) are studied, the strategy problem can essentially be cast in business strategy terms. However, in more complex industries the problem becomes more difficult.

When developing theory, strategy researchers must move away from research based upon choices of "convenient" industry settings towards studying firms which operate in multiple businesses. Given the increasing trend towards corporate diversification (Chandler, 1990), it is important to understand the strategic groups concept in the context of complex firms and complex industries. These typically involve diversified firms which compete across industry boundaries and often possess strong financial resources derived from operations in other business areas (McGee and Thomas, 1986, 1989).

Third, earlier work on strategic groups focused more upon *a priori* classifications ("rule of thumb" strategic mapping) than on empirical approaches (such as multivariate analysis) as bases for identifying strategic groups. Now that the empiricists have exhausted the data-driven route, there is a renewed focus upon understanding industries and mapping and interpreting strategic groups based upon better defined strategic dimensions (Porter, 1980; McGee and Thomas, 1989). It is now clear that empirical grouping analyses must be performed with care and certainly only after careful definition of strategic dimensions.

Further, there is much interest in using strategic groups to understand industry dynamics. For example, Oster (1982) examined dynamic aspects of strategic groups and concluded that there was a low level of movement between strategic groups and relatively stable group membership over time within the industries she studied. Mascarenhas (1989) and Fiegenbaum, Tang and Thomas (1990) found similarly low levels of mobility in the oil and insurance industries. Ramsler

(1982) used the strategic groups derived from the 100 largest non-US banks to predict the entry strategies adopted by banks in entering the US market. In the same vein, McGee and Segal-Horn (1990) predict the long-term dynamics in the European food-processing industry. Thus, the identification of strategic groups can lead both to predictions about future competitive behaviour and better understanding of current competitive behaviour.

## Research Observations

(1)  No industry is homogeneous: firm and group level strategies are important.

Most studies appear to have as their first (and, in some cases, the only) goal to establish that the chosen industry (or industries) is heterogeneous and that distinct groupings can be identified through clustering in terms of a set of appropriate strategic characteristics. The typical approach is as follows. Consider a particular industry (often defined in terms of national boundaries, usually the USA), identify a set of strategic dimensions, obtain data on those dimensions (either through objective, secondary sources or through perceptual measures provided by managers), employ one of the data reduction techniques, obtain a set of groupings, interpret them in the light of their scores along the dimensions used for the clustering procedure, and provide rather weak interpretations of the meaning of the groups for theory or practice.

Given the natural concern of industrial organization research to investigate the level of heterogeneity within an industry, we are not surprised that several studies have sought to demonstrate the existence of groups, i.e. "structures within structures". However, from a contemporary strategic management perspective, this may be a non-issue! Most of us at least implicitly subscribe to a view that firms differ in their strategies (Wernerfelt, 1984), but not to an extent that all are so unique that they cannot be sorted into homogeneous classes. Indeed, the notion of generic strategies (Miles and Snow, 1978; Porter, 1980) builds on this view. Hence, any empirical demonstration of the mere existence of some grouping within an industry is not a significant research result within strategic management unless the observed grouping structure can be related to the expected grouping structure through extant theory.

(2)  Industry boundaries are porous and "fuzzy", especially where globalization is taking place.

The second observation pertains to the definition of an "industry". Strategic groups researchers have defined their sample frames in terms of classical industry categories, largely limited to national boundaries. While this may have been acceptable in the past, it is now becoming increasingly evident that a global perspective on strategic groups research would enrich the research studies considerably (e.g. McGee and Segal-Horn, 1990). Defined in terms of the Standard Industrial Classification (SIC) scheme, the "industry" has been for a long time the generally accepted unit and level of analysis in industrial organization (Bain, 1956; Scherer, 1980). Yet even economists (Chamberlin, 1951; Robinson, 1956) have questioned the imprecision of the industry definition and the "fuzziness" of industry boundaries in economic environments characterized by product differentiation and technological change.

In general, given that strategic management is concerned with the efficient and effective process of alignment between the organization and its environment (Andrews, 1980; Venkatraman and Camillus, 1984), it is appropriate neither to be bound to an SIC scheme that mainly reflects product variations nor to one which limits the sample frame to national boundaries. It may be more appropriate to regard the concepts of market, industry, and nation as complementary and to adopt a more comprehensive definition of business and competition that captures variations in product, market, and technology (Abell, 1980) and also reflects competition in input markets, process (technology) and the more conventional notion of output-based competition in a global perspective (Hout, Porter and Rudden, 1982).

A move away from the constraint of industry boundaries is the use of the concept of "environmental types", which reflects patterns of competition across groups. This can be seen in the recent attempts to identify groups of firms (or business units) that are following "similar" strategies but are situated in environments that cut across the boundaries of industries. In this stream, the aim is to identify strategic taxonomies (akin to strategic groups) within a homogeneous environment (akin to an industry). This approach is useful for theory building, namely for evaluating strategy–performance relationships within and across different environmental profiles (see Hambrick, 1983, 1984; Miller and Friesen, 1978; Prescott, Kohli and Venkatraman, 1986).

(3)    There is no consistent pattern in strategic group characteristics.

There does not appear to be any consistent pattern in the characteristics of groups across the different studies reviewed here. In other words, the conceptualization of the characteristics of strategic groups varies significantly across the studies. We attribute this mainly to non-uniformity in the choices of variables used for the definition of groups. In some studies, the groups are developed on size differences only (for example Porter, 1979), others are based on geographical coverage (Hatten and Schendel, 1977; Schendel and Patton, 1978), while some others are based on specific features of the product market (for example Hayes, Spence and Marks, 1983). Thus one cannot meaningfully compare and aggregate the results across different studies.

Had the studies been anchored around a common theme of operationalizing strategy (such as Porter's generic types or Miles and Snow's types, or using a more precise definition of groups that reflect an asset-oriented set of strategy dimensions such as scope and resource deployment) it would have been possible systematically to see patterns across studies. We are not advocating the use of any one particular typology for all strategic groups studies, but, rather, we are in favour of relating the choice of strategy dimensions to previous studies so that a cumulative perspective can be brought to bear.

(4)    There is a lack of clarity in the description of groups.

The most disappointing observation in this review is that the extant studies do not provide strong evidence of "descriptive validity"—i.e. descriptions of the strategic groups in a way that establishes that groups are internally homogeneous and maximally different from other groups. Although there are no well-established criteria for describing the groups, it is generally accepted that the major characteristics are: (i) each group is composed of firms (or businesses) that follow similar strategies; (ii) firms within a group resemble one another more closely than they resemble firms outside the group; and (iii) firms within a group are more likely to respond similarly to a market opportunity (or threat). Support for the first two criteria may be provided through cluster analysis results. But the third criterion, which reflects an important theoretical issue, is usually not tested. However, no empirical research study has developed groups in such a way as to satisfy all the criteria. It is possible that when the groups are defined *a priori* through in-depth analysis of the industry, researchers might have taken these criteria into account, but empirical demonstration of them is lacking. The implication is that groups may reflect nothing more than statistical homogeneity, at best. This requires a clearer articulation of the theoretical reasons for the existence of groups that are grounded in the nature of competition within the domain (see Tang and Thomas, 1991).

(5)    There is only weak evidence of performance variations across groups.

A complementary theme to "descriptive validity" is that of "predictive validity", namely the use of the structure of the groups to predict systematically an external criterion such as performance. Performance is of central concern in strategic management for two reasons. First, if distinct groups show statistically significant variations in performance, the results support the theory of performance variations attributable to strategy. Second, if performance differences do not exist, then they either imply a rejection of the hypothesis of a structure–performance linkage (following industrial organization) or support the view that alternative "generic" strategies with equal performance effects are operative.

The latter implication is a serious one and needs to be backed with a clear articulation of the reasons for the observance of equally effective (but different) strategies (i.e. the well-known equifinality principle). If adequate theoretical reasoning cannot be brought to bear in favour of equifinality, the rejection of the performance differences hypothesis implies that attention should be focused on "within group" differences in performance, and hence on the differential set of skills and assets of the different players. Prahalad and Hamel (1990) have coined the term "core competences" to characterize the unique resource bundles owned by different corporate entities.

Within existing research on performance differences, two patterns are evident. One is that many studies have indeed observed some differences across groups. Thus some preliminary support for the predictive validity of group structures is available. The other pattern—perhaps a more important one—is that performance is treated in the somewhat narrow terms of profitability as opposed to a broader conceptualization to include both financial and operational measures. Given that performance measurement is a thorny issue in strategic management (Venkatraman and Ramanujam, 1986), it is important that multiple measures of performance are incorporated into strategic groups analysis. Thus, measures and key trade-off issues can be evaluated within a simultaneous equation framework. It is therefore encouraging to note that recently more strategic groups studies are reflecting the use of multiple performance measures (e.g. Dess and Davies, 1984) as well as risk-adjusted measures (see Cool, 1985; Fiegenbaum, 1987). Given that performance is not a unitary concept, it needs to be recognized that the strongest support for the predictive validity of strategic groups will only be found through the use of multiple indices of performance reflecting both financial and operational criteria (e.g. Cool and Schendel, 1987; Fiegenbaum and Thomas, 1990).

# PROGNOSIS AND FUTURE DIRECTIONS

## Prognosis

One main area of confusion in current literature is the linkage between strategic groups and the strategic management of firms (the view of the firm as a unique bundle of strategic resources). For this reason, it is important to restate the main theoretical explanations and uses advanced for the strategic groups concept.

Porter (1979) provides three main explanations for the formation of strategic groups:

(1)   Investments in building mobility barriers are risky and firms have different risk-aversion postures; this leads to different groups defined in terms of the R&D and advertising outlays as defensive mobility barriers.
(2)   Business units which differ in their relation to a parent company may differ in goals in ways that lead to strategy differences.
(3)   Historical development of an industry (nature of demand, production

technology, product characteristics, etc.) bestows differential advantages/ disadvantages on firms.

A fourth possible explanation, relegated by Porter (1979, p. 217) to a footnote, is exogenous causes such as technological change:

> Changes in the structure of the industry can either facilitate group formation, or work to homogenise groups. For example, technological change or changes in buyer behaviour can shift industry boundaries bringing entirely new strategic groups into play in the industry by increasing or decreasing product substitutability and hence shifting relevant industry boundaries.

By occupying an intermediate level of analysis between firms and industry, strategic groups are helpful for identifying issues about an organization's competitive position (e.g. Who are the direct competitors? What are the competitive forces? What are the distinctive competitive assets?). Indeed, the key to understanding industry evolution lies in the ways in which firms change their asset structures, in other words, the ways in which mobility barriers change and redefine the strategic groups thus enabling predictions about future industry evolution to be advanced.

As noted by Hatten and Hatten (1987, p. 329), strategic groups provide potentially powerful tools in the armory of the strategic analyst in the following areas:

(1) Groups can be used to preserve information characterizing individual firms which is typically lost in industry studies using averaged and aggregated data.

(2) Because groups allow us to investigate multiple firms concurrently, they allow us to assess the effectiveness of their strategic actions over a wider range of variation than a single firm's experience affords.

(3) Group analysis can be used to summarize information to bring key dimensions into high relief, for example to facilitate an assessment of the consequences of a collective movement by many firms into similar competitive postures or to verify similarities of strategic direction across an industry.

Yet, many questions remain concerning the overall role of strategic groups and firm linkages in strategic management research. It is argued here that, at a minimum, the following issues should be addressed.

## Suggested Directions

These have been divided for ease of exposition into methodological and theoretical issues.

## Methodological issues

### (1)   Explicit rationale for expected groupings

An important area for future theorizing pertains to the development of a strong, explicit rationale for expected groupings. Given any data matrix (a set of firms or businesses along a set of variables), it is not difficult for numerical taxonomic methods to derive statistically significant groupings. Thus, the power of any research study is not determined by a demonstration of a set of strategic groups, but rather through their interpretation in terms of the theory that guided the grouping exercise. Given that the demonstration of the heterogeneous nature of industry is not the prime focus, there should be clear reasons for expecting groupings. Thus the focus should be on deductive theorizing about the number of groups and their differential characteristics rather than simply on the exploratory derivation of any set of groups.

This issue is particularly significant given the inherent bias in cluster analytical methods in favour of uncovering groups. If we consider cluster analysis, for example, several methods are available for evaluating the "number of clusters" (Milligan and Cooper, 1985). But they typically focus on the evaluation of the superiority of an $n1$-cluster solution over an $n2$-cluster solution. In other words, they provide a statistical indication of the superiority of a three-cluster solution over an alternative five-cluster solution. However, they are limited in providing support for the critical test of assessing the appropriateness of an $n1$-or an $n2$-cluster solution against a zero-cluster solution.

We recognize that the *ex ante* specification of the criteria for the grouping structure is a difficult but challenging task. Its challenge is derived from the fact that cluster analytic methods should not be the main route for theory development, especially as the field matures. While exploratory derivation of cluster analytic-based strategic groups is acceptable in pioneering studies, we feel that it is time to adopt a confirmatory mode. Researchers should recognize the value of the multidisciplinary perspective of strategic management in theorizing about strategic groups. For example, theories from industrial organization may provide useful approaches for understanding market structure and thereby posit reasons for expecting heterogeneity. Further marketing concepts related to product-market definition, customer needs and wants as well as choice preference and buyer behaviour may provide insights into the existence or absence of groups. similarly, the literature on organization theory and administrative sciences provides useful pointers in relation to the differences in organization structure and management systems as well as organizational culture issues that may have close relationships to strategic choices and actions.

In a somewhat different role, population ecology and notions of organizational species (McKelvey, 1978) provide useful pointers and arguments as to why groups form and the correlates of stability over time. The challenge from a strategic management perspective is the reconciliation of these somewhat competing viewpoints towards an explicit rationale that can be used as the starting point for the future generation of research studies. If this is accomplished, the future research can examine not only the evidence of groups at a single point in time but also the evolution of groups over time.

*(2)   Richer operationalization of strategy*
Strategic groups research is handicapped by inadequate attention to operationalization and measurement issues. Most studies have used surrogates like size to reflect strategy (see Hunt, 1972; Newman 1978; Porter, 1979) or finance (e.g. Baird and Sudharsan, 1983). If we subscribe to a view that the strategy concept is truly integrative and extends beyond that of a single functional area, then we should seek to develop operationalizations that reflect the interrelationships among the functional strategies rather than the individual functional strategies *per se*

By richer operationalizations we mean those that are powerful enough to reflect the complexities of the competitive situation, that is, by defining strategies (and strategic groups) in terms of firm-level investments in asset structures and distinctive competences (Rumelt, 1984; McGee and Thomas, 1989). A welcome trend is seen in the strategic groups studies by Cool (1985), Fiegenbaum (1987) and Fombrun and Zajac (1987). It is well accepted that the concept of strategy is complex and it is naive to expect that the complexities can be captured using simplistic schemes without sacrificing properties of validity and reliability. Our call for a richer and systematic operationalization of strategy for strategic group development is parallel to McKelvey's (1978) call for development of organization types using multiple dimensions, and to Hambrick's (1984) as well as Miller and Friesen's call for the development of strategy gestalts. Our call also builds on Venkatraman and Grants's (1986) discussion calling for improvements in the measurement of strategy in general.

*(3)   Enlarge the sample frame across national borders*
This stream of research has been marked by its limitation to examination of strategic groups within particular national boundaries. This may be appropriate if the competition is itself limited in this way, but given the increasing trend towards globalization of markets, future research should evaluate the appropriateness of defining the sample frame to include multiple nations within one study. Thus, if the automotive market is truly international with participants organized on a global basis, then a rich study of strategic groups would have to focus on the entire marketplace rather than conduct separate studies of US strategic groups, UK strategic groups, etc. Such a direction would lead to the identification of strategy differences across countries as well as shedding light on multipoint global competition.

### Theoretical issues

*(1)    View strategic groups as a means towards the end*

Our last and perhaps the most important suggestion is to view the formation of strategic groups as a means towards addressing a set of important strategy research questions (Fiegenbaum, 1987). In industrial organization, strategic groups serve to demonstrate the heterogeneous nature of an industry and to explain intra-industry variations in performance. In strategic management research, its role should be to offer insights into important questions and issues that *may not otherwise* be forthcoming (Ghazanfar, 1984; Steffens, 1987).

Possible sets of issues that can be framed within a strategic groups perspective are:

(a)    *Determinants of grouping structure.* It is interesting that very little work has been done to explore the question of the formation of groups, and more importantly to identify the key determinants for the structure of strategic groups. This issue needs to be addressed in a manner that goes beyond the industrial organization explanation and needs to incorporate relevant concepts from disciplines such as marketing, organization theory, and population ecology. If we believe that the concept of strategic groups is more than intra-industry variation in conduct but truly reflects both strategic behaviours and strategic choices, then these issues need to be addressed systematically in the context of a strategic theory of the firm (Rumelt, 1984). Otherwise, there is a real danger that strategic groups may become nothing more than an economic or analytical construct (see also Tang and Thomas, 1991).

(b)    *Stability of grouping structure.* Little is known about the stability of the structure (but see Fiegenbaum, 1987). We define stability in two ways. One pertains to stability across variations in the dimensions used to develop the structure of strategic groups. For example, what would happen to the groups if we added or subtracted a strategy variable used for constructing the groups? The other is temporal stability. What determines the stability of groups over time? What external and internal factors (idiosyncratic to the sample frame) might change the structure significantly? What is the relationship between movement of firms across groups and performance changes?

(c)    *Predictive ability of group structure.* It is essential that the groups be used to predict either further strategic behaviour and/or performance, failing which the results have minimal use.

# CRITERIA FOR AN EFFECTIVE DESIGN OF A STRATEGIC GROUP STUDY

In addition to the suggestions above, we offer what we believe to be an important set of criteria for designing future studies in this area. We do not expect that all the criteria will be satisfied in every design but we offer them as a set of broad guidelines.

## Justification of the Sample Frame

An SIC-based industry definition (restricted to a single country) that has routinely served to demarcate the sample domain in previous studies should not be implicitly accepted. The concept of the business strategy level—which focuses on competitive superiority in a marketplace—is *not* isomorphic with the definition of product-based industry boundaries (Porter, 1980). For instance, the boundaries between the various financial services industries have blurred in recent years due to technological, regulatory, and global factors. Consequently, the justification of the sample frame emerges as an important design criterion.

## Operationalization of Strategy

Particular care must be taken to ensure that the operationalization of strategy en route to identification of the group structures covers the following issues:

(a) It matches the key bases of competition or core competences in the marketplace (i.e. key success factors that form the basis for effective strategy development and which can be confirmed by industry experts)
(b) It bears a strong relationship to some of the common theoretical discussions on strategy types so that a cumulative perspective can be developed
(c) It follows basic measurement criteria of reliability, validity, and replicability

A move in this direction would contribute greatly to the usefulness of strategic groups for theory building.

## Theoretical Anchors

Any study should be anchored in theoretical positions that reflect the reasons for the expected dimensions of groups. We do not advocate the complete abandonment of exploratory data-driven analyses. However, we do believe that it is necessary to pay particular attention to prior theorizing as well as *post hoc* reconciliation of the discovered groupings with extant work. In the absence of theoretical frameworks (in this area of research as well as elsewhere) we could be empirically demonstrating a set of findings without sound reasoning as to why they occurred in that particular form!

## Data-Analytic Issues

We do not intend to provide any primer on multivariate statistical methods and issues except to note that internal stability of the cluster-analytic results is essential. Since cluster analysis is an exploratory data-analytic technique, it is important to be particularly sensitive to issues such as the number of clusters and the need to cross-validate the solution within subsample analyses. A related note is the possibility of moving towards confirmatory approaches (including structural equation models) to test *a priori* structure.

## Interpretation of Groups

Interpretability concerns whether the strategic groups observed make sense to strategists and other interested parties. This can be achieved at two levels—one through an evaluation of the dimensions used to develop groupings by the concerned managers or industry experts, and the other through an assessment of the output, namely the group configuration observed. We do not advocate any particular approach at this stage, as long as some attempt is made to incorporate managerial perceptions. Too often, the research has been characterized by "far-removed" secondary analysis of the observed groups.

## Link to an External Criterion

We have already stressed the need to use strategic groups as a starting point in strategy research rather than as an end in itself. Thus, it is important to position the identification of strategic groups into a larger strategy issue to which the group configuration makes a significant input. We suggest two possibilities. One is the use of performance measures (in their multidimensional form) to discern strategy–performance and structure–performance links (see Venkatraman and Ramanujam, 1986, for a recent discussion on measurement of performance issues in relation to strategy research). The other candidate is future strategic behavior that can be predicted from the group composition. Here, one should be able to establish that the group configuration serves to condition the repertoire of possible future behaviours.

Our expectation is that an explicit consideration of these criteria would go a long way in enhancing the quality and usefulness of strategic groups research. Before summarizing our conclusions, we thought it appropriate to provide examples of the types of future intra-industry studies which will advance understanding of industry dynamics and evolution of competition.

# STRATEGIC GROUPS, COMPETITIVE EVOLUTION, AND INDUSTRY DYNAMICS

A major theme of this chapter is that strategic groups be applied to problems of real significance as opposed to questions of mere classification and taxonomy. One such real problem is the understanding of the nature of change in industries and the process by which it takes place. Strategic groups ideas can have a major role in exploring the dynamics of industries in terms of understanding structure changes and ensuing changes in competitive conditions in regard to both prior changes in asset structures and key competences of firms. This section gives an overview of two recent studies in which a strategic groups methodology has been used to this purpose.

One study concerns the development of the competitive positions of European firms in the US pharmaceutical market (Bogner and Thomas, 1991). The second discusses the prospective development of the food processing industry in Europe following the development of the European Single Market (McGee and Segal-Horn, 1990, 1991). An explicit strategic groups approach is used in each case although the underlying economics of the two industries is fundamentally different.

## The Pharmaceutical Industry

The pharmaceuticals analysis looks at competition in the US pharmaceutical market between the years 1969 and 1988. It focuses on the external environmental events which disrupted existing patterns of intra-industry competition and on the ensuing patterns of competition that then developed. In particular, it looks at the position of European firms in the strategic groups identified, how those competitive positions changed over time and suggests a rationale for the variations in competitive strategies between firms based on differences in their accumulated asset structures. The strategic groups were defined in terms of variables covering (i) the scope and breadth of market posture (including product market scope, new drugs introduced, and relative measures of new product development), and (ii) the nature of R&D (including short-term and longer-term measures of R&D spending and concentration of R&D by research classes).

An historical analysis of the industry enabled the identification of four periods of stability with three intervening breaks. A grouping analysis was conducted for each stable period revealing four distinct strategic groups. A statistical analysis of each break identified which of the grouping variables "caused" the breaks in each of the four stable periods. Different variables (i.e. assets) can be seen to dominate the ensuing periods of stability following a break in the established order. The analysis then goes on to show how the European firms moved across the groups as their US strategies evolved and as they became better able to deploy their European-based assets in the US market. The results show how European firms are pursuing very different global strategies, but also evident is the way in which these reflect underlying firm asset stocks and key competences. The latter periods show the role of merger and acquisition in enabling firms of modest size and strength to develop the size necessary to compete with the largest firms. The authors comment in conclusion:

> First, firms enter and improve competitive position in the market in an established sequence (of moves through strategic groups). Second, firms' upward movement through strategic space is limited by the scope and strategic asset structure of the multi-national parent.

## The Food Processing Industry

The papers on the European food processing industry were basically concerned with the possible emergence of a pan-European food industry from the existing mosaic of separate nationally focused industries, i.e. a transnational emerging from a multidomestic structure. This possibility was mooted in the context of the single European Act in 1987, which was expected to reduce the costs of access to separate European markets and along with expectations about increasing homogeneity of consumers across Europe constituted external triggers for structural change.

The approach to this was to develop a model of "strategic space" onto which the prospective movements of firms could be mapped. An historical overview enabled the identification of periods of stability and the conditions causing breaks between periods. On the basis of this history key variables were identified as the basis for strategic group identification. These were market scope (territories covered), marketing intensity and brand strength, manufacturing focus, and R&D intensity (the latter two were not statistically validated). These were used to identify the strategic group configuration in 1990, enabling the identification of at least four distinct groupings. However, the real strength of the configuration lay in the specification of the mobility barriers between the groups. The strategic space idea is the converse of the strategic group, i.e. why is there no group present in a particular location on the $n$-dimensional map. The first possible answer is that some spaces are currently infeasible and the asset structures implied by that space are competitively dominated by other asset structures. The second possible answer is that some spaces have never been entered because the construction of the implied assets was not thought to be competitively viable. This second insight allowed the analysis of certain empty spaces to suggest that certain assets could technically be constructed (e.g. European marketing systems and brands) and that changing market conditions might yield a payoff for those new asset structures. Thus the strategic groups/space analysis allowed the juxtaposition of a changing market situation in Europe with a lowering of mobility barriers between existing groups and the empty spaces. The conclusion drawn is that certain kinds of new asset structures of firms are very likely to be constructed and that these will fall into two or three key new groups. The processes by which this might happen can be identified, including a wave of mergers and acquisitions. The consequences for competition both in the transition period and for a period of subsequent stability can be analysed, although the time period over which the transition will take place could not be identified. The analysis is distinctive in that it is almost entirely prospective in character, laying out a methodology for analysing future change in the industry. The authors conclude:

> First, two major new strategies are ... likely to emerge, the pan-European own label supplier and the pan-European brander. Second, the strategic space analysis tells us something about the pathways to achieving these positions. Third, it also tells us something about the nature of competition both en route and in the new structure. This approach does not tell us how long the process of change will take, nor does it say who will be the winners and losers. It does, however, say a great deal about the characteristics of the winners and losers.

## Common Features

There are a number of common features in these two papers which, we argue, can be extended to other studies of dynamics. The *first* is the interpretation of industry history in terms of periods of relative stability punctuated by external disturbances or triggers which cause realignments and restructuring. Eventually there is a transition into another period of stability within which firms compete within well-understood rules and assumptions. The periods of stability enable the identification of stable strategies and therefore stable groups. The *second* commonality is the use of the experience and data of these stable periods to identify the dimensions of the groups in contrast to the *ad hoc* theorizing from first principles which has marked so much analysis hitherto. The pharmaceutical study was particularly explicit in using statistical procedures on objective data whereas the food study relied more on a synthesis of a wide range of industry material and experience. The *third* feature is the careful definition of strategic groups dimensions according to asset and resource characteristics. The essence of groups is the use of asset "inputs" rather than "output" variables like performance. Thus, product and market scope variables, research intensity, and economies of scope variables are variables of direct interest. *Fourthly*, the dimensions are validated against a longer-run historical perspective in order to assess the ways in which change is rooted in long-term accretion of tangible and intangible assets. This is an explicitly theoretical check on data-driven variables to avoid errors arising from misspecification of the time-frames of recent history.

The *fifth* feature is that the analysis allows the emergence of multiple groups showing very diverse strategic approaches. This confirms the utility of a strategic

group approach in "fuzzy" industry sets where boundaries can be very difficult
to draw. With this approach the boundaries are set by the strategies themselves
and the interaction within groups and between unlike groups can then be
analysed in terms of the alternative applications in the marketplace of their asset
sets. This approach also has the merit of providing an explicit definition of the
mobility barriers (as long as the dimensions have been identified correctly, see
two previous sections). Thus the asset investments required for change can be
directly identified. The pharmaceutical study shows this *ex post*, and the food
study *ex ante*, but the procedure is identical. Therefore, *six*, the analysis of
mobility becomes possible. The pharmaceutical study tracks the shifts across
groups by European firms as they build up strength to compete in the US market.
The food study uses the idea of feasible strategic space to show areas where new
groups can develop given the external triggers for change. Both show the role of
mergers and acquisitions, pharmaceuticals in retrospect (with payoffs yet to
come), food in seeing them as a key process in restructuring the asset sets. The
difference in the two studies here lies in the evolutionary nature of the
pharmaceuticals industry compared to possible revolutionary changes taking
place in food.

A further, *seventh*, similarity is the analysis of a piece of the industry against a
global context. Thus, pharmaceuticals shows the evolution of European firms in
the US market but the backdrop is the global industry. The food study looks only
at Europe but acknowledges the importance of the changing global context. In
other words, a strategic groups approach does not necessarily require a full
specification of the complete model in order to analyse the phenomena of interest
as long as the interactions between the partial and the full model can be captured
in the understanding of how the asset structures operate in the market. However,
both studies do need to provide a rather fuller description of the global context in
order to fully defend this proposition.

The payoff to both studies is:

(1)    A richer interpretation of the current market structures and the interaction
       of asset structures and key competences with the conduct of intra-industry
       competition;
(2)    A framework for analysing change which is replicable both over time and
       across industries;
(3)    A language for interpreting change in terms of changes in asset structures
       of firms (i.e. their strategies) and the ensuing effects on competition. In this
       approach change is analysed in terms of the inputs (assets) which lead
       eventually to outputs (nature of competition). This is a substantial change
       from the *ad hoc* rapportage of changes in competitive conditions.

# SUMMARY AND CONCLUSIONS

Strategic groups pose a number of interesting research challenges. The first to be explored, and the most obvious one, is the contribution it makes to the market structure–performance debate. Of more promise are other areas: the existence and evolution of group structures and their relationship to firms' asset investments and the evolution of industries, their contribution to the theory of entry in terms of the queue of potential entrants and the alternative entry paths, the patterns of rivalry in oligopolistic markets, and our understanding of the growth and evolutionary patterns of firms and industries, particularly in increasingly global markets as characterized by our food industry and pharmaceuticals examples.

The emergence of the strategic groups concept and the increasing research attention being paid to the boundary areas between industrial organization, strategic marketing, administrative behaviour, and strategic management suggests closer attention to the firm as the unit of analysis (Rumelt, 1984; Seth and Thomas, 1991). The difficulty of applying rigorous research techniques in the area of strategic decision-making is extreme. The problems of controlling for exogenous variables, the lack of comparability among the units of analysis, and the disparate nature of these units together with the changing nature of the opportunity sets and the environment generally restrict the ability of researchers to make causal connections between sets of variables. All these problems are compounded by the lack of suitable databases for research. There may well be a continuing trend towards in-depth studies of firms and their industry settings in an attempt to apply control procedures to fewer variables and to explore the character and texture of strategic choices in ways impossible for statistical analysis to achieve. The effect of strategic groups is to restore strategic decisions to the centre of the structure and performance arena and to reemphasize the firm as an important unit of analysis.

# NOTE

This chapter draws strongly from the authors' previous research papers and reviews in the field, particularly McGee (1985), McGee and Thomas (1986, 1989), Thomas and Venkatraman (1988) and Fiegenbaum and Thomas (1990). Its structure, however reflects the authors' current views on the subject.

# REFERENCES

Abell, D. F. (1980) *Defining the Business*. Prentice-Hall, Englewood Cliffs, NJ.
Andrews, K. R. (1980) *The Concept of Corporate Strategy*. Irwin, Homewood, Illinois.

Bain, J. S. (1956) *Barriers to New Competition.* Harvard University Press, Boston.

Baird, I. S. and Sudharsan, D. (1983) Strategic groups: A three mode factory analysis of some measures of financial risk. Working Paper 931, University of Illinois at Urbana-Champaign.

Bogner, W. C. and Thomas, H. (1991) Competitive positions of European firms in the US pharmaceutical market. Paper given at the Academy of International Business Annual Meeting, October 17–20.

Caves, R. and Porter, M. (1977) From entry barriers to mobility barriers. *Quarterly Journal of Economics,* '91.

Chamberlin, E. H. (1991) Monopolistic competition revisited. *Economica,* 343–362.

Chandler, A. D. (1990) The enduring logic of industrial success. *Harvard Business Review,* March–April, 130–140.

Cool, K. O. (1985) Strategic group formation and strategic group shifts: A longitudinal analysis of the US pharmaceutical industry 1963–82. Unpublished doctoral dissertation, Purdue University.

Cool, K. O. and Schendel, D. E. (1987) Strategic group formation and performance: US pharmaceutical industry 1963–82. *Management Science,* 33, 1102–1124.

Cool, K. O. and Schendel, D. (1988) Performance differences among strategic group members. *Strategic Management Journal,* 9, 207–223.

Dess, G. G. and Davis, P. S. (1984) Porter's (1980) generic strategies as determinants of strategic group membership and organisational performance. *Academy of Management Journal,* 27, 467–488.

Fiegenbaum, A. (1987) Dynamic aspects of strategic groups and competitive strategy: Concepts and empirical examination in the insurance industry. Doctoral dissertation, University of Illinois at Urbana-Champaign.

Fiegenbaum, A. and Thomas, H. (1990) Strategic groups and performance: The US insurance industry 1980–84. *Strategic Management Journal,* 11, 197–215.

Fiegenbaum, A., Tang, M. J. and Thomas, H. (1990) Strategic time periods and strategic group research: Concepts and an empirical example. *Journal of Management Studies,* 27, 133–148.

Fombrun, C. and Zajac, E. (1987) Structural and perceptual influences on intra-industry stratification. *Academy of Management Journal,* 30(1), 33–50.

Galbraith, J. R. (1973) *Designing Complex Organisations.* Addison-Wesley, Reading, Mass.

Ghazanfar, A. (1984) An analysis of competition in the reprographics industry in the United Kingdom 1980–1981. Unpublished doctoral dissertation, University of London.

Hambrick, D. C. (1983) An empirical typology of mature industrial product environments. *Academy of Management Journal,* 26, 213–220.

Hambrick, D. C. (1984) Taxonomic approaches to studying strategy: Some conceptual and methodological issues. *Journal of Management Studies,* 10, 27–41.

Hatten, K. J. and Hatten, M. L. (1987) Strategic groups, asymmetrical mobility barriers and contestability. *Strategic Management Journal,* 8 (4), 329–343.

Hatten, K. J. and Schendel, D. E. (1977) Heterogeneity within an industry: Firm conduct in the US brewing industry 1952–71. *Journal of Industrial Economics,* 26, 97–113.

Hayes, S. M., Spence, A. M. and Marks, D. V. P. (1983). *Competition in the Investment Banking Industry.* Harvard University Press, Boston.

Hout, T., Porter, M. E. and Rudden, E. (1982) How global companies win out. *Harvard Business Review*, September–October, 98–108.

Howell, R. D. and Frazier, G. L. (1983) Business definition and performance. *Journal of Marketing*, 47, Spring, 59–67.

Hunt, M. (1972) Competition in the major home appliance industry, 1960–70. Unpublished doctoral dissertation, Harvard University.

Mascarenhas, B. (1989) Strategic group dynamics. *Academy of Management Journal*, 32, 333–352.

Mascarenhas, B. and Aaker, D. A. (1989) Mobility barriers and strategic groups. *Strategic Management Journal*, 8 (5), 475–486.

McGee, J. (1985) Strategic groups: A useful linkage between industry structure and strategic management. In *Strategic Marketing and Management* (H. Thomas and D. M. Gardner, Eds). Wiley, Chichester.

McGee, J. and Segal-Horn, S. (1990) Strategic space and industry dynamics: The implications for international marketing strategy. *Journal of Marketing Management*, 6 (3), 175–193.

McGee, J. and Segal-Horn, S. (1991) Will there be a European food processing industry? In *Europe and the Multinationals* (S. Young and J. Hamill, Eds). Edward Elgar Publishing.

McGee, J. and Thomas, H. (1986) Strategic groups: Theory, research and taxonomy. *Strategic Management Journal*, 7 (2), 141–160.

McGee, J. and Thomas, H. (1988) Making sense of complex industries. In *Strategies in Global Competition* (N. Hood and J. E. Vahlne, Eds). Routledge, Kegan & Paul, London.

McGee, J. and Thomas, H. (1989) Strategic groups: A further comment. *Strategic Management Journal*, 10 (1), 105–107.

McGee, J. and Thomas, H. (1990) Analysis of sequential entry paths: Entry theory, technological change and industry dynamics, unpublished (under review).

McKelvey, B. (1978) Organisational systematics: Taxonomic lessons from biology. *Management Science*, 24, 921–933.

Miles, R. E. and Snow, C. C. (1978) *Organisational Strategy, Structure and Process*. McGraw-Hill, New York.

Miller, D. and Friesen, P. H. (1978) Archetypes of strategy formulation. *Management Science*, 24, 921–933.

Milligan, G. W. and Cooper, M. C. (1985) An examination of procedures for determining the number of clusters in a data set. *Psychometrika*, 30, 159–179.

Newman, H. H. (1973) Strategic groups and the structure–performance relationship: A study with respect to the chemical process industries. Unpublished doctoral dissertation, Harvard University.

Newman, H. H. (1978) Strategic groups and the structure-performance relationship. *Review of Economics and Statistics*, 60, 417–427.

Oster, S. (1982) Intra-industry structure and the ease of industry change. *Review of Economics and Statistics*, 64, August.

Penrose, E. (1959) *The Theory of the Growth of the Firm*. Basil Blackwell, Oxford.

Porter, M. E. (1979) The structure within industries and company performance. *Review of Economics and Statistics*, 61, 214–227.

Porter, M. E. (1980) *Competitive Strategy*. Free Press, New York.

Porter, M. E. (1986) *Competition in Global Industries*. Harvard Business School Press, Boston.

Prahalad, C. K. and Hamel, G. (1990) The core competence of the corporation. *Harvard Business Review*, May–June, 79–94.

Prescott, J. E., Kohli, A. K. and Venkatraman, N. (1986) The market share profitability relationship: An empirical assessment of assertions and contradictions. *Strategic Management Journal*, 7, 377–394.

Primeaux, W. J. (1985) A method for determining strategic groups and life cycle stages of an industry. In *Strategic Marketing and Management* (H. Thomas and D. M. Gardner, Eds). Wiley, Chichester.

Ramsler, M. (1982) Strategic groups and foreign market entry in global banking competition. Unpublished doctoral dissertation, Harvard University.

Robinson, J. (1956) The industry and the market. *Economic Journal*, 66, 360–361.

Rumelt, R. (1984) Towards a strategic theory of the firm. In *Competitive Strategic Management* (R. B. Lamb, Ed.). Prentice-Hall, Englewood Cliffs, NJ, pp. 566–570.

Ryans, A. B. and Wittink, D. R. (1985) Security returns as a basis for estimating the competitive structure of an industry. In *Strategic Marketing and Management* (H. Thomas and D. M. Gardner, Eds). Wiley, Chichester.

Schendel, D. and Patton G. R. (1978) A simultaneous equation model of corporate strategy. *Management Science*, 24, 1611–1621.

Scherer, F. M. (1980) *Industrial Market Structure and Economic Performance*. Rand-McNally, Chicago, Ill.

Seth, A. and Thomas, H. (1991) Theories of the firm: Implications for strategy research. *Journal of Management Studies*, forthcoming.

Steffens, J. (1987) Entry behaviour and competition in the evolution of the United States personal computer industry. Unpublished doctoral dissertation, University of London.

Tang, M. J. and Thomas, H. (1991) The concept of strategic groups: Theoretical construct or analytical convenience. *Managerial and Decision Economics*, forthcoming.

Thomas, H. and Venkatraman, N. (1988) Research on strategic groups: Progress and prognosis. *Journal of Management Studies*, 25(6), 537–556.

Venkatraman, N. and Camillus, V. C. (1984) Exploring the concept of "Fit" in strategy research. *Academy of Management Review*, 9, 513–525.

Venkatraman, N. and Grant, J. H. (1986) Construct measurement in organisational strategy research: A critique and proposal. *Academy of Management Review*, 11, 71–87.

Venkatraman, N. and Ramanujam, V. (1986) Measurement of business performance in strategy research: A comparison of approaches. *Academy of Management Review*, 11, 801–814.

Wernerfelt, B. (1984) A resource based view of the firm. *Strategic Management Journal*, 5 (2), 171–188.

# 5

# TRENDS IN DATA COLLECTION AND ANALYSIS: A NEW APPROACH TO THE COLLECTION OF GLOBAL INFORMATION

President, SIS International

## INTRODUCTION

With the rapidly changing political and economic events worldwide, research executives are currently faced with the need for translated, synthesized and analyzed information from the various countries throughout the world. As a result of this "new world order", several companies will plan to expand the marketing of their products and services. Consequently, they will have a need for the collection of published information as well as the need to collect quantitative data. During the nineties, senior management will seek answers to specific questions, such as "Is the Eastern European consumer ready for X, Y, or Z product?" rather than reading large market research reports which do not specifically answer their questions.

On a global basis, there are several obstacles to the collection of published information (e.g. from newspapers, the media and journals). Following a detailed discussion of these obstacles, this chapter discusses a methodology for the scanning, synthesis, translation and analysis of published information. Within this methodology, the chapter is organized into eight parts as follows:

Part 1   Obstacles to the collection of published information on a global basis
Part 2   The solution: the need for ongoing tracking systems for published information
Part 3   How to define your published information needs
Part 4   Sources of international business intelligence
Part 5   Design of the database
Part 6   Internal staffing versus outsourcing
Part 7   Determining the cost/benefits of the system
Part 8   Strategic importance of these systems to the unification of Europe

The chapter concludes with a discussion of how international research managers will experience an increasing need for market trend, competitive intelligence and new product activity information as new trade agreements evolve within and outside of the European continent. It also includes a discussion of research needs for Eastern Europe. In summary, the chapter focuses on the development of new cost-efficient systems to process this information, rather than utilizing older labor-intensive methods. It provides readers with a "how to" develop these systems along with the specifics for costs and staffing.

## PART 1: OBSTACLES TO THE COLLECTION OF PUBLISHED INFORMATION ON A GLOBAL BASIS

During the past year, we have seen a dramatic change in worldwide political and economic events. With the eruption of the Gulf crisis, the demise of communism and the liberation of several Eastern Bloc countries, the demand for access to credible worldwide business and political information has increased. European research professionals are now asking themselves: "How can I provide management with accurate and timely answers to their international information requests?"

Each country has a wealth of information or business intelligence which is reported in their daily newspapers, general business journals and various industry and market publications. The challenge is to capture this information on a timely basis, translate the information, and synthesize and digest the information which can be used for market intelligence or research briefs, newsletters or reports.

## THE LANGUAGE BARRIER

First and foremost, research professionals, regardless of the country in which they are located, will be faced with language barriers throughout the world. While

English is becoming the accepted language for business throughout Western Europe, the research professional is faced with the challenge of capturing information from the following worldwide geographical regions:

USA and Canada
Western Europe (including Scandinavian countries)
Eastern Europe
USSR
Mexico, Latin America, South America
Middle East
Far East
Australia
Africa

Even within these geographical regions, the diversity of languages can be complex, such as in Western Europe. This challenges the research professional to either increase his or her knowledge and/or fluency in other foreign languages or to locate information providers and/or commercial database vendors who offer translated information. This chapter will focus on a methodology from which research professionals can develop their own system to track international published sources.

## USA and Canada

The USA has a sophisticated, if not mature, market offering of business and technical commercial databases. Both Japan and Western Europe are rapidly following us with the recent development of commercial database offerings during the past three–five years. Fortunately for the USA or English user, many of these databases are translated into English for access using English commands.

In Western Europe, some databases do exist in specific languages (e.g. German). As the software technology improves, we will expect that these databases will be able to be translated into the local language of the users. Various publishers of international directories are searching to locate the local commercial databases available for access and it is anticipated that more of these global database directories will be published as the world moves toward a global economy.

## Western Europe

Similar to the USA, Great Britain has a sophisticated market for commercial databases (both scientific and business). With the unification of Europe by 1992, however, the challenge is to develop databases which capture and report the local business and scientific information from each of the countries and then synthesize and digest the information into a structure which can offer the information as a Western European segment.

Within the EEC, select countries have sophisticated information-reporting systems along with commercial database offerings. The user, however, is faced with the obstacles of differing telecommunications systems and networks. As the unification progresses, data-reporting standards and telecommunications access to local country databases will be necessary to enable the information professional to search local database information. Both Reuters and Datastar currently have the largest systems or networks to deliver European technical and business information.

In spite of the rapid growth of Western European databases and distributors, a significant amount of business information still resides in local market research firms or in corporate libraries. For example, local branch offices and affiliates of large European companies gather business information and provide it on demand to local or international management or just simply file the information in file drawers. This type of local intelligence is typically in the local language and is collected by a research professional. The research professional is faced with the challenge of developing a system which can capture this information and organize customized databases from the material.

## Eastern Europe/USSR

The situation is more pronounced in Eastern Europe and the USSR. I term these regions "virgin" territory for database development. Whereas Western Europe has had a sophisticated structure for research and information reporting or publishing, Eastern Europe and the USSR have had to rely on state controlled agencies to gather and collect data (scientific and business). Despite this fact, local market research firms and state agencies have had some type of data-reporting methodology even without the technology.

In some countries, these local "intelligence networks" are quite sophisticated and the challenge is to locate these firms and to develop a business relationship whereby the information can be automated and disseminated to worldwide users. Clearly, the development of databases from these countries will be slow as they are still undergoing economic and political changes. Until the reporting and publishing systems improve in several of these countries, the integrity of the published material will continue to be questioned.

At present, the sources of strategic and market information are contained in private, newly developed local market research firms or in state agencies. Several local consulting firms have developed in Budapest, Prague and Warsaw. Database publishing is starting to evolve and can be found in the USSR and in Bulgaria. Again, due to their previous communistic regimes, published business intelligence information is minimal. Interestingly enough, most of the business intelligence resided in the minds of industry experts. The challenge is the transference of this industry and market intelligence into high-quality databases and published reports.

## Mexico, Latin America, South America

Similar to Eastern Europe and the USSR, this region of the world has not had a sophisticated publishing or research network. While some government agencies collect and publish data, local business intelligence (e.g. industry, market and competitive data) is lacking. Once again, the challenge is to develop databases from credible sources. One of the best sources for local market intelligence is the local affiliate or distribution offices in this region of the world. The challenge is to motivate the local offices to forward the information to a centralized library for input into the corporate intelligence system.

It is significant that this region of the world does not possess the plethora of business publications such as in the USA or Western Europe from which to scan, research and abstract the material. Therefore, researchers who require information from Latin America will have to depend more on local intelligence gathering for input into their system.

## Far East

As mentioned previously, Japan has the most sophisticated systems and commercial database products in the Far East. While they have been long-time users of European and USA databases and reports, they have recently expanded the distribution of their databases (translated into English) to the USA and European Community. Other countries such as Korea, Taiwan and Singapore are making strides to develop commercial databases and open up distribution of other international databases into their country. Here again, much of the existing data are not in electronic format nor are they published material. Similar to Eastern Europe, much of the valuable information is in the affiliate offices and local libraries. The challenge is to capture this information on a systematic basis and disseminate it throughout one's organization.

Several large market research firms have valuable data in Australia. During recent years, Australia has made strides to use and disseminate electronic information. With the increased use of telecommunications technology, it is expected that the research professional will be able to locate strategic market information from this region of the world through either electronic commercial databases or published global market intelligence directories.

## Fragmentation of the Information

As we begin the nineties, research executives must be able to view their competition on a worldwide basis. Specifically, they must have rapid access to translated, digested and analyzed information. More importantly, the information must be credible. While Western Europe research executives have been gathering information and analyzing their own domestic markets over the past four decades, they are now faced with the fragmentation of published information on a worldwide basis.

We suggest that research professionals approach organizing their research information by geographical region, by industry, by market, by products and by competitors. While this may appear to be a simplistic approach, databases can be built which can systematically obtain the information from local affiliates and can detect "holes" in the data.

## Timeliness of the Information

Information which is local to the country or termed "domestic" can usually be obtained rapidly. However, the research professional must still have a system which systematically scans the domestic publications, determines which articles are strategic or have a high degree of impact on the business and digests the articles to be input into a system.

This challenge is augmented when publications from other European countries and from other geographical regions of the world must be scanned, digested and abstracted. Global information, even when it is structured and captured on a consistent basis, still has to be translated, formatted and input electronically for transmission. During the next five years, I believe that software and telecommunications technology will make its greatest developments in this area.

During the nineties, research executives will require worldwide news information on a daily basis and digested published information which is no older than a week. Over this decade, executives will demand "answers to specific questions" rather than piles of information or voluminous reports or outputs from database searches. As information professionals, we have to be ready to deliver against these difficult orders.

## PART 2: THE SOLUTION—THE NEED FOR ONGOING TRACKING SYSTEMS FOR PUBLISHED INFORMATION

Despite the advances in software, computer and telecommunications technology, the information capturing process and translation process, electronic input is, for the most part, manual. This will continue to be the case for the next few years, particularly in developing countries. The research executive is faced with the following challenges:

- The need for an efficient method or system which will scan and digest the relevant newspapers and business and technical journals in the domestic country and then expand this to the other countries
- The need for this information to be scanned daily, translated, digested, abstracted and input into electronic format for a market intelligence system

● The need to expand this coverage to other regions of the world

Within the USA, several large corporations have developed a corporate or market intelligence system to accomplish this task. In effect, senior management has made a "top down" commitment to invest in this type of system to enable management throughout the organization to be kept abreast of the industry, the market, the competition and the products on a global basis. Typically, these systems are managed or staffed by the strategic planning or market research department. The information is distributed by this department to senior management and to managers throughout the organization.

As the world economies evolve, much of the valuable information will be found in published articles and journals. Unfortunately, most of this information is kept in "pockets" within the organization or is resident in other countries. Shared corporate information networks break down these barriers and enable managers throughout the organization to obtain the information cost efficiently. The role of the research professional is to be aware of these systems and to be knowledgeable as to the execution of them.

During the nineties, we will experience the rapid growth of corporate intelligence networks which are centralized systems which integrate information internal to the firm, synthesized external information and information from the field (e.g. plants, affiliates, brokers, or sales personnel). Typically these systems have "top down" or senior management support and are implemented by an "internal champion". The internal champion must have credibility and be a good implementer and sales person. The internal champion can come from strategic planning, corporate marketing or from the information systems department. An organization must be created under the internal champion to assume the quality control function for the information.

Content is the key to the successful implementation of the corporate intelligence system or network. Therefore, these systems require contracted services to synthesize and digest the multiple feeds of information that enter the system. Clearly, the objectives of corporate intelligence systems are not to automate all of the file drawers within a company, but to actually distill and sift through the maze and glut of internal and external global information. As a result, it becomes necessary to define your published information needs.

## PART 3: HOW TO DEFINE YOUR PUBLISHED
## INFORMATION NEEDS

### THE STRATEGIC INFORMATION AUDIT

Within your own firm, I recommend that you initially survey your management and the recipients of your research to assess the utility of the published journals they are currently receiving. I term this procedure a "strategic information audit", as the survey accomplishes the following:

- An assessment of the level of usage of current publications
- The "flow" of the information within the company (both formal and informal)
- The degree of duplication of subscriptions within the organization
- Determines the timeliness of the information and the effectiveness of "routing lists"
- Determines the cost and usefulness of newsletters, research publications and reports
- Determines which managers are using computers and what form of communications they use the most
- Enables you to draw an "information blueprint" of your organization
- Enables you to assess the respondent's wish list, which eventually becomes the optimum information network for the organization

The strategic information audit should be conducted by a task force with representatives from the market research department, the library, the information systems department and a representative from a business unit (no more than four or five representatives). The procedure should entail approximately 30–50 interviews of key suppliers and end-users of information within the organization. The audit should clearly define the utility of the published information within the company and should sumamarize the needs of the users. The summary of the results should list the most needed published matter and determine the international scope of the literature, the optimum timeliness and format of the information, and if an electronic system or hard copy process is the best way to deliver published business intelligence to the recipients. A copy of a sample questionnaire is included below:

SIS international audit questionnaire
_____

Date of interview:

Department:

Interviewee:

Interviewer:

*Information sources*
(1)    What information sources do you use to obtain market intelligence or competitor intelligence?

(2)  How satisfied are you with these information sources as they pertain to your job function?
(3)  What is your budget on information sources?
(4)  What publications do you subscribe to? What is the total cost of subscriptions?
(5)  What publications that you do not receive should be acquired?
(6)  What elements would make your current information sources more valuable (for example, more timely information)?

*Information distribution*
(7)  In addition to your own department, to what other departments do you distribute information?
(8)  How frequently do you circulate information to other departments?
(9)  What information sources gathered by your group would be appropriate to put into a shared information network?

*Critical information issues*
(10)  What type of information would you look for on a systematic or routine basis?
(11)  How would you like to see information indexed (by competitor, line of business, markets of interest)?
(12)  What emerging technologies, competitors, or businesses might threaten the market position of your group or even cause your group to be divested?

*Time factors, expectations, and format*
(13)  How often would you like to see the information updated (daily, weekly, monthly, quarterly)?
(14)  What are your initial expectations of a business intelligence network? How will it benefit your role in the organization and your line of business?
(15)  In what format would you like to see the data of a business intelligence network? Would you rather have summarized abstracts, abstracts with analysis, or full text of a document?
(16)  How would you like to access this information (hard copy or floppy disk)?

*Other*
(17)  What are the future needs of a business intelligence network (for example, should it focus on regional markets, opportunities overseas, more competitive policies rather than actual products/services)?
(18)  What other marketing services would benefit your department and job function (for instance, qualitative research)?
(19)  Who else would you recommend we interview?
(20)  Which consulting firms have you hired over the past few years? What services have they performed and what did each firm charge?

# PART 4: SOURCES OF INTERNATIONAL BUSINESS INTELLIGENCE

Within Western Europe and the USA and Canada, numerous published sources of business and technical information exist. Unfortunately, executives and managers do not have the time to scan and digest all of the available publications which impact your business on a daily basis, much less on an international scale. In addition to published material, a wealth of strategic business and technical information is published in conference proceedings and in sales personnel trip reports. This published material should also be considered for input into a corporate intelligence system. The following lists sources of international business intelligence:

- National and regional (local) newspapers
- Business and scientific journals
- Conference proceedings
- Sales personnel trip reports
- Published newsletters
- Syndicated and customized market research reports
- Internal business and marketing plans
- Internal memoranda
- Legal proceedings
- Research and development reports both internal and external to the organization

With the globalization of our economies, the collection, translation, analysis and dissemination of published material is essential to develop new marketing and product development plans. Clearly, it is impossible for a research department to scan all of the publications from the member EEC countries on a daily basis, translate the material, analyze the information, and input the information on an electronic network on a daily or weekly basis. This situation becomes more complex if Western European companies wish to remain abreast of the rest of the world's publications (Eastern Europe, USA, Latin America, Far East, etc.). The following section therefore discusses a solution to the problem with the development of a process or system within the company to handle this information.

## PART 5: HOW TO DEVELOP PROTOTYPE SYSTEMS

# DESIGN OF THE DATABASE

Following your completion of the strategic information audit and definition of the published information which is relevant for tactical and strategic decision-making, it is necessary to develop a low-cost prototype of the system. Effectively, the design of the database should "fall out" from the needs of the users from the strategic information audit. The following outlines a sample design of a database which organizes the published information by geographical region.

Organization by geographical region

| Topic areas | Industry | Market segments |
| --- | --- | --- |
| Industry trends | | |
| Political trends | | |
| Economic developments | | |
| Market activity | | |
| Competitive activity | | |
| New product development activity | | |
| Use of technology | | |
| Future trends | | |

Clearly, the design of the database should reflect the wishes of the survey respondents. It should be noted that no two competitors view their products and markets in the same manner. The database can also be organized by competitor X, Y, Z in a competitor profile format as charted on page 110.

# FORMAT OF THE DATABASE

Market intelligence systems which capture published information also require easy-to-use menu screens which enable users to select the information they wish to view. The published data can be organized by geographical region, by competitor and by topic. In other words, the system can include several different ways to view or access the information.

Published information can be presented in three ways:

(1)   Abstracts of articles, with opinions and references added (refer to the Appendix)

Organization by competitive activity

| Topic areas | Company overview | Competitor X | Competitor Y | Competitor Z |
| --- | --- | --- | --- | --- |
| Overall strategic direction | | | | |
| Company organization | | | | |
| Market position | | | | |
| Market share | | | | |
| Competitive position | | | | |
| Advertising and promotion | | | | |
| Financial performance | | | | |
| Distribution strategy | | | | |
| Research and development | | | | |
| Strategy | | | | |
| Investment | | | | |
| New product development activity | | | | |
| Use of technology | | | | |
| International strategy | | | | |
| Potential mergers, acquisitions, divestitures | | | | |
| Future projected strategy | | | | |

(2)  Report format with summary analysis or textual information
(3)  Full text of the information

Most market intelligence systems which capture published information provide abstracts of key relevant articles, which are abstracted daily and updated in
the system weekly. They may also include two- or three-page newsletters and
quarterly reports. Many of these systems also include information from the
"field", or rumor information from the field sales force or from plant personnel.
Our experience indicates that field intelligence is not useful in the formation of
anecdotal rumors by itself. When this information is analyzed and verified by
published information or by expert opinion, it is then suitable for inclusion in a
market intelligence system. The following suggests preliminary screens for the
prototype market intelligence system.
Our experience indicates that the information which is published from these
systems should be analytical. Most users can read factual information from the
literature itself. It is necessary to add the value of analysis both to the abstracts
and to the report information.

Corporate market intelligence system
_____

Menu items
_____

Abstracts
Newsletters
Quarterly reports
Field intelligence
_____

# HOW TO DEVELOP THE PROTOTYPE

Following agreement on the design and format of the database, the coordinator
for the market intelligence system will have to select software and computer
equipment. For a prototype, we recommend developing the databases on a
personal computer with a text-retrieval package.
Following evaluation by a select group of users, and if the response is positive,
we then recommend transporting the database to a mainframe or mini-computer
which can store the information and which can be accessed by multiple users
throughout the organization (on both a domestic and worldwide basis).
We recommend software packages which can provide full-text search capabilities along with graphics capabilities. Additionally, telecommunications software
and data lines should be installed for users to dial up to the information on an
international basis or from remote terminals from their homes. (A sample data
architecture is illustrated in Figure 5.1.)
It should be noted that both the content of the published material and the

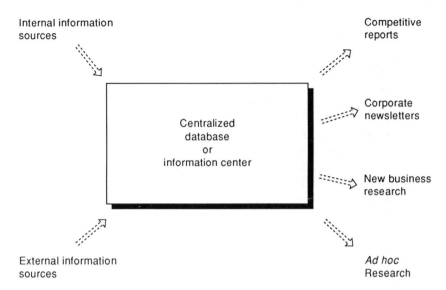

**Figure 5.1**   A simple system architecture

system's operational capabilities should be evaluated every six to 12 months. As the international business environment continues to change, so should the market intelligence system. This implies that the topic areas could change as frequently as quarterly or semiannually. The overall system architecture, however, should reflect the strategic thinking of management for the next three to five years.

## PART 6: INTERNAL STAFFING VERSUS OUTSOURCING

Clearly, the development of market intelligence systems which capture published information and provide it to the organization needs an "internal champion" or a person from the research department who is willing to head up the strategic information audit effort and work with the information systems department to design the database and implement the system. Our experience indicates that it is important for the internal champion to have "top down" support from senior management. Moreover, a budget must be established for the strategic information audit, the development of the prototype, the authoring of the information, or the procurement of the information into electronic format and the acquisition of software, computers and telecommunications equipment.

The internal champion should be the system architect as well as the corporate salesperson, or the person who sells the benefits of the system to internal management and research personnel. Additionally, the person should have a technical person on his or her staff to support the database and a customer service person to "hold the hands" of the users and obtain continual feedback on the database.

With regard to the decision of whether to produce the databases using the existing research staff or to contract out to a supplier to publish the databases, the following questions serve as guidelines:

(1) Does the research department have a sufficient staff of research analysts to publish the information? Do they have the time to scan publications, clip the material, translate and summarize the material and put it into database format?

(2) Does the department have the skills and/or the time for database publishing? Would the time of the research analysts be better spent analyzing the data from the database and publishing analytical reports or newsletters for senior management?

(3) Can the research department absorb the cost of the publications or can they utilize the publications from the corporate library? The cost and translation of international publications should also be considered.

(4) Compute a cost per abstract or quarterly report. Is it cheaper to outsource this work? Consider the quality issues. Perhaps it is more efficient to contract out the lower-level abstracting and have the research analysts access the database and analyze this material to produce senior level management reports or marketing plans.

The internal champion should conduct a "make versus buy" analysis as follows:

|  | Annual costs ($US) |
| --- | --- |
| *Internal department* | |
| Staffing 3–4 research analysts | $200 000 – $250 000 |
| Translation fees | $30 000 – $50 000 |
| Publications | $30 000 – $50 000 |
| Total annual costs | $260 000 – $350 000 |
| # of abstracts per year | 1200 – 2400 |
| Cost per abstract | $216 – $145 |
| *Outside supplier* | |
| Total annual contract | $100 000 – $150 000 |
| # of abstracts per year | 1200 – 2400 |
| Cost per abstract | $83 – $63 |

In most cases, it is more cost-efficient to contract with an outside supplier. The issue remains, however, whether the outside supplier can quickly, or over a period of time, develop the perspective you need so the abstracts and reports will add value to your analysis. Several companies with successful marketing intelligence systems contract to an outside supplier to publish the abstracts or quarterly summaries, and then their internal research analysts "manage the system" and utilize the information to publish more detailed analytical reports or answer key senior management questions or *ad hoc* requests.

## PART 7: DETERMINING THE COST/BENEFITS OF THE SYSTEM

In this current period of economic and political uncertainty, with tight budgets, investment in this type of system must clearly prove value or impact the corporation. The following outlines a typical budget for a market intelligence system which captures published information:

| | |
|---|---|
| Internal champion, technician, customer service rep | $250 000 |
| Outside contract supplier | $100 000 |
| Total labor and materials costs | $350 000 |
| Personal computer software | $1000 |
| Mainframe software (if do not have in-house) | $100 000 |
| Additional costs of computers (if do not have in-house) | — |

Note that companies have very successfully developed very low-cost systems on personal computers for minimal costs. Here again, content is the key to the success of these systems. The systems often include executive briefing reports, competitive intelligence tracking systems, market and product tracking systems and company profiles. They are either stand alone on text retrieval or database software or are part of a distributed corporate intelligence network. In the latter case, the information is resident on the corporate mainframe and can be accessed by remote PCs. In some cases, companies have integrated both textual and numeric information in these systems. It should be noted that these figures represent large corporate investments in systems which can be accessed worldwide by staff personnel.

After a period of one to two years, management will want to quantify the benefits of the system. If management can answer "yes" to any of the following questions, the systems has paid for itself:

(1)   Has the company increased (or protected) its market share or revenues as a result of decisions made from the material in the system?

(2)   Has the company developed new products or repositioned existing products as a result of direct usage of information from the system?

(3)   Has the company identified new business or market opportunities as a result of usage of the system (e.g. expanded into new markets—Eastern Europe, mergers, acquisitions, etc.)?

(4)   Has the company been able to reposition itself with respect to the unification of Europe more quickly or efficiently through the use of the system?

(5)   Can the company's worldwide affiliates make decisions more rapidly as a result of published information being translated, synthesized and made available in electronic format on a timely basis?

## PART 8: STRATEGIC IMPORTANCE OF THESE SYSTEMS TO THE GLOBAL BUSINESS EXECUTIVE

During the nineties, it will be necessary for corporations to have access to the published business intelligence of companies throughout the world. While a plethora of publications may develop, international research executives will still need business intelligence which is local to the member and non-member countries. Moreover, countries will need business intelligence from Eastern Europe, the USA, Soviet Union, Far East, Latin America and other parts of the world. Strategic decisions are made from published information in addition to non-published information. The need exists for a firm to offer a global intelligence network which provides a synthesis of public information throughout the world in addition to the use of field experts throughout the world.

On a regional basis, the USA has a very mature information industry and will be searching for strategic information from other parts of the world to maintain their world position. Information from Mexico and South America will be critical to their expansion of free trade within the Americas. On the other hand, Europe, has the challenge of obtaining strategic information within the EC and facing up to the global challenge. Eastern Europe will face an explosive growth in the demand for high-quality and reliable market data from their countries. The challenge, here, is the quality and timeliness of the information.

Interestingly enough, the Asian sector will experience the most rapid rates of growth economically and will need to develop strategic information systems to provide market and product data for western firms interested in investing in these countries. I foresee the capturing and delivery of this global information on an internal corporate intelligence network. These networks must be implemented in a tight cost-control environment and contain quality information. Information providers and research firms which have extensive global capabilities will become major information content suppliers into these networks. Alternatively, corporations who implement these systems and utilize these suppliers should evolve into the winners in the nineties.


# APPENDIX: EXAMPLES OF ABSTRACTS*

## A: Industry Trends

### Financial services industry

Consumer rates have declined sharply since the June 5, 1989 prime rate cut by major banks. Many lenders have reduced their fixed mortgage rates below 10%, as CD, MMA, and consumer credit rates also decline.

- *Bank Rate Monitor* suggests that the accelerated pace at which consumer rates declined in the week following the prime rate cut indicates the beginning of a downward cycle.
- A reduction in inflationary pressure and a spate of economic reports that showed the economy to be slowing have allowed the Fed to reduce short-term rates for the first time since February 1987. Banks responded by cutting their prime lending rate, after six consecutive increases.
- Major banks reduced their one-year CD rate by as much as 0.5% in the week following the prime rate move. Adjustable rate loans will be affected by the prime rate cut, since many of these vehicles are tied to the prime.
- The decline in rates has allowed such major mortgage lenders as Sears to reduce their fixed mortgage rates below 10%. Sears is currently charging 9.675% (with a charge of two points) for its 30-year vehicle. Sears Mortgage reported a 50% surge in originations over the past several months thanks to the lower mortgage rates.

*Implications:* The move toward lower rates may be complicated by the 0.9% surge in the May wholesale inflation rate. However, the continued advance in dollar price may cause the Fed to directly intervene in the market with a discount rate cut.

---

*A through G represent a series of abstracts that are examples of organized and analyzed information from external sources. These abstracts encompass various topic areas that are typically used to effectively segment information for searching and retrieval purposes. The material in the Appendix is reprinted by permission of the publisher, from *The Intelligent Corporation* by Ruth Stanat. Copyright © 1990 AMACOM, a division of the American Management Association. All rights reserved.

*References*
1. Downcycle may be under way. *Bank Rate Monitor*, June 12, 1989, pp. 1,4.
2. Mortgage rate drop heats up housing market. *USA Today*, June 13, 1989, p. B1.

*Key words*
Interest rates

### Automotive industry

Falling new car sales and higher marketing costs are expected to translate into lower profits for the Big 3 US automakers this year.

- Initially, many forecasts called for 1989 new car and truck sales to fall about 500 000 below last year's strong showing of 15.8 million.
- GM Chairman Roger Smith expects sales to fall to about 15 million.
- In addition to economic uncertainties, higher interest rates, a saturated market, and higher auto prices, other factors are involved in declining sales.
- According to the so-called multiplier effect, each job in an auto assembly plant generates five to eight additional jobs elsewhere. However, with sharp declines in production, the impact of the downturn in sales will be more severe on a regional basis.

*Implications:* Any downturn will also affect everyone from brake manufacturers to steel suppliers, as well as organizations that have automakers as key service clients (computer firms, engineers, and so on).

*References*
1. Auto slump could send tremors through softening US economy. *Investor's Daily*, June 9, 1989, p. 32.
2. Dark clouds gather over sated car market. *Investor's Daily*, June 9, 1989, pp. 1, 32.

*Key words*
Smith, GM

# B: Environmental Trends

### Automotive industry

The Environmental Protection Agency (EPA) is asking President Bush to support mandatory requirements for the use of cars and buses that use fuel other than gasoline.

- To date, the idea has been met with stiff opposition.
- A prototype bill features proposals favored by the EPA to require 50% of new cars and buses in the 25 most polluted US cities to run on methanol, ethanol, or compressed natural gas beginning in 1995.
- Henson Moore, a deputy secretary with the Department of Energy, is against this requirement, claiming that the economic costs would be higher than the EPA estimates.
- Automakers and the oil industries oppose any requirement for fuel switching. They cite problems with methanol. The American Petroleum Institute warns that it would cost $18 billion to $24 billion to build about 60 new methanol plants to supply fuel under the EPA proposal.
- In addition, energy industry analysts note that extra natural gas needed to make the methanol would have to be imported from the Middle East, posing the same national security threat as imported oil.

*Implications:* The prospects of pressures for manufacturers to produce vehicles that use alternative fuels may represent the most sweeping changes in the history of automobile and petroleum industries.

*References*
1. Clean air costly, automakers say. *Washington Post,* June 14, 1989, p. F1.
2. Carmakers pressed to radically re-engineer autos. *Investor's Daily,* June 29, 1989, p. 31.

*Key words*
EPA, Bush, Department of Energy

**Chemical industry**

At a meeting of the United Nations Environment Program in Helsinki, 80 countries signed a declaration to stop all production and consumption of chlorofluorocarbons (CFCs), which damage the ozone layer, by the year 2000. The 80 nations also supported establishment of a global fund that would aid Third World nations in developing alternatives to CFCs.

*Implications:* Manufacturers should begin to search for a solution to the CFC problem before they find their products banned in many nations. Sales are bound to drop dramatically if bans are placed into effect.

*References*
1. Eighty countries support CFC ban. *Chemical Week,* May 10, 1989, p. 16.
2. EC Ministers agree to ban CFCs by 2000. *HAPPI,* April 1989, p. 10.

*Key words*
United Nations Environment Program, Helsinki, CFC

*Food industry*

Consumer activists at a House hearing called for tougher laws against pesticide residues in food and suggested that Congress ban the use of any pesticide that could cause cancer.

- Agricultural groups complained that the "negligible risk" standard proposed in a House bill is too extreme because it does not take into account the benefits of chemical use, without which food production would suffer.
- The "negligible risk" bill, sponsored by Rep. Henry Waxman, would bar the use of chemicals if they carried a risk of one cancer case per one million people.
- A poll by the Food Marketing Institute showed consumer confidence was shaken by the scares over the tampering with Chilean grapes and the possible health effects from Alar, which regulates the color and firmness of apples.
- Representatives of the Natural Resources Defense Fund, Public Citizen, and the Public Interest Research Group said that no cancer-causing chemicals should be allowed in agricultural use at all.
- The agricultural groups said that the economic benefits of farm chemicals should be taken into account. The bill could block the use of fumigants needed to keep grain in top condition and prevent infestation by crop pests.

*Implications:* Stiffer but realistic pesticide laws should be proposed to Congress. Although agricultural groups may suffer economically from chemical restrictions, this minimal loss cannot compare with the health hazard chemicals pose to the population, not to mention the drop in sales for specific food products due to a poison scare. In addition, chemical manufacturers should attempt to find safer products without compromising effectiveness.

*References*
1. Consumers call for stiffer pesticide law. *Investor's Daily*, June 11, 1989, p. 13.
2. Alar campaign steps up. *Chemical Marketing Reporter*, May 15, 1989, pp. 7, 12.
3. The pesticide scare: Changing public perception. *Chemical Week*, May 2, 1989, pp. 28–30.

*Key words*
Congress, Rep. Henry Waxman, Food Marketing Institute, Alar, Natural Resources Defense Fund, Public Citizen, Public Interest Research Group.

# C: Legislation

*Financial services industry*

The Federal Reserve has expanded banks' securities powers to include corporate debt underwriting. The central bank applied several restrictions and limitations to this ruling. Many in Congress vocally opposed the ruling, which will allow banks to underwrite speculative debt, citing the mounting volume of LBO debt held by commercial banks and the S&L crisis—which many lawmakers argued grew out of the deregulation of the thrift industry.

- According to executives quoted in the *American Banker*, major banks plan to quickly enter the corporate debt markets.
- The Fed previously ruled that banks could underwrite commercial paper, mortgage-backed securities, municipal bonds, and several other types of collateralized issues in 1987.
- The latest ruling applies the same restrictions that were placed under these previous rulings. These limitations include:
  (1) Underwriting must be conducted through a separate subsidiary of the bank's holding company.
  (2) Revenue derived from underwriting must not exceed 5 % of the unit's total revenue.
- The ruling grew out of requests from five major banks: Citicorp, Chase, J. P. Morgan, Bankers Trust, and Security Pacific.
- Banks that plan to exercise corporate debt underwriting powers must submit a proposal outlining how the bank will capitalize underwriting subsidiaries in order to assure that the capital of the bank holding company will not be depleted.
- In an important contingent to the ruling, the Fed cleared the way for banks to enter the equities underwriting market in one year. The one-year period is designed to allow Congress an opportunity to enact legislation covering various underwriting issues.

*References*
1. Fed moves to allow banks to underwrite corporate debt; equity powers withheld. P. Duke, *The Wall Street Journal*, January 19, 1989, pp. A3, A4.
2. Banks get nod on corporate debt. *American Banker*, January 19, 1989, pp. 1, 16.

*Key words*
Federal reserve, corporate debt underwriting

**Automative industry**

The NHTSA will require rear-seat lap and shoulder belts in new passenger cars, effective January 1990.

- According to the agency, 16 % of all rear-seat passengers currently use the lap safety belts. The agency maintains that if this level were 100 %, 600 additional lives would be saved.

- The regulation is not expected to have a negative effect on US automakers, who already planned to make shoulder belts standard for rear-seat passengers in 1990 models. The foreign automakers will be saddled with most of these costs.
- The rule applies to all new passenger cars except convertibles. Vans, utility vehicles, and light trucks are exempt from the regulation, but the NHTSA said it is investigating whether to extend the rule to cover those vehicles.

*References*
1. Rear-seat shoulder belts are ordered for new cars. *The Wall Street Journal*, June 13, 1989, p. C19.
2. New rule requires belts in back seats of 1990-model cars. *The New York Times*, June 15, 1989, p. A24.

*Key words*
NHTSA

### Chemical/detergent industries

The future of sodium tripolyphosphate (STPP) is cloudy as legislation ponders its use in heavy-duty laundry detergents. Eroding demand, offset to some degree by the success of new powder/bleach formulations, is expected to continue throughout 1989, as bans in Ohio and Pennsylvania take effect the first of next year.

- Legislation is also pending in Georgia, South Carolina, Idaho, and Oregon. Lewis Furman, director of marketing for the phosphorus division at FMC Corporation, says the threat of bans exists in nearly 10 states and asserts that producers will begin to question the benefit of powders with STPP.
- The introduction of Tide With Bleach and testing of Clorox Super Detergent helped the powder market by taking from liquids. Liquids are growing at a much slower rate than in past years.

*Implications*: Manufacturers of products containing STPP would be wise to consider different formulations excluding this chemical. Though bans are currently on a limited basis, nationwide publicity of this issue could generate undesired repercussions. In addition, the chemical may become difficult to attain and manufacturers will be unable to purchase needed quantities.

*References*
1. STPP producers brood over phosphate bans. *Chemical Marketing Reporter*, May 1, 1989, p. 33.
2. Henkel moves to P-free detergents. *HAPPI*, June 1989, p. 24.

Key words
STPP, Tide With Bleach, Super Detergent, Clorax, FMC Corporation, Lewis
Furman

Phosphorus producers are considering the pitfalls of investing too much of
their product in the heavy-duty laundry detergent market. Although companies
will continue to fight legislation, it is inevitable that the trend toward enacting
bans will also continue, according to a business director for phosphorus and
derivatives at Monsanto Chemical Company.

• During a press briefing, Monsanto executives pointed out that only 3 % of
  the phosphorus buildup in the nation's rivers, lakes, and streams is contributed by detergent phosphates. The remaining 97 % emanates primarily from
  animal and human waste and agricultural runoff.
• The alternative that producers such as Monsanto have arrived at is not total
  defeat, but rather a gradual movement away from phosphorus production for
  use in detergents. This means putting roughly one-third of its phosphorus
  into areas such as food, intermediates, and industrial and institutional
  cleaning.
• The director of marketing for the phosphorus division at FMC Corporation
  projects that US demand for phosphates over the next three years will be flat
  and will most likely decline by 5 % or more.

*Implications:* It is understandable that phosphorus producers would oppose a
ban on phosphorus use in detergents. However, if it is true that 97 % of the
buildup derives from the sources mentioned, such a ban on detergents alone
would, in effect, be futile. Sewage treatment methods and farming chemicals need
to be evaluated in tandem with phosphate use in detergents.

References
1. STPP producers prepare for the inevitable. *Chemical Marketing Reporter*, May
   29, 1989, p. 23.
2. FMC reduces STPP pricing. *Chemical Marketing Reporter*, August 7, 1989,
   p. 27.

Key words
Monsanto Chemical Company, FMC Corporation, phosphorus

**Pharmaceutical industry**

The FDA has approved use of a genetically engineered drug that can help reduce
anemia in patients suffering from kidney failure. Developed under the agency's

orphan drug program, erythropoietin (EPO) will be marketed by Amgen, Inc. under the trade name Epogen.

• Amgen becomes the second biotechnological company to market a drug, after Genentech, Inc. The company will be allowed to market the drug immediately.

• The cost of EPO is $4000 to $6000 per patient annually. It is expected that patients will receive government assistance.

• The FDA approval, however, appears to complicate Amgen's ongoing dispute with Johnson & Johnson. Amgen is licensed to sell EPO for dialysis patients in the United States, but J&J has all rights elsewhere and rights for other indications in the United States.

• J&J filed suit against Amgen claiming that the company has reneged on its responsibility to submit predialysis clinical data in its FDA application.

• Although Amgen salespeople cannot promote EPO for nondialysis use, doctors will be allowed to prescribe it as they wish.

• A J&J spokesman said Ortho will start marketing EPO when the dispute with Amgen is settled. J&J still hopes that Amgen will supply the drug, although its own plants could produce it. The FDA has yet to approve labeling for Ortho's version of EPO, called Eprex.

• Amgen's EPO sales are still potentially threatened by the company's patent dispute with Genetics Institute, which holds competing patent rights.

*Implications:* It is important that these companies resolve their disputes as soon as possible because although they apparently have time to spare, kidney failure patients do not. EPO would allow patients to live a more normal life. Constant dialysis treatments and frequent transfusions drain the blood of necessary nutrients and minerals. Because EPO stimulates the growth of red blood cells, more oxygen can be transported throughout the body.

*References*
1. Anemia drug okayed. *Chemical Marketing Reporter*, June 5, 1989, p. 7.
2. FDA approves Amgen's new biotech drug. *Investor's Daily*, June 2, 1989, pp. 1, 30.

*Key words*
FDA, EPO, Amgen, Inc., Epogen, J&J, Eprex

# D: Competitor Activity

## Automotive industry

GM will give its "big car" manufacturing group responsibility for all of the company's domestic small-car production. This is a shift that reverses a major goal of GM's massive reorganization plan of 1984.

- Clearly, the idea of this is to realize further cost savings.
- As per this new strategy, the engineering and manufacturing of the compact cars (Chevrolet–Pontiac–GM of Canada) are being transferred to the big-car group (Buick–Oldsmobile–Cadillac).
- The big-car group already controls production of GM's other two compact car lines (the J and N body cars).
- The idea behind the shift is that it will make it easier for GM to carry out plans to merge the three separate small-car platforms into one small-car platform that can share common parts and allow production of several different models in a single plant.

*Implications:* Although the decision makes sense on the basis of cost, the decision to consolidate these functions may baffle some observers. For one, the Buick–Olds–Cadillac group consists of decentralized units that already have increased quality and have cut costs better than the centralized small-car group (Chevrolet–Pontiac–Canada operation).

*References*
1. GM to consolidate big, small car roles for cost savings, reversing revamp goal. *The Wall Street Journal,* June 7, 1989, p. A4.
2. GM sets a major realignment. *The New York Times,* June 7, 1989, p. D4.

*Key words*
GM, Chevrolet, Pontiac, Oldsmobile, Cadillac

Tenneco will restructure its automotive parts unit, including the sale of its automotive retail division and the acquisition of a Georgia brake manufacturing plant.

- The restructuring is designed to strengthen Tenneco's presence in the parts business.
- Under the plan, Tenneco Automotive will sell its retail division (Toronto) to a group of Canadian investors led by Stanley Goldfarb and Fred Karp, chair of Speedy King Muffler.
- The divested unit, which accounted for $260 million of the automotive

division's $1.7 billion in sales revenues, operates 709 muffler shops in five countries.

- The automotive division, which accounts for about 21% of Tenneco's earnings, is one of the corporation's most profitable and includes the Monroe Auto Equipment Company. Monroe manufactures more than 50% of the shock absorbers made in the United States.
- Tenneco has also completed the acquisition of a nonasbestos brake manufacturing plant in Cartersville, Georgia, from Interfriction USA for an undisclosed sum.

*Implications:* As vertically integrated as Tenneco is, the company is looking to streamline its automotive division and redeploy capital in automotive markets that are growing and less dependent on shifts in the economy.

*References*
1. Tenneco revamping auto parts subsidiary. *Investor's Daily*, June 13, 1989, p. 8.
2. Tenneco to reorganize auto parts business. *The New York Times*, June 13, 1989, p. D5.

*Key words*
Tenneco

## Packaging/detergent industries

Procter & Gamble, in conjunction with some of its packaging suppliers, has unveiled new plastic packaging for some of its detergent products that will aid in the nation's solid waste disposal efforts.

- Bottles of Downy fabric softener, Liquid Tide, and Liquid Cheer will now be made from 20 to 30% recycled high-density polyethylene (HDPE). The three-layer bottles made by Plastipak Packaging, Inc. incorporate scrap HDPE into the layers.
- The containers are believed to be the first of their kind and are recyclable. Incorporating reycled HPDE is much more complex than using polyethylene (PET).
- Last fall, P&G announced the development of a Spic & Span bottle made from 100% postconsumer recycled PET.
- P&G uses over 100 million pounds of HDPE annually in its plastic bottles. Its goal is to develop a system that can use HDPE from any source, including P&G's own detergent bottles.

*Implications:* The concern displayed by P&G over the environment will probably spur consumers to purchase these products. Indeed, with competitive products being so similar in composition, companies will need to resort to extraordinary ways of creating uniqueness. Social and environmental issues will probably dictate the marketability of products in the near future.

*References*
1. Procter & Gamble unveils recyclable plastic packaging. *Supermarket News*, May 1, 1989, p. 52.
2. How P&G does it. *Chemical Marketing Reporter*, April 24, 1989, pp. 7, 21.

*Key words*
P&G, Downy, Liquid Tide, Liquid Cheer, polyethylene

### Chemical/detergent industries

Texaco Chemical Company has taken a major step toward its stated objective of becoming a broad-based supplier in the $3.5 billion US *laundry* detergent market.

- Under a joint agreement just signed with Ethyl Corporation, Texaco will take linear alcohols from Ethyl's Houston facility, ethoxylate them, and market the products under its established Surfonic trade name.
- Nonylphenol ethoxylates, a market in which the company is fully integrated and in which it has a $50-million-plus market share, have been relegated largely to industrial applications and are not a major thrust in that market area.
- In addition, the company's impact on the total surfactant business is obscured by the fact that its significant ethoxylation operation is seldom publicized.
- Texaco's total ethoxylation capacity is rated at 200 million to 250 million pounds annually, making the company second only to Shell Chemical Company.
- Texaco will offer eight different products based on three alcohols. The products will be 1- to 10-mole ethoxylates, with the largest volume expected to be in the 3- to 6-mole range.
- Alcohol ethoxylates, used directly as nonionic surfactants in laundry products, generally contain 6 to 12 moles of ethylene oxide (EO) per mole of alcohol; those used for production of alcohol ether sulfates contain 1 to 3 moles of EO.
- US demand for alcohol ethoxylates is estimated to have been about 400 million pounds last year, with another 400-million-pound requirement for the ether sulfates, out of a total 4-billion-pound surfactant market.

*Implications:* The inevitable reduction of phosphorus use in detergents will create the need for replacement chemicals. It is possible that this void will be filled with ethylene-based materials, thus increasing the market share for this product. Texaco's increased production of alcohol ethoxylates will provide tremendous profits in the near future.

References
1. Texaco recasts its role in big US detergents mart. *Chemical Marketing Reporter*, June 5, 1989, pp. 3, 23.
2. Ethyl and Texaco in surfactants deal. *Chemical Marketing Reporter*, May 29, 1989, p. 4.

*Key words*
Texaco, Shell, alcohol ethoxylates, surfactants, ethyl

# E: Product Development

### Financial services industry

Many Pennsylvania banks are targeting mature individuals with retirement center branch locations. According to Ezekiel Ketchum, CEO of Meridian Bank, retirement center branches are shifting in branching strategy from a mass market approach to an effort to target specific market segments.

- The $9.7 billion bank, based in Reading, Pennsylvania, has opened an office at the Highlands, a retirement community in an upscale suburb of Reading.
- Generally, retirement center branches are staffed by two individuals and operated on limited hours, often opening four hours per day, three days per week. Employees are typically mature, sensitive, and empathetic individuals, according to Kathryn Donahue, a senior vice-president at First Fidelity. She also stated that residents expect service and can be demanding.
- The draw for banks in opening retirement center locations is that older people generally have money. According to Robert Stevens, president of Bryn Mawr Bank, the branches are a "nice, solid, traditional deposit business for banks". Bryn Mawr, a $280 million bank based in Pennsylvania, has two retirement center locations. The bank is planning to open a third branch in a new retirement center that was opened by the Marriott Corporation near its headquarters in Bethesda, Maryland.
- Retirement center locations are so desirable that First Fidelity, the super-regional based in Newark, New Jersey, prepared a 40-page prospectus and a 50-page operating manual, complete with testimonials, in attempting to beat out the competition for a retirement location.
- Several banks often vie for the right to open branches at any one retirement center.

References
1. Philadelphia banks tap older market. *American Banker*, June 15, 1989, p. 10.
2. Senior programs: marketing efforts up. *Bank Advertising News*, July 3, 1989, pp. 3, 8.

*Key words*
Retirement center branches

# F: Merger and Acquisition Activity

### Financial services industry

Security Pacific has agreed to sell a 5 % stake in its nonbanking operations to Mitsui Bank of Japan in a deal worth $100 million. The transaction puts the value of SecPac's consumer and commercial services operations at 15 times operating earnings. This is a high premium considering that SecPac's stock is trading at just seven times 1988 earnings on the New York Stock Exchange.

- Mitsui is Japan's seventh largest bank with assets of $210 billion. The transaction will give the bank a stake in SecPac's international insurance, consumer and commercial finance, leasing, and other nonbanking operations, which contributed a combined $153 million to SecPac's bottom line last year. This equals a 1.2 % return on the operation's $12.6 billion asset base. Mitsui has the right to purchase an additional 5 % of these operations at the same price.
- SecPac and Mitsui are also partners in a commercial financing unit located in Japan. Security Pacific's CEO, Richard Flamson, and Mitsui's CEO, Kenichi Kamiya, have a close personal friendship.
- The sale was made in an effort to increase the value of SecPac's stock, which is trading at a multiple far below that of the market average. The market has valued the stock of major banks at a low multiple because of several problems, including the S&L crisis, the less-developed country debt situation, and the uncertain regulatory environment. Several of the most profitable and healthy banks, including SecPac and Fleet, have been negatively affected by market perceptions.
- Therefore, deals such as the SecPac-Mitsui joint venture are expected to become a standard for regional banks that have strong balance sheets and are seeking to increase their market value.

*References*
1. Security Pacific to sell stakes to Mitsui Bank. *The Wall Street Journal*, June 14, 1989, p. A2.
2. Mitsui Bank to buy stake in Security Pacific Unit. *American Banker*, June 14, 1989, pp. 3, 23.

*Key words*
Security Pacific, Mitsui

## Automotive/car rental industries

Chrysler announced that it will acquire Thrifty Rent-A-Car System for $263 million. The deal is significant because it would make Chrysler the last of the Big 3 to take a stake in a major rental agency. Thrifty, based in Tulsa, Oklahoma, buys about 40 000 cars a year from *Chrysler*.

- On the average, Chrysler cars represent 75 % to 80 % of Thrifty's fleet. Clearly, however, this percentage will increase.
- The cash tender offer comes to about $27.75 per share for all of Thrifty's stock.
- Because GM and Ford hold large shares in the Big 4 rental car agencies (Hertz, Avis, Budget, and National), Chrysler was in danger of being edged out of the daily car rental market, which buys 10 % of the total US car production annually.
- Thrifty reported $79.3 million in revenues and $9.1 million in net income for the fiscal year ended June 30, 1988.
- The agency has an estimated 5.3 % market share in the United States and has 357 locations in the United States and 301 abroad.

*Implications:* Clearly, the purchase of Thrifty by Chrysler will solidify its relationship with the car rental agency and possibly increase fleet sales. These sales have become an increasingly important factor in overall automotive sales, considering the expected downturn in the market. In addition to fleet sales, Chrysler should expand awareness of the agency through promotional tie-ins with its product lineup.

*References*

1. Chrysler to buy Rent-A-Car Company. *Ward's Automotive Reports*, May 22, 1989, p. 165.
2. Thrifty buy is Chrysler's rental shield. *Automotive News*, May 22, 1989, pp. 1, 57.
3. Chrysler to buy car rental firm for $263 million. *The Wall Street Journal*, May 19, 1989, p. C16.
4. Chrysler agrees to pay $263 mil. for Thrifty Rent-A-Car purchase. *Investor's Daily*, May 19, 1989, p. 31.
5. Chrysler to buy Thrifty car rental. *USA Today*, May 19, 1989, p. B1.
6. Chrysler to buy Thrifty Rent-A-Car. *The New York Times*, May 19, 1989, pp. D1, D3.

*Key words*
Chrysler, Thrifty

# G: International

## Automotive industry

Environmental concerns have moved to the center stage of EEC politics as the ministers continue to embrace tough emission standards for automobiles.

- The new standards can cut pollution from small cars by an estimated 70 %.
- Under the ministerial decisions, emission standards equivalent to those in force in the United States since 1983 will apply in the EEC to cars with engines of under 1.4 liters as of July 1, 1992, for new models, and six months later for other new cars.
- The EEC is allowing governments to offer tax incentives for the low-pollution cars between now and the end of 1992.

*References*
1. Pollution curbs for cars are set by EEC Ministers. *The Wall Street Journal*, June 12, 1989, p. A11.
2. Europe sets tough small-car pollution curbs. *Investor's Daily*, June 12, 1989, p. 26.

*Key words*
EEC, emissions

West Germany's auto industry continues to disprove pessimistic forecasts of declining revenue and flat earnings.

- Many analysts have recently taken a more favorable view of BMW, Volkswagen, Daimler-Benz, and even Porsche AG.
- Earnings declines for BMW, VW, and Porsche are viewed as an unavoidable consequence of the auto industry's cyclical nature.
- During the first four months of 1989, new auto registrations in West Germany jumped 7.4 % to 1 million units, and were about 9 % in Italy, Britain, and France.
- Recently, BMW reported that group sales surged 23 % in the first four months of 1989, and that pretax profits rose 6.9 % to DM 990 million ($500.9 million).

*Implications:* Although the long-term prospects for the West German auto manufacturers may look optimistic, the fact remains that the Japanese represent a competitive threat to these manufacturers, particularly in the EEC markets and the United States. These competitive dynamics should affect BMW the most as it continues to rebuff diversification. Daimler-Benz, a company that is more of a conglomerate, has a thriving aerospace business, so it should be less vulnerable. Although Porsche has addressed its problems and is now less dependent on the US market, many say that the company's only chance of long-term survival may be to merge with another company. Currently, it appears as though Volkswagen is in the best position (on a global basis) of all the West German auto manufacturers.

*References:*
1. The West German auto makers' pace in '89 defies bears. *The Wall Street Journal*, June 12, 1989, p. 9C.
2. Mercedes, BMW stepping up competition in home market. *Investor's Daily*, June 22, 1989, p. 29.

*Key words*
Volkswagen, Porsche, Daimler-Benz, BMW

### Chemical/detergent industries

As of January 1, 1989, Henkel discontinued its production of phosphate-built detergents in West Germany. For the past 15 years Henkel has been working on finding phosphate substitutes, and as early as 1983 the company had introduced phosphate-free detergents in Germany and Switzerland.

- Switzerland has banned usage of phosphates in detergents completely, and phosphate-built products now account for about 10 % of the West German market.
- Between 1975 and 1985, use of phosphates in detergents fell from 276 000 tons to 160 000 tons in West Germany, and by 1987 it amounted to only 80 000 tons.
- Henkel has also replaced PVC bottles will polyethylene bottles for its liquid detergents and cleaners in response to public concern over dioxin emission during incineration of PVC bottles.
- Other innovations in this area include using a 5-liter carton lined with a thin plastic skin that, when empty, can be folded and the carton treated like any other paper waste.

*Implications:* Other manufacturers would be wise to discontinue phosphate-built detergents abroad as well as domestically. Now more than ever, environmental concerns are beginning to affect producers and product sales.

*References*
1. Henkel halts STPP detergent production in Germany. *Chemical Marketing Reporter*, May 15, 1989, p. 23.

2. Henkel moves to P-free detergents. *HAPPI*, June 1989, p. 24.

*Key words*
Henkel, phosphate, West Germany, Switzerland, PVC bottles

### Cosmetics industry

The US import restrictions on Japanese cosmetics would jeopardize efforts at establishing US–Japanese cooperation, the Cosmetic, Toiletry and Fragrance Association (CTFA) said at a US Trade Representative (USTR) hearing on May 24.

● The USTR, after determining that Japan had committed unfair trade practices in the telecommunications trade, drafted a list of candidates for increased duties or import restrictions. The list includes beauty or makeup preparations, skin care, and sun care products.
● Japan is the US cosmetic industry's third-largest foreign market. Exports to Japan increased 86 % from 1986 to 1988, and imports from Japan rose 98 % in the two-year period.
● The trade association noted that US 1988 cosmetics sales in Japan were $877 million, representing 9.6 % of the $9.2 billion total cosmetics sales in Japan.
● Max Factor sales in Japan reached $300 million in 1988; Avon totaled $224 million; Estée Lauder volume was $171 million; Revlon reached $79 million; Helene Curtis totaled $52 million; and Bristol-Myers realized $51 million.
● In addition, increased trade restrictions would harm US companies that import Japanese ingredients and components. About $9 million worth of Japanese ingredients were imported in 1988.

*Implications:* If trade restrictions are increased, retaliation can be expected. Japanese firms and consumers will probably boycott US cosmetics. The unfair telecommunications trade practices conducted by the Japanese do not affect the cosmetics industry. It is difficult to understand then how this action can do anything but cause further damage in an already difficult situation.

*References*
1. US retaliatory import restrictions on Japanese cosmetics. *FDC Reports Rise Sheet*, May 29, 1989, p. 2.
2. Cosmetics may suffer in trade war. *Chemical Marketing Reporter*, May 29, 1989, pp. 7, 16.

*Key words*
CTFA, USTR, Max Factor, Avon, Estée Lauder, Revlon, Helene Curtis, Bristol-Myers

# 6

# EXPERT SYSTEMS TO SUPPORT STRATEGIC MANAGEMENT DECISION-MAKING

## Robert J. Mockler

*Professor of Business, St John's University, New York*

## and D. G. Dologite

*Professor of Computer Information Systems, City University of New York*

Expert (knowledge-based) systems have been built to replicate the thinking processes involved in strategic management. They not only assist in making strategic management decisions, but also serve as useful learning tools for those studying strategic management. By examining the knowledge bases of these systems, it is possible to analyze in detail how planners think. In addition, by using the systems, it is possible to observe how these processes are put to work in making specific decisions.

## COMMERCIALLY AVAILABLE SYSTEMS

Several commercially available expert (knowledge-based) systems are briefly described below:

International Review of Strategic Management.
Edited by D. E. Hussey. © 1992 John Wiley & Sons Ltd

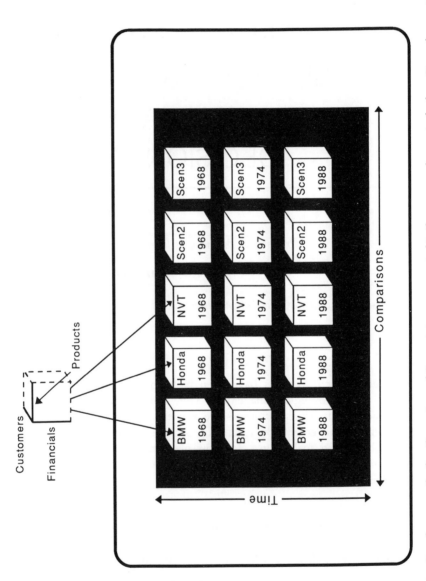

**Figure 6.1** Sample screen: the five dimensions of Competel are represented in the program by a set of cubes. One cube consists of a set of financials broken out by products and customers

*Alacrity* appears to have been the first commercially available knowledge-based system designed to assist in strategic company planning (Cook and Sterling, 1989). The Alacrity integrated system is made up of several components, which can be used separately or in combination and include the following:

Alacrity strategy provides a framework to think through key strategic issues.
Alacrity report writer provides a set of outlines to help managers organize strategic and marketing reports.
Resource allocation uses decision matrices to compare potential investments, projects, products, and businesses.
Competitive advantage quantifies and compares fundamental cost drivers of the user's and the competitors' businesses in order to analyze costs, complexity, and pricing issues.
Knowledge seeker statistically analyzes databases using intelligent cross-tabbing to look for important relationships.

*Compete!* is another knowledge-based, decision support tool that models financial data in five dimensions (for example, financial, markets, product line, regions and time) while maintaining the relationships among the data. This multidimensional feature is imperative in business situations where users need to track more than the traditional two dimensions available in spreadsheets. The effects of key decisions on the overall company performance can be tracked as they ripple through the business operations (Berman and Kautz, 1990).

With Compete!, a user manipulates cubes, not rows and columns. The system's prestructured models cover financial analysis, product line analysis, market (customer) analysis, and competitive analysis over time. Necessary cross-dependencies are initially established, but can be modified by the user as needed. The system automatically updates associated relationships when any one relationship changes.

Figure 6.1 shows the five dimensions of Compete!. An individual cube represents three of these dimensions for one company at a single point in time, segmenting a business by two criteria—products and customers—and the financial results of the business. Additional cubes add the dimension of time (one cube for each time period), which are shown by the vertical columns of cubes in the figure. The final dimension, comparisons (the rows of cubes), uses the scenario cubes to show comparisons among competing companies.

A user begins by opening the screen of cubes and tables through the "Business" menu. The screens in Figure 6.2 (A and B) show how data are displayed from different "slices" of the same cube. Each of the five dimensions is represented on the right-hand side of the screen, i.e. the table. For example, in Figure 6.2A, the rows of the table are the "product" dimension (types of motorcycles) and the columns are the "customer" (or region) dimension. Across the top of the table are three boxes. The first, NVT, represents the "comparisons"

The same table for different years can be viewed by clicking this double-headed arrow

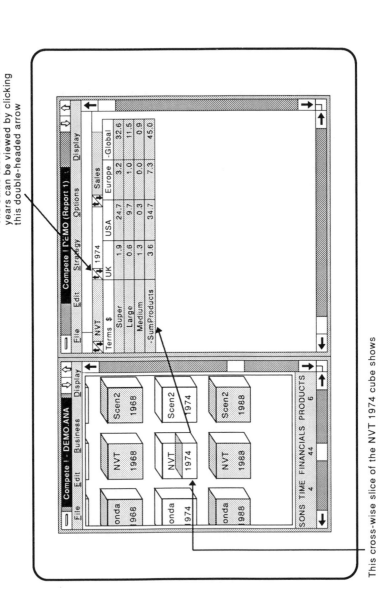

This cross-wise slice of the NVT 1974 cube shows product (super/large/medium motorcycles) versus region (UK/USA/Europe/global)

**Figure 6.2** Compete! sample screens for viewing and manipulating data. (A) a view of NVT Company sales in a product by customer (region) matrix

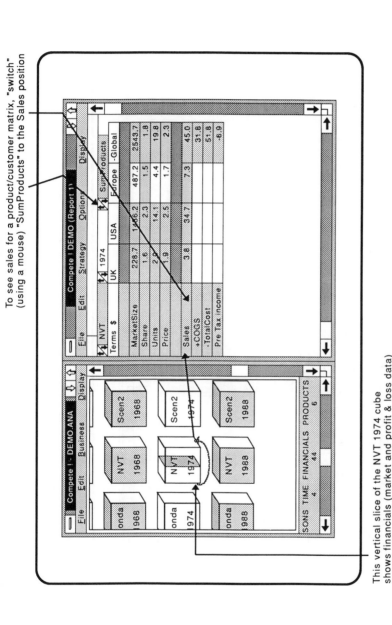

137

To see sales for a product/customer matrix, "switch" (using a mouse) "SumProducts" to the Sales position

This vertical slice of the NVT 1974 cube shows financials (market and profit & loss data) versus region (UK/USA/Europe/global)

**Figure 6.2** *Continued*   (B) a view of NVT Company for financials by customer (region). This is a different "slice" of the same cube as the previous screen

138

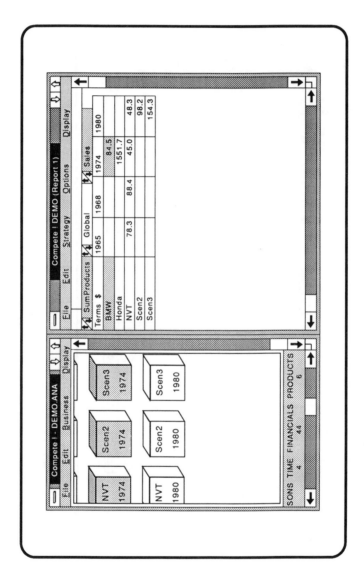

**Figure 6.2** *Continued* (C) a comparison scenario view of NVT Company and its competitors over time. This view is like looking at one sales cell from each cube, as shown by the dots in the center of the cubes

dimension, the second is for "time", and the last represents financials (in this case, sales).

By clicking a mouse on the appropriate icon (cube), such as NVT 1974, a user can quickly move from one dimension to another, viewing the data from different perspectives. In Figure 6.2A, a "cross-wise" slice of the selected cube is examined, displaying a table of financial results of product (super, large, and medium motorcycles) by region (UK, USA, Europe, and global). To view the same table for a different year, a user simply clicks a mouse on the "time" (year) box above the table.

Figure 6.2B displays data from the same cube, but uses different dimensions. In this case, the vertical slice of the NVT 1974 cube shows financials (market and profit & loss data) by region.

The third screen of this figure (6.2C) uses the comparisons dimension to view sales by scenario over time. The table shows a scenario that compares NVT Company with its competitors, displaying sales financials for all products over all time periods. This view is like looking at one sales cell from each cube, as shown by the dots in the centers of the cubes.

Compete! is also able to predict performance with its goal-seek option. If the user wants sales for 1980 at $45.0 million, the goal-seek option is used. After setting the goal, the user chooses the "seek" command and Compete! calculates the variable(s) that need to change in order to achieve the goal.

A "terms feature" in Compete! allows comparison of products with vastly different characteristics by converting all figures to a common format, such as per cent of sales. In addition, the software contains an array of graphic tools and specialized functions, such as forecasting, scales economies, and activity-based costing.

Another system, *Finexpro*, is an expert system planning tool developed by Paris-based EXPERTeam. This software enables accountants, consultants, bankers and others to produce financial reports. Reports are based on answers a user supplies during a consultation session with five parts: an analysis of financial activity; judgements of the company's future profitability; financial equilibrium evaluation; risk analysis; and comments and proposed strategic plans. Finexpro also has a simulator to plan for future years.

## PROPRIETARY COMPANY SYSTEMS

Many companies have developed proprietary knowledge-based systems for their own use. A review of some of these proprietary systems is given in *Intelligent Systems in Business* (Richardson, Jeffrey and DeFries, 1990), *The Rise of the Expert Company* (Feigenbaum, McCorduck and Nii, 1988), *Expert Systems 1990* (Walker and Miller, 1989), *Expert Systems in Business and Finance* (Watkins and Eliot, 1991), and *Innovative Applications of Artificial Intelligence* (Schorr and Rappaport, 1989,

Vol. 1; Rappaport and Smith, 1990, Vol. 2; Smith and Scott, 1991, Vol. 3). A few select examples from the above and other sources are discussed here.

In London, The Aries Club (Alvey Research in Insurance Expert Systems) has developed two expert knowledge-based systems in the field of insurance (Butler and Chamberlin, 1989). One, *Fire Risks Underwriting System*, assists in the planning process for commercial fire risks selection. The other, *Equity Selection Investment Advisor*, assists in the strategy formulation process for equity selection for the life insurance portfolio. This system has two different parts: a statistical analysis of the company in question on which key opinions can be based and a judgemental analysis which leads to "buy" or "no buy" decisions. Figure 6.3 gives a summary outline of the system.

---

I.  Statistical analysis—both numerical and qualitative data are input to reach a conclusion. These could be expressed as:
- P/E ratio is very high
- Credit control is erratic
- Share price performance is strong
- Gearing is moderately high

II. Judgemental analysis—questions are asked to obtain information about key factors in share selection, such as:
- Industry and company prospects
- Management and ownership
- Financial situation
- Professional opinions in the City

III. Once the main areas have been analyzed, the system will come to a possible recommendation to buy the given share (or not) on four possible grounds:
- Growth
- Recovery
- Income
- Discount to assets

IV. The main method used is for a user to weight the market P/E ratio of the share according to the user's opinions, and to compare this moderate value with the actual P/E. If the result is favorable, then a Buy recommendation is given, with a reason. If none of the four grounds is satisfied, then a No Buy recommendation is made.

V.  A price range within which the results hold is given—for example:
- Buy provided the price is less than X, or
- Do not buy if the price is more than Y

---

**Figure 6.3**   *Equity Selection Investment Advisor.* System outline. Adapted from Butler and Chamberlin (1989)

In addition to a widely publicized *ExperTAX* expert system for corporate tax accrual and planning (Shpilberg, Graham and Schatz, 1986), Coopers & Lybrand have developed an expert system for the volatile area of international taxation (Gleeson and West, 1989). *CLINTE* applies both national and international tax planning strategies and regulations to partial corporate models. It attempts to optimize the tax position of corporations within the bounds of user-defined constraints. This has major implications for forward planning, merger and acquisitions, and financial management.

The CLINTE user interface consists of five "windows" as shown in Figure 6.4A: a command menu window at the top; the company structure graphics window; the country icon window; the company icon window; and the system command window at the bottom. The different dimensions of CLINTE are shown in Figure 6.4.

Corporation models are developed by selecting company types from the company icon windows. Once created, the attributes (financial information, name, location, parent, etc.) are input via a template menu shown in Figure 6.4B. The corporation is displayed graphically, as shown in Figure 6.4C, with the parent company at the root and its subsidiaries beneath it.

The system then runs by making all necessary international tax calculations and corporate tax calculating for each company in each country. It also makes recommendations on other facets of the corporate situation.

## RESEARCH

The potential for using knowledge-based systems to support strategic management decision-making is demonstrable, as the above examples indicate (Ashmore, 1989; Bidgoli and Attaran, 1988). More research and development is needed, however, before the full potential of such systems can be realized.

Considerable research work is being done to model strategic management processes and develop prototype knowledge-based systems for strategic planning based on these models. Andersen Consulting, a division of the accounting firm of Arthur Andersen & Co., and IBM, for example, have modelled strategic planning processes as part of their research into developing enterprise-wide generic strategy planning knowledge-based systems (Rowe, 1989).

Andersen Consulting has worked with Jeff Williams of Carnegie Mellon University to develop the "competitive spectrum" model. This model, which isolates major competitive types of companies and identifies a specific company's strengths and weaknesses in relation to other companies in the competitive market, is the basis of a knowledge-based system which has been successfully tested at several major companies (Hiddings, 1989; Williams, 1988). The system is based on "objects" which represent competitive success principles. Object-based KBS show great potential for replicating strategic management decision-making (Mayberry, 1990).

142

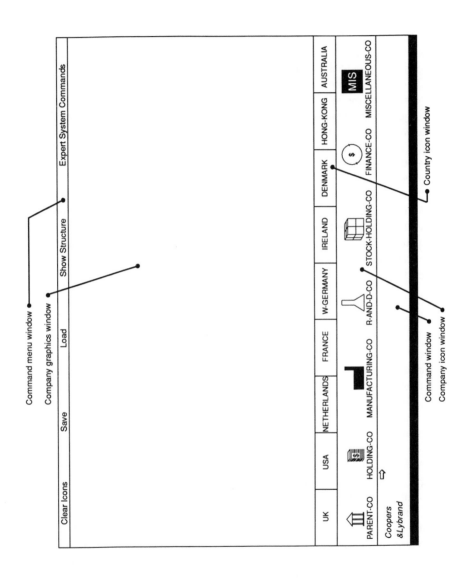

**Figure 6.4** CLINTE. (A) the user interface

143

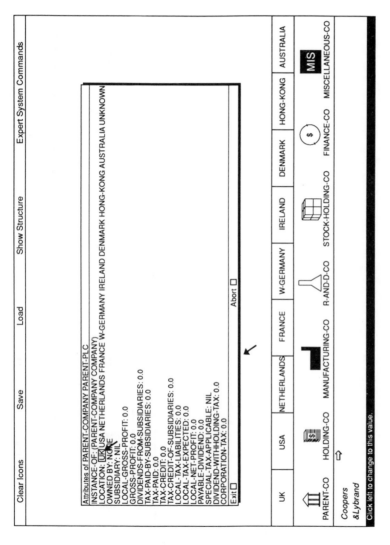

**Figure 6.4** *Continued* (B) template menu for attribute input

144

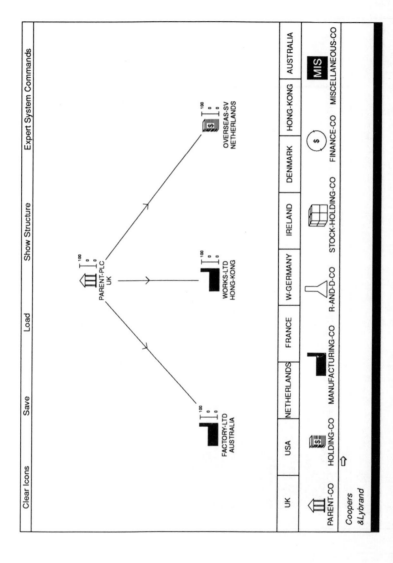

**Figure 6.4** *Continued*  (C) typical corporation structure. Each icon in the structure has a "thermometer" associated with it which is used for displaying one of the various numeric values which are held as attributes of the company

The *Business Strategy Advisor (The Strategist)* is an experimental prototype of an expert system that has been developed at the IBM Los Angeles Scientific Center (LASC). It is intended mostly for use in the manufacturing industry (Schumann *et al.*, 1990). It helps users analyze an organization's existing or planned products and suggests appropriate business strategies for the products.

Although the potential competitive benefits of applying information technology are generally recognized by business and information systems executives, there is a great gap between recognizing such value and applying the technology effectively. To help bridge this gap, a group at IBM Los Angeles Scientific Center has developed a knowledge-based system facilitator, called *S∗P∗A∗R∗K*. The system is designed to help business and information systems managers identify competitive applications of information technology and create a range of alternative strategies using information technology.

University researchers are also at work defining and modelling strategic planning processes. For example, a project at the University of Massachusetts focuses on product planning processes (Abraham, 1990). Another at Stanford Research Institute (SRI) focuses on analyzing company, market and technological factors, and recommending competitive market strategies in the polyfins (a special kind of plastic) industry (Syed and Tse, 1987). Work is being done at Rensselaer Polytechnic and the California Institute of Technology on a system called *Pleiades*. It creates interactive software that allows evaluation of automated assembly operations (Sanderson *et al.*, 1990). Work is also being done at Wharton School of Business, Georgia State University, University of Michigan, Gonzaga University, the Technical University of Brno, Czechoslovakia, and James Madison University, among other centers of research activity. The authors' research work being done in this area is described in several works (Mockler, 1989a, b, 1990, 1991).

According to a survey of *AI Expert* readers, corporations consider the potential for KBS applications in the strategic management area to be very high (Philip and Schultz, 1990).

## THE FUTURE: INTEGRATED SYSTEMS TOOLS

Many KBS are integrated with conventional computer systems—especially database and spreadsheet-based systems, and financial analyses, modelling (or simulation of activities), forecasting and reporting systems. According to many, such integrated or imbedded use of KBS is where their growth in business will be (Chapnick 1988).

The commercial loan screening system outlined in Figure 6.5 is an example of this. Strategic planning affects decision-making using this system in three ways:

(1)   In the purpose segment, strategic company policy limitations control what loans are considered.

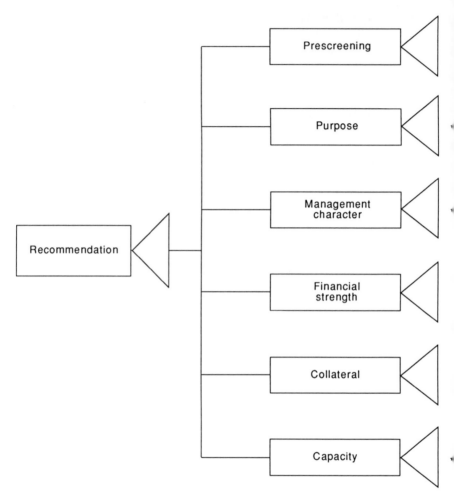

**Figure 6.5**  Overall dependency diagram: commercial loan screening system (initial prototype). *Integrated KBS. Copyright © by R. J. Mockler. Reprinted with permission

(2)    In the management character segment, long-term personality predictors of performance are examined.

(3)    In the capacity segment, the strategic factors affecting a prospective company's long-term future are examined

Similar strategic planning segments are part of several commercial systems, for example Syntelligence's *Lending Advisor, Underwriting Advisor,* the early versions of *Alacrity,* and *Operations Planner.* KBS are also found embedded in many marketing decision support systems. In addition, KBS are being used as integrated segments of group strategic planning sessions at Ronin Corporation and the University of Arizona. While not commonly employed for strategic planning in business today, KBS systems appear to show promise of becoming a useful technology for strategic management, especially for key functional areas, in addition to their usefulness today for training and learning purposes.

# REFERENCES

Abraham, T. (1990) Market advisor: An expert system for product development. PhD Dissertation, Amherst, University of Massachusetts.

Ashmore, M. (1989) Applying expert systems to business strategy. *The Journal of Business Strategy*, September/October, 46–49.

Berman, S. J. and Kautz, R. F. (1990) Compete! A sophisticated tool that facilitates strategic analysis. *Planning Review*, July/August, 35–39.

Bidgoli, H. and Attaran, M. (1988) Improving the effectiveness of strategic decision making using an integrated decision support system. *Information and Software Technology*, June, 278–284.

Butler, A. and Chamberlin, G. (1989) The Aries Club—experience of expert systems in insurance & investment. *British Computer Workshop Series: Research & Development in Expert Systems IV*, Ed. D. S. Moralee, pp. 246–257.

Chapnick, P. (1988) MIS is not the enemy. *AI Expert*, April, 5–6.

Cook, D. A. and Sterling, W. (1989) Alacrity: Software that asks shrewd questions. *Planning Review*, November/December, 22–29.

Dologite, D. G. (1991) Developing knowledge-based systems: A survey of its impact on graduate MBAs. *Expert Systems with Applications: An International Journal*, 2. 175–186.

Dologite, D. G. (1990) Software selection: A knowledge-based system approach. *Journal of Microcomputer Systems Management*, 2(1). 15–24.

Dologite, D. G. and Mockler, R. J. (1992) *Knowledge-Based Systems: An Introduction to Expert Systems*. Merrill, Columbus, Ohio.

Feigenbaum, E., McCorduck, P. and Nii, H. P. (1988) *The Rise of the Expert Company*. Times Books, New York.

Gleeson, J. F. J. and West, M. (1989) CLINTE: Coopers & Lybrand International Tax Expert System. *British Computer Society Workshop Series: Research & Development in Expert Systems IV*, Ed. D. S. Moralee, pp. 18–31.

Gongla, P. *et al.* (1989) S*P*A*R*K: A knowledge-based system for identifying competitive uses of information technology. *IBM Systems Journal*, 28(4). 628–637.

Hiddings, G. (1989) Expert systems and the competitive spectrum model. Center for Strategic Technology Research, Andersen Consulting, Seminar, New Orleans, LA. Decision Sciences Institute, November 22.

Mayberry, M. T. (1990) Knowledge-based simulation of strategic planning: Closing the gap. AAAI Workshop on AI and Business, Boston. MA. American Association of Artificial Intelligence, July 30.

Mockler, R. J. (1989a) *Knowledge-Based Systems for Management Decisions*. Prentice-Hall, Englewood Cliffs, NJ.

Mockler, R. J. (1989b) *Knowledge-Based Systems for Strategic Planning*. Prentice-Hall, Englewood Cliffs, NJ.

Mockler, R. J. (1990) *Cognitive Modelling for Strategic Planning*, a research monograph. Business Research Institute, St Johns University, Jamaica, NY.

Mockler, R. J. (1991) *Strategic Management*. D & R Publishing Company, New York.

Philip, G. C. and Schultz, H. K. (1990) What's happening with expert systems? *AI Expert*, November, 57–59.

Rappaport, A. and Smith, R. (Eds) (1990) *Innovative Applications of Artificial Intelligence 2*. AAAI Press/MIT Press, Cambridge, MA.

Richardson, J. J. and DeFries, M. J. (1990) *Intelligent Systems in Business: Integrating the Technology*. Ablex Publishing Corporation, Norwood, NJ.

Rowe, A. (1989) Expert systems in strategic management. Presented at the Decision Sciences Institute 20th Annual Meeting, New Orleans, LA, November 20–22.

Sanderson, A. C. *et al.* (1990) Assembly sequence planning. *AI Magazine*, Spring, 62–81.

Schorr, H. and Rappaport, A. (Eds) (1989) *Innovative Applications of Artificial Intelligence*. AAAI Press/MIT Press, Cambridge, MA.

Schumann, M. *et al.* (1990) An expert business strategy advisor. *Expert Systems*, Winter, 32–39.

Shpilberg, D., Graham, L. E. and Schatz, H. (1986) ExperTAX: An expert system for corporate tax planning. *Expert Systems*, July, 136–151.

Smith, R. and Scott, C. (Eds) (1991) *Innovative Applications of Artificial Intelligence 3*. AAAI Press/MIT Press, Cambridge, MA.

Syed, J. R. and Tse, E. *Proceedings of the 7th International Workshop on Expert Systems and Their Applications*, Avignon, May 13–15, p. 689.

Walker, T. O. and Miller, R. K. (1989) *Expert Systems 1990: An In-Depth Assessment of Technology and Applications*. SEAI Technical Publications, Madison, GA.

Watkins, P. and Eliot, L. (1991) *Expert Systems in Business and Finance*. Wiley, New York.

Williams, J. R. (1988) I don't think we're in Kansas anymore. Work in Progress No. 20–86–87. Carnegie Mellon University, Graduate School of Industrial Administration, Pittsburgh, PA.

# 7

# CHARTING STRATEGIC ROLES FOR INTERNATIONAL FACTORIES

### Kasra Ferdows

*Professor of Technology Management, INSEAD*
*Professor Business Administration, Georgetown University*

The volume of world trade in manufactured goods has increased 15 times in the last three decades, and this long-term trend is not slowing down. (*The Economist*, 1987). More products manufactured in one country are finding their ways into other countries. These products are not just finished goods; they are also components, intracompany transfers, and processed materials.

No company can stay indifferent to this trend. The competitive threats posed by foreign manufacturers should, of course, be constantly monitored, but, looking at this trend more positively, all companies should examine more vigorously the cost/benefits of establishing or expanding their own manufacturing base internationally. Variations in tariffs, fluctuations in currencies, proximity to markets, and access to foreign technology are but some of the reasons why the existence of an international, manufacturing base would provide a company with more room to manoeuver. Without an international network of factories, a firm has simply fewer strategic options, and given the trend in global competition, the consequence of this limitation in options is becoming more dire.

The decision to establish, expand, or change an international network of factories is complex. A large number of factors should be taken into account, many of which are intractable, unmeasurable, or unpredictable. Consequently, the

International Review of Strategic Management.
Edited by D. E. Hussey. © 1992 John Wiley & Sons Ltd

decision-making process is usually long and costly. Rightly so, because such decisions bind the firm for a long time and there are many pitfalls on the way. So experience is particularly important here, and given the accelerated pace of internationalization of manufacturing called for at present, a prudent company would be looking around hard to learn more about how to go about making these decisions.

But where should one look? Who are the ones to provide the lessons for the internationalization of manufacturing? The answer is simply those that have been at it for a long time, and they do not include many Japanese firms. They are mostly American and European multinationals. This is one area in manufacturing management where the Japanese have not matched the strength of Americans and Europeans.

The American multinational companies have been setting up foreign manufacturing facilities rather aggressively in the last four decades. Thanks mostly to them, the total foreign manufacturing base of the United States is larger than that of any other nation (*International Herald Tribune*, 1988). German, British, and other European companies also already have a large manufacturing base outside their countries. The Japanese multinationals have started this more recently but are on an accelerated course (*Economist*, 1988).

How have some of the experienced multinational companies developed their international factory networks? How have they divided work among different plants? What stategic roles have they assigned to each? In short, how have they managed the process of internationalizing their manufacturing operations, and what general lessons can be derived from their experience?

These were the questions which prompted this investigation. The answers are not found easily. My research to date has yielded a model which, essentially through reduction of complexity, helps the search for the answers. Specifically, what I report in this chapter is a model for (a) identifying the strategic role of each plant in the firm's international network of factories, and (b) suggesting a pattern for evolution of these strategic roles through time.

The research leading to this chapter consisted of analysis of an international factory network of eight large multinational companies in the electronic industry. Five were American, one Dutch, one Italian, and one Japanese (see Note 1). For most of them, I focused on their European factories. I have also drawn on the data collected from multinational manufacturers in other industries—both through publicly available documents and personal observations—to show that the model I propose in this chapter applies more generally.

The model has two important limitations which I should point out at the outset. First, it covers only factories which are essentially owned and/or operated by the firm itself; joint ventures, contract manufacturing, technological partnerships, long-term supply contracts, non-integrated affiliates and other forms of engaging in manufacturing activity in a foreign country have not been included. This is not because these other forms are less important than own manufacturing;

rather, it only reflects my choice in keeping the scope of this research manageable.

Second, only the long-term decisions are addressed. Day-to-day operational decisions are not covered here. Management of operations of an international factory network is complicated and needs further work. Nevertheless, the model I propose in this chapter provides an insight into how the network of international factories should be organized and has a few direct implications for the communication links among factories and between factories and headquarters.

# PATTERNS OF INTERNATIONALIZATION OF THE MANUFACTURING BASE

If a typical manufacturing company in the industrially advanced region of the world were to follow the "product life cycle" model proposed by Vernon (1966) and modified by Wells (1972) and Stobaugh (1968), one would expect to see a shift in the manufacturing base of its more mature products from developed to developing countries. Applied to an American company, a simplistic version of this model (as proposed in the early 1970s) would predict five phases in the shift of the manufacturing base as a new product moves towards maturity: in phase I, when the new product is just introduced, all manufacturing is done in the United States; in phase II, production is started in Europe; in phase III, production in Europe is expanded to export also to the developing countries; in phase IV, production is started in the developing countries and Europe also exports to the United States; and finally, in phase V, the developing countries start exporting to the United States.

Even if we adjust for the changes in the industrial power and economic growth of different countries since the early 1970s, still the model has little explanatory power for the evolution of the manufacturing base at the firm level. In fact, Vernon himself states:

Neither the theory of international trade nor the theory of international capital movements has much to offer in explanation of *managerial decisions* to invest in production facilities abroad. (Emphasis added)

(*Gruber, Mehta and Vernon, 1972*)

The main problem, as I see it, is that these theories assume only a subset of possible motivations for a company to locate a manufacturing facility in a new country. Access to cheap production input factors and proximity to market form the foundation of these theories. Both are valid and important motivating forces. But since companies have more than just these reasons for putting a factory abroad, these theories lose their explanatory power.

They also lose their normative power, because the key for answering *how* a company should expand its manufacturing base internationally is simply in the *why*. In other words, the reasons for establishing a factory abroad determine the way the company should plan, design, construct, and commission that factory. What is the strategic role of the factory—that is the starting question.

Later in this chapter I suggest a simple framework to differentiate among a set of generic strategic roles for factories in the firm's international manufacturing network. The premise of this framework is that a factory's strategic role is defined to a large extent by two variables: (a) the primary reason for establishment of the factory, and (b) the extent of "technical activities" planned for that site. In the next section, I describe five categories of primary reasons for establishing a factory in a new country. By "technical activities" I mean a selected set of activities which go beyond the mere production of the product—activities such as procurement, process engineering, product engineering, product development, warehousing and distribution, finance, aftersale service, and the like. More on this is also explained later.

# MANUFACTURING IN A DIFFERENT COUNTRY

There are always a combination of different reasons why a firm puts a factory abroad. I suggest most of the reasons can be grouped into five categories:

- Access to low-cost production input factors
- Proximity to market
- Use of local technological resources
- Control and amortization of technological assets
- Preemption of competition

Brief descriptions of these categories follow.

## Access to Low-Cost Production Input Factors

Economists have long argued that the primary reason for locating manufacturing abroad is exploitation of low-cost production factors. Of the four factors, labour, materials, energy and capital, the foremost has been, of course, labour. Proximity to cheaper raw materials and energy, too, has provided compelling reasons in certain industries. However, the fourth factor, capital, has seldom been a *primary* reason for locating manufacturing facilities abroad. Availability of cheaper capital (in the form of grants or low-interest loans) seem to be a factor in choosing among alternative manufacturing sites, but not the driving force behind internationalizing the manufacturing base of the firm.

## Proximity to Market

Existence of a manufacturing base often allows a better customer service—particularly in product customization and delivery—and enhances customer confidence in the company. Some of the ideas put forward by Vernon's product life cycle model (Vernon, 1966)—stipulating movement of manufacturing base from developed to developing countries as the product matures and the size of the market reaches certain thresholds—are such market-driven reasons.

Davidson (1980), in a study of US-based multinationals, suggested that the primary reason for locating manufacturing abroad has been essentially to serve a new market or to reduce financial and trade restriction risks. When a national market is served from a manufacturing base in the country, production costs and sales revenues are denominated in the same currency, reducing uncertainty related to currency and price fluctuations; furthermore, by being inside, the rise of trade barriers would in fact enhance the position of the company. Many observers suggest that the current rush of the Japanese automobile and electronics companies to set up manufacturing facilities in North America and Europe is mainly due to these reasons.

## Use of Local Technological Resources

A manufacturing base can be an effective way to tap into local technological resources. If keeping up-to-date with technology is critical to a company, then proximity to universities, research centers, and sophisticated suppliers, competitors, and customers assume strategic importance. Having a manufacturing base not only increases the frequency of interactions with the environment, but may be the most efficient way to distill the available information and experience into useful knowledge for the company.

A primary reason for establishing manufacturing facilities in Silicon Valley, in Japan, or in many industrially advanced European countries, among other places, falls into this category.

## Control and Amortization of Technological Assets

By using its own processes in foreign manufacturing, a company may earn better returns on its technology than would be possible through licensing. Moreover, by expanding internationally, a firm may benefit from scale economies. Flaherty (1987) found these to be among the important reasons for internationalization of the manufacturing base in the five companies she studied.

The same is true for many other European manufacturers, particularly those coming from smaller countries such as Holland, Denmark, Belgium, and Sweden. For many of the manufacturers in these countries, access to international markets, especially the United States market, is crucial. Without that they simply would not be able to afford the resources which are needed to establish and maintain a technological leadership. Desire to control the knowhow can be a strong reason why they may establish their own factory as opposed to entering into partnerships, joint ventures or licensing agreements, even though the latter may be cheaper.

## Preemption of Competition

In a developing country with an underdeveloped market, a company may establish a manufacturing base in order to preempt the competition. The goal is to expand as the market grows, and through government permits, accumulated local experience, and customer dependence and confidence, maintain a high barrier to entry for others. Many tobacco factories in the African and South American countries are illustrative cases; so are tire factories, breweries, artificial textile fibers, and automotive component plants.

In oligopolies, the necessity to establish a manufacturing base in some of these countries goes beyond the potential returns to be earned in that country: there is also a motivation to deny competitors an incubation zone to grow and become strong. Car manufacturers are a case in point. By going to the Federal Republic of China, Volkswagen and Peugeot not only benefit from the potential growth in that market, but also they may be preempting other competitors from growing strong there and attacking other markets. One may argue that if Ford and General Motors had kept or reestablished their manufacturing facilities in Japan after World War II—as they did in Europe—the shape of the car industry in the world today would have been very different.

Some of these reasons are, of course, more frequently encountered than others. In my research, I found the first three to be more prevalent than the last two. For simplicity, in the framework that I suggest in the next section, I consider only the first three categories. If necessary, the framework can be extended to include all five.

# IDENTIFYING STRATEGIC ROLE OF THE FACTORY

Identifying the role of a particular factory in the competitive strategy of the company is indeed a complex task. Every case seems to be special, meaning that a unique set of factors are dictating the role which is assigned or played by the factory. Is there a way to reduce this complexity? Is there a way to categorize the strategic roles of various factories in a firm's international manufacturing network?

My research suggests that looking at the primary reason for establishing the manufacturing site together with examination of the extent of technical activities currently planned for that site provide significant clues for understanding the strategic role which is assigned to the factory (or if such assignment is not done

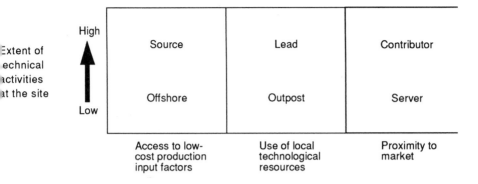

**Figure 7.1**    Generic roles of international factories

consciously, the role actually being played by the factory). Figure 7.1 shows a framework which incorporates this, and suggests six generic strategic roles: offshore, source, server, contributor, outpost, lead.

## Offshore Factories

These are factories which are there essentially to utilize local cheap production input factors and supply components or final products to the home plant.

The basic characteristic of these plants is that managerial investment in the plant is kept to the minimum essential to run the production. Usually no real engineering work—product or process related—goes on at the site; procurement decisions are reduced to managing day-to-day order follow-up; accounting and finance primary purpose is to provide data for the management in the home country; the pattern of shipments out of the plant is kept simple and essentially out of the control of the plant management.

Many factories in the Far East established by American and European so-called "high-tech" companies fall in this cateogry. During the 1970s almost all producers of integrated circuits shipped their wafers to the Far East to be assembled into a microchip. Other examples can be found in the Mexican Free Zone (*Maquiladoras*), where in the last decade the number of factories set up by mostly American companies to take advantage of low Mexican wages have increased several fold. The outputs of these factories are essentially all exported to the US.

## Source Factories

The primary reason for establishing these factories, too, is access to cheap production input factors. But they are given a more substantial strategic role than the offshore factories. They become a focal point for a company's efforts for specific components, products, or production processes. More managers and technical support staff are housed at the site, and the factory is given a greater autonomy in procurement, production planning, process changes, and distribution.

Apple Computer's factory in Singapore is such a factory. For a long time it supplied assembled printed circuits to other Apple factories in the United States and Ireland. The factory specialized in this, and some of the advanced engineering work for this production process (burn-in, for example) was done at this site. Similarly, the Hewlett-Packard memory board plant in Puerto Rico and the Philips plant in Singapore (producing a variety of small electrical appliances such as irons and hair dryers) are source plants in the sense that they carry responsibility for development and production of specific products or components—even if these products or components may be relatively minor ones—for worldwide distribution.

## Server Factories

These factories are to serve specific national or regional markets. Like the offshore category, the investment in managerial talents at these sites is kept to a level deemed essential to run the production efficiently. There is, however, more autonomy at the site for managing the flow of material and information between the factory and its suppliers and customers.

Best examples are the soft drinks bottling plants and tobacco factories spread over many developing countries. Many factories set up by the Japanese in Europe and the United States are essentially servers—at least in the early phases before transfer of some engineering work. Many of the companies trying to get into the Chinese market are doing so with server factories.

## Contributor Factories

These plants serve a specific national or regional market, but their assigned role goes beyond just supplying products. Like source factories, they become focal points for certain company-wide activities. They compete even with the company's home factories to be the test bed for the newest process technology, newest computer system, and for the introduction of new products. In short, they are given explicit roles to develop and contribute knowhow for the company—going beyond the normal financial contributions expected from the server factories.

Nestle's plant in Singapore (serving the south east Asian markets), Apple Computer's plant in County Cork, Ireland (serving the European markets), Baekart's (world's largest producer of steel wires for tires) plant in Japan, Volvo in Belgium, Waertsila's (Finnish producer of large diesel engines) factory in

Singapore are all examples of contributor factories. All have a role which goes beyond just serving their designated markets.

## Outpost Factories

Their main role is to collect information. They are located in areas where technologically advanced suppliers, competitors, customers, or research laboratories are situated. The premise for their establishment is that a factory would provide an efficient mechanism to collect useful information. In my research, I have not come across outpost factories. Therefore this category is perhaps only a theoretical possibility.

The companies which want to be present in technologically advanced areas seldom set up a whole new factory. Instead, they seem to prefer acquiring an existing one, or going into a joint venture. For example, Philips' acquisition of Signetics in Silicon Valley, Ciba-Geigy's acquisition of a biotechnology firm in the same area, Ford's purchase of 25 % of Mazda in Japan, have been mostly driven by the desire to establish an outpost for collecting data.

## Lead Factories

These factories serve as partners of headquarters in building strategic capabilities in the manufacturing function. They tap into local technological resources not only to collect data for headquarters, but also to use these resources themselves. Companies would depend on lead factories for development of specific manufacturing capabilities. Often they would be the sole or major producer of certain products or components for the companies' global markets.

Hewlett-Packard plants in France, Germany and the United Kingdom are good examples. They are situated in areas with a good supply of engineers and in close proximity to other high-tech factories. Each plant has responsibilities for many technical activities beyond production; often at the same site one finds centers for development of certain products for worldwide applications. The same is true for some of the European plants of IBM. These plants are often the "prime sites" for worldwide supply of new products and processes.

Factories of Corning Glass in France, the United Kingdom and Germany can also be considered as lead factories. The four plants in France specialize in specific products (such as lenses and television screens), and by being in close proximity to Corning's European research center, have pioneered many new products and processes for Corning worldwide. The two plants in the United Kingdom have specialized in various other products, including tableware. The German plant is where most of the work in fiber optics is going on. Almost all these plants have significant roles in developing manufacturing competence for Corning Europe.

# INTERNATIONAL FACTORY NETWORK IN A NEW PERSPECTIVE

Even though the boundaries of the above categories are not sharply defined, the model allows a company's factories to be viewed in a new perspective. This perspective is useful in three ways: first and most important, in tracking the patterns of changes in the strategic role of each factory through time; second, in the choice of the appropriate communication system for the factory network; and third, in the organization design for a firm's international network of factories. These are explained below.

## Changes in Strategic Role of Factory

New factories generally start with clear strategic roles. Factories located abroad usually start as servers of offshores. (Outpost is another possibility, but, as mentioned before, I have not come across any outpost plants.) A company may choose to keep the factories in these roles for a variety of reasons. Many global companies have highly centralized organizational structures and choose to keep all technology development near domestic operations. However, it should be noted that those offshore and server plants which do not gradually change to source and contributor plants provide little benefit to the rest of the company in terms of locally generated technological knowledge. Moreover, there is a danger of stagnation and falling behind in technological progress in such factories. Not having the necessary human resources and organizational latitude, the factory is likely to be slow in improving its operations in transferring knowhow and technology from the company's central staff. The net result is a deterioration of performance.

One way to avoid these risks is to build technical capabilities within plants. Process improvement, product customization, making more decisions for procurement and distribution, and ultimately product development are examples of technical tasks which can be relocated at the manufacturing site. Expanding a factory's responsibilities for these tasks implies a change in the strategic role assigned to the factory in the international network. This can be depicted more clearly in Figure 7.2.

Figure 7.2 is a more detailed version of Figure 7.1. The movements shown are the natural ones in an evolutionary sense; they increase the chance of survival of the factory. The scale of "technical activities at the site" in Figure 7.2 is meant as an illustration, and should be adjusted for relevant tasks in the specific company or industry being analyzed by this model.

The arguments for the specific moves suggested in Figure 7.2 are threefold:

First, as mentioned above, server and offshore plants, by being essentially occupied with mere production and lacking slack resources, may fall behind

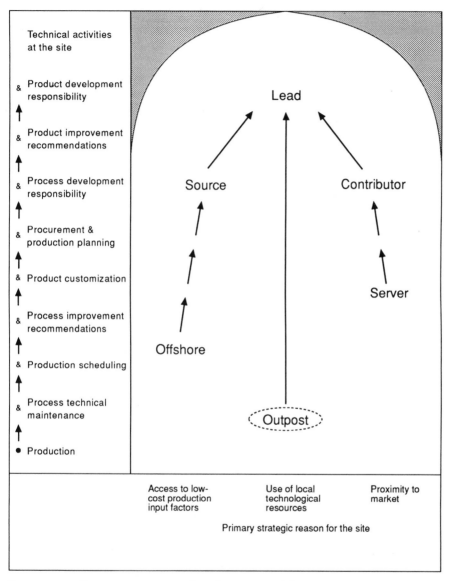

**Figure 7.2**    Changes in strategic roles of international factories

technological progress. Lack of excitement in the plant is likely to drive the talented managers and engineers away; hence performance is likely to deteriorate and the site would become increasingly more dependent on central staff for long-term survival.

Second, reducing the time to market for introduction of new products encourages moving the offshore and server factories towards source and contributors and eventually some of them to lead plants. Reducing time to market requires increasing efficiency and speed of problem-solving in the design of both the product and the process. Shortening the communications link between design and production and allowing them to be done more in parallel (instead of sequentially) are effective methods for achieving these. Hence, putting more of the firm's technical resources physically close to the factories is helpful in this process. For the server factories, the shortening of the cycle applies also to customization of products to fit the local market needs, and sometimes to compliance with local government pressure for increasing local contents. As product technology matures, markets begin to segment and local substitution occurs. For sophisticated products, customers start demanding local changes to the product. As volumes increase, governments and local industry structure put pressure on factories to have more local contents. Thus, with time, there is more pressure to increase the extent of technical activities at the site.

A third reason, and the principal one to move towards lead factories, is to tap into local technological resources. Existence of a manufacturing site seems to be an important means for attracting local talent to join the company. Such talent would then be underutilized if the factory is not given the broad strategic scope of a lead plant. To keep successful managers sufficiently motivated, and to use the factory as an effective learning vehicle for the organization, the company must let such factories grow in complexity and scope. Additional functions must be added once production becomes routine. These factories should be given the chance of competing for the company's new products and processes. They should have the resources to carry projects forward and transfer knowledge to the rest of the company.

All this implies that moving towards source, contributor, and lead factories is desirable. As the model in Figure 7.2 suggests, there are specific paths for the development of these types of factories. Moreover, certainly not all factories in a multinational company can or should be turned into lead plants. Some plants might be kept as contributor or source plants and remain effective. Of those, only the plants which are situated in technologically advanced environments—for example in certain parts of Germany, France, Japan and the United States—are in a good position to move into the lead position.

In the sample of eight multinational companies studied in this research (Note 1), in almost all cases the international factories had been started in offshore or server roles, and after a while some of them had moved to source, contributor or lead plants. The Apple plant in Singapore started as an offshore but moved to become a source; the H-P plants in Germany, the UK, and France started as servers, but then developed into contributor and lead plants. Through the years, these plants have built up organizations which have become competence centers for development of specific systems, products, and processes for the company's worldwide operations.

To recap, lead plants, and to a lesser extent contributor and source factories, must have management teams and technical skills capable of learning from their environments and of using the knowledge effectively and innovatively in creating new products and processes. They must as well be continually striving for efficiency and flexibility within their plants to respond quickly to changing customer needs. This requires a charter sufficiently broad at the outset to attract the quality of employees needed to spur innovation and to manage complexity. Site location is important, hence a plant with such a mandate must be strategically located, even though the site may look expensive for the early phases during which the factory has a simpler strategic role.

Why should a company go through all the trouble of spreading its technical resources in manufacturing sites around the world? The answer simply is because the abilities to learn from one's employees worldwide, to tap centers of excellence in various countries, and to be more responsive to changes in different parts of the global market are becoming more important.

These arguments have been put forth by many, most recently by Bartlett and Ghoshal (1987), who state them eloquently and convincingly. If we were to apply Bartlett and Ghoshal's findings here, the successful multinational corporations are those which maximize learning from their international factory network by investing in local resources—i.e., in the context of Figure 7.2, moving from offshore and server positions up. Bartlett and Ghoshal would also advocate not staying in the outpost position, because an outpost factory is neither effective for the purpose of timely information collection nor efficient in the use of resources. In fact, the outpost factory fits what they call a "black hole".

## Communication Within Factory Network

Many speak of installing sophisticated telecommunications and management information systems within the international factory network. These include computer-aided design links, materials management links, engineering systems links, worldwide project teams, and uniform cost management reporting systems, among many others. Aside from the expense and irreplaceable management time which successful implementation of these systems demands, a persistent risk is that if not properly chosen, the information system may in fact be harmful! Too much data transfer reduces the ability of the management to sort out the useful information. Mere measurement of certain variables may send the wrong signals to some factories in the chain. In short, choosing an appropriate communication system for an international factory network is clearly not an easy task. Albeit only modestly, the model in Figure 7.2 helps determine the needed information links to and from each factory in the network.

The premise is a simple one: the communication links between a factory and headquarters and the other factories in the network depend on the strategic role of the factory. This looks obvious, but it often gets buried in the complexity of each factory being considered as a special case. The usual result is that either the factories are left to develop their own systems or, paradoxically, senior management forces a common system for all. These might be good solutions in certain cases, but certainly not in all.

If all foreign factories of a firm are essentially offshores, or all are servers, aiming for a common system of communications would not be a problem. But if some are offshores and some are contributors and source factories, then a common communication system would be a mistake. Again, the reasons are obvious. Information exchange with offshore and server factories is relatively limited in scope and flows mostly in one direction. The contributor and source plants, on the other hand, require a broader band for communication, more intensive and frequent exchanges, and need connections not only with the central staff but also with other plants. In the same vein, if the plant network contains lead factories, then the entire communication system in the network—including the links with the offshore and server factories—becomes more complicated.

To be more specific, networks containing source, contributor, and lead factories need complex yet efficient communication systems not only for transmitting the routine data—production plans, output, costs, engineering change notices, product documents, and the like—but also for frequent exchange of views and ideas on product and process designs. Personal contacts and informal channels become as important as the formal channels. De Meyer's (1988) comments on formal and informal communication flows between international R&D facilities summarize well the communication needs within such factory networks:

> The need for excellent communication between sites is critical for the effective transfer of technology. Much of the information that must flow to headquarters and between different sites can be routinized and one can rely on impersonal media, such as electronic mail, reports and global database networks. But for many stages of the innovation cycle, the personal face-to-face communication remains of primordial importance. Personal contacts play a preponderant role in the diffusion of knowledge between sites and in the exploitation of research results. Lateral informational flows must be stimulated. Tools available include:
>
> • A policy to stimulate travel and constant telephone contacts between managers and technological experts (both DEC and Ford have private planes for shuttling employees daily between their European sites)
> • Regular formal meetings with extensive informal "appendices"
> • Company culture stressing open informational exchange

- Organization of international working groups or project teams leading to intense interaction between employees from different sites
- An active policy of job rotation between sites
- Language training

The extent and the level of sophistication of the communication links in an international network of factories has thus less to do with the number in the network or the geographical spread of the factories and more with the variety of strategic roles assigned to the factories. A bottling or a tobacco company with factories spread in 50 countries probably needs a simpler communication system than a car company that designs and manufactures in five.

All the eight companies in the sample, being very large multinational companies, had factories in almost all the categories of Figure 7.2 (except fully owned outposts). The communication systems in their factory networks were thus quite complex. Even so, one could discern the strong influence of the factory's strategic role in the design of the communication system. In Philips, for example, the lighting division had a distinctly different communication system from the electronics division.

In the lighting division, Philips operates server factories for markets outside of those supplied by lead plants in Holland. All lighting R&D is performed in Philips' Holland labs and first transferred to the lead factories nearby for process development and validation. Mature products and processes are then transferred to its server factories worldwide. In contrast, the consumer electronics division has mostly contributor and lead factories spread over the world. Most product and process development tasks are housed in these factories. The intensity and nature of communications among the factories in these two divisions, as one expects, are vastly different. In the lighting division, the flow of the data to and from its mostly server factories is rather routine, vertical (i.e. hierarchical) and reasonably regular. In the electronics division, the communication between the factories consists more of sharing knowledge and experience. More tools for stimulating lateral information flow—such as more face-to-face meetings, job rotations, international work groups or project teams—are employed in the electronics division.

Another example of extensive use of these tools is in Hewlett-Packard. The international factory network of H-P consists of mostly source, contributor and lead factories, and a wide range of tools—from electronic mail, to regular meetings and "retreats", and job rotations—are employed to create and keep multiple lines of communication between factories. Travel expenses seem to be a significant amount of each factory's budget. Had H-P had mostly offshore or server factories, one could question the need for all this. But with lead, contributor and source factories, such investment in communications becomes a necessity.

## Organization of Factory Network

Organizationally, the choice of reporting system in an international network of factories has been confounded by many factors. The usual solution is a matrix organization where geography, product, or technology has shaped the decision. In addition to these three axes of differentiation, the strategic role of the factory is certainly another important axis which in some cases should perhaps prevail over the other three. Identifying the current and planned strategic roles for each factory should lead to a better choice for the worldwide manufacturing organization.

The premise here is that there are benefits in putting the factories with similar strategic roles in the same organizational units—even if they are scattered in different corners of the world. Because a contributor, server, and an offshore factory belong to the same business unit and happen to be, say, in Europe or the Far East, they should not be necessarily put under the same organization.

The ways in which these factories need to communicate with each other, with the rest of the international network, and with central manufacturing and development staff are vastly different. While the server factories and perhaps offshores can be organized on a geographical basis, source, contributors, and lead plants need more direct and frequent access to units outside their region. Performance measure, too, would be different for these factories depending on their strategic roles. Whereas cost efficiency is important in an offshore plant, or profit margin in a server one, the measure for outpost, source, contributor, and lead plants is more complicated. Placing a mix of these factories in the same organizational unit increases the level of confusion, and cost allocations among factories and organizational units become a more taxing affair.

# CONCLUSION

The international expansion of a corporation's manufacturing base is becoming a necessity for survival. With diverse and sometimes conflicting forces driving this expansion, the absence of a clear strategic map for the role of each factory within the firm's international manufacturing network can have dire consequences. Establishment of a plant is a binding and generally irreversible decision, locking the firm into long-term constraints, and there is no guarantee that a series of such decisions made incrementally would yield an optimal network. Moreover, once the factory is established, its development should be guided strategically, even though the operational considerations may seem overwhelming.

The model I suggest here (Figure 7.2) helps clarify the strategic role of each factory within the international network. Using it for analysis of factory networks provides a fresh perspective and yields a few insights. I suggest three as follows:

First, development of lead plants in the network is a strategy that stimulates innovation and provides effective access to globally developed technology. No one nation has a monopoly on manufacturing strength now, and a multinational manufacturer without such plants would be at a strategic disadvantage. The building of these types of plants requires a large commitment and takes a long time. Seldom is it practical to establish a lead factory from scratch. The usual way is to start with a server, source, or even offshore factory, and build up technical resources and capabilities at the site. Turning an outpost into a lead factory seems to be less practical probably because, without a clear staple production or market, it is difficult to justify investment of technical resources in outpost factories.

Second, in analyzing the international network of factories of a company, the existence of lead, source, and contributor plants indicates sophisticated international production experience, and potential for achieving lasting competitive advantage through worldwide manufacturing. Conversely, gaps in a company's network of international factories can raise new questions. Sheer numbers of international factories may give the wrong impression. Many offshore plants or server plants but no source, contributor, or lead plants are not signs of a mature network which can make long-term contributions to the competitive position of the firm.

Third, in the choice of the organizational structure for the international factory network, an important criterion is the current and future strategic role of each factory as defined from the perspective of this model. Often for international factories, geographical, product or technological criteria seem to shape the worldwide organization. The strategic roles defined here can be a new and powerful source of differentiation in the choice of grouping of the international factories in a company. Similarly, the choice of communication systems among factories, and between them and the central staff, can be helped by differentiation among the strategic roles of the factories.

There are those who view the setting up of factories in foreign countries as the export of jobs and eventually export of production knowhow. They argue that internationalization of the manufacturing base can lead to the "hollowing" of the firm because it shifts production away from the home base. They may be right if a firm sets up only offshore and server factories and keeps them in such roles. They are wrong, however, if a firm charts broader strategic roles for its international factories—roles which include source, contributor, and lead.

# ACKNOWLEDGEMENTS

I thank David Sackrider for his help throughout this research, particularly during the fieldwork. I also thank Scott Marquardt, Arnoud De Meyer, and Sumantra Ghoshal for their valuable comments on the earlier drafts of this chapter.

# NOTES

1. The companies studied were: Apple Computers, Digital Equipment Company, Hewlett-Packard, IBM, LSI Logic, Olivetti, Philips, Sony (France).
   Data were collected through company documents, field visits and interviews with directors of these companies. Interviews were held during winter and spring 1988.
2. An earlier version of this chapter was published in *Managing International Manufacturing*. K. Ferdows (Ed.), North Holland (1989). Used with permission.

# REFERENCES

Bartlett, C. A. and Ghoshal, S. (1987) Managing across borders. *Sloan Management Review*, Summer and Fall.

Davidson, W. H. (1980) *Experience Effects in International Investment*. UMI Research Press, Ann Arbor, MI.

De Meyer, A. (1988) *Internationalisation of Research and Development*. INSEAD, Fontainebleau.

Flaherty, T. (1987) Coordinating international manufacturing and technology. *Competition in Global Industries* (M. E. Porter, Ed.). Harvard Business School Press, Boston.

Gruber, W. H., Mehta, D. and Vernon, R. (1972) The R&D factor in international trade and international investment of United States industries. In *The Product Life Cycle and International Trade* (L. T. Wells, Ed.). Harvard University Press, Cambridge MA, p. 126.

Stobaugh, R. E. (1968) The product life cycle, US exports, and international investment. Unpublished doctoral dissertation, Harvard Business School, Cambridge, MA.

*The Economist* (1987) GATT as reported on September 26, p. 78.

*The Economist* (1988) August 20, p. 62.

*The International Herald Tribune* (1988) US Commerce Department, as reported May 21–22, p. 13.

Vernon, R. (1966) International investment and international trade in the product cycle. *Quarterly Journal of Economics*, 80. 190–207.

Wells, L. T. (1972) International trade: The product life cycle approach. In *The Product Life Cycle and International Trade* (L. T. Wells, Ed.). Harvard University Press, Cambridge MA, pp. 3–33.

# 8

# THE KNOWHOW COMPANY: STRATEGY FORMULATION IN KNOWLEDGE-INTENSIVE INDUSTRIES

**Karl Erik Sveiby**

*Publisher of Ledarskap*

## PURPOSE OF THE ARTICLE

Why has so little strategy development occurred outside the world of manufacturing industry? When reading through any strategy or management journal one gets the impression that it is only the manufacturing industry that needs strategy. Or—that strategy in the service industry is the same. Or—that the service industry is uninteresting to professors?

The implicit message of the management profession seems to be: if you are a CEO of a non-manufacturing company, try to behave as if you produce products and everything will turn out all right.

Is this why the present strategy formulation of service industry seems a blueprint of manufacturing industry?

However, two-thirds of OECD country CEOs work in non-manufacturing companies! In the EEC countries, 62 % of employment is in the service sector.

The purpose of this chapter is to suggest an alternative route in strategy formulation for knowledge-intensive organizations. I call it "the knowhow company", an expression coined by myself and my coauthor Tom Lloyd in our book *Managing Knowhow* (1987).

International Review of Strategic Management.
Edited by D. E. Hussey. © 1992 John Wiley & Sons Ltd

In most developed countries, some two-thirds of the GNP is made up of services. However, strategic planning and concept development are still focused on solving problems for the manufacturing industry. They are, with few exceptions, manufacturing companies with their roots in the nineteenth century. The only new service industry in which strategy concept makers have shown any interest is financial services, especially banking. Again, big banks are an integrated part of the world of big global manufacturing industrials.

Is it because of this poor state of knowledge that almost the only service company that has had any impact on general strategy formulation is the fast food chain McDonalds? The success of McDonalds is based on a simple and effective strategic formula: standardization of service into a package of the smallest detail, strict quality control and cost-effective production by young, cheap, unskilled workers supervised by managers on the shopfloor. The growth comes from franchising out this concept and the name to entrepreneurs.

What you see behind the desk of any McDonalds restaurant is an almost perfect industrial system, a conveyor belt in an environment which is inadvertently designed as a blueprint of the traditional manufacturing organization in the factory as it was conceived by F. W. Taylor and his successors at the beginning of this century.

As an employee, you don't even have to like the work. The McDonalds concept is so successful that it can handle a personnel turnover of more than 100 % a year, a rate that would grind any car manufacturer to a halt. At McDonalds the system is greater than the individual, the tasks of the employees simplistic. Many are the successful followers of McDonalds. But can it be true that "McDonaldization" is *the* strategy formula for the future in services?

No, I suggest that it is a far too simple way of looking at the dynamic and fast-changing world outside the manufacturing industries—people-intensive and people-dependent.

Is it possible that we are looking at the non-manufacturing organizations with the eyes of a world that has passed by, just as the farmers experienced the first manufacturing companies at the beginning of the 1800s—as another kind of farm?

I suggest that in order to develop truly original strategy concepts for the non-manufacturing companies one should try to turn the traditional logic of manufacturing "upside down". Instead of basing our conceptual thinking on 100-year-old doctrines based on the notion of the one-product factory, I suggest that we should look away from the manufacturing industry, very far away.

Why not learn from the organizations which are not only people-intensive but also people-dependent, i.e. dependent on their employees? What can we learn from companies where the employees are very skilled, very highly educated and thus have true power? The answers are interesting, not only for the knowledge-intensive industry itself but also for the manufacturing industry. What was a car

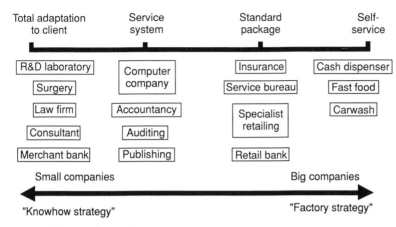

**Figure 8.1**  The service sector

manufacturer yesterday is more and more becoming an industry that is entrusting its complex production machines to fewer and fewer very skilled people. Look at Figure 8.1.

# THE SERVICE SECTOR

The service sector is not a discrete phenomenon but rather a spectrum of company types, ranging from those organizations totally adapted to their customers to organizations that have refined and packaged their output. The latter have more in common with manufacturing companies.

In the companies on the far right, service has become industry; the key to profitability lies in efficient, industrialized preprogrammed production aimed at a mass market. The McDonald's fast-food chain exemplifies this type, where even the smile you get as a customer is preprogrammed in the employee's manual.

The knowledge of a McDonalds company is totally structured and supervised by management. Even if the service package is delivered in a "moment of truth" (Normann, 1963) by an employee, little or no room is left for individual initiative. The success comes from standardization and the economy of scale resulting from it. In fact, too much initiative might disrupt the fine-tuned system and make it less effective.

The knowledge is in the hands of the organization. Image, manuals, routines, experience, control. The standardized service factory has a high structural capital.

Thus, the customer knows what he or she can expect when entering a McDonalds restaurant. No surprises, either negative or positive. The customer buys security.

# THE KNOWLEDGE-INTENSIVE SERVICE SECTOR

The companies at the far left of Figure 8.1, however, are their opposite. It is to the left that we find what we might call the sector of the knowledge industries. The "service" emerges as an ongoing problem-solving process between the customer and the producer. There is no standardized service package. The customer often does not know what he or she is asking for. The service provider is an expert and the customer wants the problem solved by the expertise of the expert. The knowledge industry therefore has to treat its customers as individuals. Their close relationship is sometimes even revealed in their language. Who has not heard a lawyer say "We decided to plead guilty" or ridiculed a doctor claiming "I believe we've got fever". The most typical firms are to be found within the professional services or business services.

The doctor or the consultant finds it hard to standardize his operations. Because he cannot force his clients to adapt to him, he must perforce adapt to them.

What characterizes a knowledge-intensive organization? It is an organization where the majority of the employees are highly educated, where the "production" does not consist of goods or services but complex non-standardized problem-solving. The problem-solving process involves a lot of information processing (not necessarily computerized) and the end result is normally a report or process delivered orally or as hard copy. The customers are treated individually and often called clients or patients.

The four main distinguishing features of the production are:

- Non-standardization
- Creativity
- High dependence on individuals
- Complex problem-solving

The companies are in any of the knowledge industries like management consulting, computer software, technical research, advertising, law, medicine, architecture, and so on. The sector is sometimes called professional services or business services but they have counterparts in the public sector, such as many of the highly specialized governmental bodies or specialized hospitals or research organizations. They also exist within big organizations as departments for R&D or laboratories.

There are very few statistics on this area. Even in Sweden, where this topic has been very "hot", the statistics are blurred. The sector has only recently been noticed by researchers and EEC officials. Even if the statistics are obscure, there are at least some facts.

According to a recent EEC Commission paper, the so-called "business service sector", which includes knowledge-intensive segments like advertising, management consulting, accountancy, PR, software, contract R&D and engineering but also companies for temporary staff, contributes about 14 % of the EEC's value added and 6 % of its GNP, which makes it a larger sector than agriculture. In Sweden, the sector (excluding temporary staff) employs 5–7 % of the total workforce, depending on the narrowness of the definition.

The sector is growing very fast. The growth rate in Sweden during the eighties was 5.5 % per annum in employment and 10.6 % in number of companies (Sveiby, 1990). The fastest growing knowledge industries are the computer consultants, the research oriented companies and the media/information companies with growth rates around 15–25 % per annum. If these growth rates continue into the nineties, the knowledge-intensive sector will employ around 11 % of the total Swedish workforce in the year 2000 (EEC Commission, 1990).

In the EEC countries, the sector's growth in current prices was an annual 14.6 % in the period 1980–1985. In Europe, statistics compiled by European Services Forum reveal the same pattern. The fastest growing companies in Europe during the eighties have been companies in the professional services, with growth rates ranging from 10 % in volume to well over 100 % in some segments (EEC Commission, 1990).

The companies in the knowledge industries are thus well worth attention—for one thing they are probably the fastest growing organizations in the world today. That they have been unnoticed so far is probably because they are so obscure, small and hidden in statistics as service companies.

A growing number of the new successful companies being formed today in the US as well as in Europe and elsewhere are probably in the knowledge industries. In the US, it is estimated that the traditional manufacturing industry will shrink down to some 10 % of the total workforce by the year 2000.

The knowledge-intensive organization is, of course, not a new kind of organization growing out of thin air. Research by the Swedish Federation of Industry has proved that some two-thirds of the growth in the service sector in the period up to 1983 originates from companies spun out of the manufacturing companies, and most of them are to be found in the knowledge-intensive sector. Very often the largest customer is their previous employer.

The knowhow companies are often founded by highly skilled professionals who constituted what might be called a "professional island" with their previous employer. (See below.)

Ever since humans lived in caves they have been living off and by their knowledge. In the old times, the majority of the skilled were craftsmen; the skilled people in non-handicraft information processing or consultancy work were rare individuals indeed. There were some—like artists or magicians or kings' advisors or diplomats—they were mostly freelancers and did not form big organizations employing thousands of them as today.

The expression "professional services" unfortunately leads our thoughts the wrong way, because these firms are not servicing their clients in the same sense as a travel agency, a washing firm, a hotel or a bank does. Their product is as intangible as a normal service company's but very different indeed! I therefore prefer the term "knowledge industry" because it is the expert knowledge of the professionals that the clients are willing to pay for, not the service.

Even if the product is intangible and the benefits often are obscure, the employees of a knowledge-intensive organization can very often show very visible results, such as an improvement in the profits of their clients, or a successful lawsuit or medical treatment.

In these circumstances, what is the output of a knowledge-intensive organization in money terms? A problem solved, which saves a client, say $10 million at a fee of $1 million. Is the output the value of the invoicing? Is it the value added in the company? Or the value added to the client's organization? Or is it the salaries paid to the consultants, $0.5 million? In the official statistics the net benefit of $59 million is shown as a profit in the client's records and $1 million as gross revenues from the business service sector, but is this the truth? What is the best mirror of the truth: to allocate the benefit to the one who asked for advice or to the one who gave it?

## THE PROFESSIONAL ISLAND

To make things more difficult, the complex and creative output of the knowledge-intensive organization and the more standardized industrial production of the service company often coexist within the same organization. Most of the companies in the non-manufacturing industries are to be found in the middle of the chart in Figure 8.1.

This doubleness of the organizations "in between" is a challenge in itself. As for the retail banks, most of us regard them as typical service organizations, which is also true to a large extent. The majority of their employees take care of routine transactions over the counter. At the same time, their colleagues in other departments might be engaged in more complex problem-solving like large credit investigations, cash management problems, corporate finance, and so on. These employees are also normally more highly educated. They are different from the majority, they know they are, and they do not want to mingle with the rest. They constitute what could be called a "professional island" within the company.

The professional island is an important and growing problem for top management in large organizations. The professionals within, say, a research department have to solve creative, non-standard problems and need a loose, creative, informal environment very much like the knowledge-intensive organization in order to be effective. On the other hand, they have to be an integrated part of the production or service system of the organization and to live by the more strict non-creative rules of that.

How does top management tackle this problem? Until the seventies it was overlooked, but it has become a dilemma for most manufacturing organizations since then. Some have tried to organize a separate research company; IBM management chose the radical solution of creating an environment outside their own when they decided to develop the personal computer. Today, Tom Peters has coined the phrase "scunk works" for the professional island and urges management to take the creative and entrepreneurial people inside the big organization seriously and invent measures to utilize their creativity.

During the eighties the capital markets all over the world flourished and new services and financial instruments were invented at almost a daily rate. The typical retail bank—originally ideally positioned for the new development—has not been able to profit from the changes but the inventions have given rise to a number of smaller organizations, investment banks, corporate finance firms, portfolio management firms and so on, i.e. knowledge-intensive companies

Where did the employees of the new companies come from? From the banks, and when their number did not suffice, straight from school. The retail banks with their large industry-like systems lost their "gold-collar workers" since they could not compete with the new companies where the knowledge-intensive people were allowed freedom, challenging tasks and a stake in the added value they created for their clients.

There seems to have developed no consensus as to how to handle the professional island yet, but I suggest that we might find some solutions if we learn some lessons from the successful knowledge-intensive organizations.

## THE FACTORY STRATEGY

The retail banks are now facing a typical industrial problem of how to get their remaining—often unskilled white-collar—workers more productive. For this, some choose a strategy towards the right in Figure 8.1.

A movement in the right direction in the diagram is one of two generic strategies open to managers in any service organization. It might be called the "factory strategy", which in short emulates the traditional manufacturing company so that well-known management methods can be applied. The "factory strategy" means:

(1)   Package the knowledge into standardized distinguishable pieces that can be sold by others than the professionals themselves
(2)   Seek economy of scale in production
(3)   Build strong brand names through marketing
(4)   Franchise out concepts

This strategy reduces the power of the individual professionals, increases the number of non-professionals and the unskilled, reduces the salary bill per employee and makes it possible to run a very large international organization by structuring it in the traditional way with business units, marketing, a sales force, etc.

It is probably the strategy most easily understood for the management of any knowledge-intensive organization today, because it makes it possible to use old-established management experience. It is thus the strategy of the computer consultant who develops a software which can be sold in multiple copies. It is also the strategy of the management guru who produces a package of videos, tapes and books plus a seminar with a price tag of $499 per package.

The successful application of the factory strategy gives a high volume in money terms and is very tempting for an entrepreneur, who can get very rich. But the strategy also almost certainly leads to a loss in professional knowledge, a reduced value added per employee, smaller job content, and opens up for price competition in the end.

The success of the factory type of companies have made many people shake their heads and predict that we are heading towards a society where the job contents are even smaller than in the traditional smokestack industry. Will this prediction come true? I find it hard to believe that the same youngsters who refuse a job on the shopfloor because of its small job content will accept a small job content in the service industry.

Some of the most challenging problems that are facing the managers of today are closely linked to the choice of strategy, and they are people problems: disenchanted employees and intensified competition for the best recruits, who are becoming ever more demanding and requiring "free" professions anywhere except on the manufacturing industry shopfloor.

The successful companies in the knowledge-intensive industries have had to tackle the problems of managing "difficult", highly skilled employees wanting to do their own thing as well as demanding customers wanting tailor-made solutions every day. In fact, it is an integral part of the lives of their managers.

One severe obstacle, however, is that there is little or no systematic research and accumulated knowledge on how to manage a knowledge-intensive organization or a service company but a lot on how to manage a manufacturing company.

## STRATEGY OF THE KNOWHOW COMPANY

Suppose we throw off our old factory glasses and look in the other direction, what strategy do we see then? I call it the "strategy of the knowhow company", (Sveiby and Lloyd, 1987).

The strategy would then be to try to emulate the successful knowledge-intensive organization (a "knowhow company"). It is an organization which moves to the left in Figure 8.1.

The knowhow company:

- Solves complex non-standard problems demanding creativity
- Has a small flat organization
- Has a high number of professional employees...
- But few non-skilled employees
- Grows organically and through alliances rather than by acquisition
- Forms private partnerships rather than goes public
- Treats its clients individually
- Builds company strength through skilled individuals
- Develops the organization through developing the knowhow of the employees
- Has managers who are formal as well as informal leaders

## THE INVISIBLE BALANCE SHEET

The manager of the knowhow company faces a very different set of problems compared to his/her colleague in the traditional manufacturing industry. Look at the comparison of the balance sheet below:

| Knowhow company | Manufacturing company |
|---|---|
| Information flow | Flow of goods |
| Human being | Machine |
| Knowhow | Capital, fixed assets |

The balance sheet of the knowhow company contains few machines except the human being. The research engineer, the programmer, the consultant or the architect is the real "machine" of the knowhow company. The computer is regarded in this respect as an extension of the brain.

The leader of a knowhow company has the same object as his or her counterpart in industry: to increase the value of the capital in the company, the assets.

However, the big difference is that the real assets are the knowledge of the employees, their formal skill, education as well as experience, and their social ability. There is also the knowledge of the "organization", the rules, the manuals, the relations with clients and suppliers. Put all this knowledge together and we find the total capital of the knowhow company. Very little financial capital is normally needed to fulfill the business idea of the consultancy firm, although there are also capital-intensive knowhow companies, like portfolio management companies. But in them too the brains of their employees are vital for squeezing an extra point of interest out for their clients.

The assets of the knowhow company are intangible and invisible to our present accounting methods, but nevertheless real. The manager of a knowhow company is no different from his/her industrial colleague. The knowhow company manager also manages the assets and tries to optimize their profitability. Only—the assets are the people.

Just imagine for the sake of argument, viewing a company balance sheet through these eyes. How would we maintain and develop the assets?

| Knowhow company | Manufacturing company |
| --- | --- |
| Education | Maintenance (of existing machines) |
| Recruitment | Investment (in new machines) |
| Research and development | Investment (in new products) |
| Departure | Disinvestment |

The capital and investment of the knowhow company does not show up in the balance sheet because we do not know how to account for it. No company accountant knows the benefits of education, but he can calculate the internal rate return of the new machine on the factory floor down to two decimal points. Neither does he know the value of the knowhow, but he can show the number of office desks on the screen of his personal computer.

Many managers are busy counting the few beans in the visible bowl, but totally forget about the giant heap of beans in the invisible bowl. Knowledge is an asset which only shows up lumped as "goodwill" in the balance sheet.

Surely that is a very unsatisfactory situation after more than 100 years of research in the accounting profession? No wonder that the managers of knowhow companies normally have great difficulty in calculating their real profitability. How many failures of company startups are due to the poor accounting methods for knowhow companies?

## THE TWO MAIN TYPES OF KNOWLEDGE

The concept of "knowledge" is very complex and many philosophers have tried to define it. I will not make an attempt here, but simply point to one aspect of knowledge which I have found fruitful in understanding the knowhow company, namely, the dichotomy between professional and managerial (organization) knowhow.

Professional knowhow is the core knowledge of the knowhow company—the essence of the business idea from which the company receives its revenues. In the law firm it is legal knowhow, in the laboratory it is scientific or chemical knowhow (an engineer, it is said, is someone who can make for 25 cents what any fool can make for a dollar, while a management consultant is someone who can do the opposite). The success of the knowhow company depends on how skilled the professionals are compared to their professional colleagues employed by their competitors. The people possessing this knowledge are called professionals, "gold-collar workers" or simply "experts" or "specialists" and they often make up 70–90 % of all the employees, so they are totally dominant both in numbers and in the company culture.

I define managerial knowhow as marketing, administration, accounting and the art of management itself. Managerial knowhow is needed, otherwise the knowhow company will not survive. The goal of managerial knowhow is to preserve and increase the value of the total organization—the total capital, i.e. mainly the invisible knowhow capital—to keep it together.

The great dilemma, the dichotomy, is that one person very seldom has both these types of knowhow. It seems a psychological fact that they even exclude each other. The professional is thus almost never a good manager, and vice versa. Just think of all the trouble a good consultant may cause a company if he is put in the chair of the CEO! Also, compare the well-known dichotomy between thinkers and doers, thinkers in this context being more similar to specialists and doers to managers.

This is a real strategic dilemma for the knowhow company, so let us look into it a little further. If we put the two types of knowhow together, we get a matrix showing the four main categories of personnel in a knowhow company (see Figure 8.2).

One of the key issues for managing a knowhow company is to understand the distinct features of these four main categories, the professionals, the managers, the clerical staff and the leaders.

The professionals have been studied by sociologists, who find some distinct features:

**Figure 8.2**   The knowhow company. Personnel categories

- They have a field of knowledge where they have developed a skill that is higher than others
- They have a special education with distinct degrees allowing them to work in the profession
- They have often formed professional associations and codes of ethics for their profession
- They have a high degree of responsibility towards their profession and their work

We have probably all encountered the typical professional. He (it is mostly a man) is intelligent, brilliant, arrogant and absent-minded. He loves his job and is a workaholic when it comes to problem-solving. But he hates the company "bureaucracy" and is seen constantly arguing with management over this bill or that expense, he is never on time and no one seems to know where he is right now. He is loyal to his organization only if he can feel proud of the professional level of it. He is both unable and unwilling to manage other people; he likes working in teams but only if they consist of skilled professionals. He is interested mainly in the freedom to develop his own professional skills and the status of the profession.

His counterpart is the manager, a person who in industry is a relatively common middle manager but who is rather lonely in the knowhow company. There are very few marketing managers (if any), no sales managers, few personnel managers (if there are any they are often called development or training officers). In fact, in many of the smaller knowhow companies, the accountant is the only traditional manager, very lonely indeed since his own profession has abandoned him in respect of tools.

The typical manager likes to work with other people, is team-oriented, likes to exert his/her influence in an organization and feels a loyalty towards the organization he or she is put to manage, since the success of it can be translated into interesting career opportunities in the future. The managers lack the professional knowhow but are strong in managing the business.

They are also normally the managers of the clerical staff, who often are in a real problematic situation. They lack the professional skill of the professionals and are prevented from developing their career structure by the usual method of moving up the ladder and becoming managers because there are very few such opportunities in knowhow companies.

The leader is the driving force of the knowhow company and is more or less irreplaceable. He or she has often founded the company and is almost always an ex-professional who has developed managerial skills and interests. It is very rare to find an accountancy firm, theatre, engineering firm or advertising agency not led by an ex-professional.

The leader must be able to handle and steer the driving forces in the knowhow company. The leader must also be able to balance conflicts between the categories of personnel, who might easily become opposed to each other if there is no leadership.

## LEADERSHIP IN THE KNOWHOW COMPANY

The power network of the knowhow company is loose, intangible and informal. It is formed by the relationships between people, the larger spots in the network being the more powerful people, most often the most skilled professionals (see Figure 8.3). They are the ones who everybody wants to relate to, to talk to and

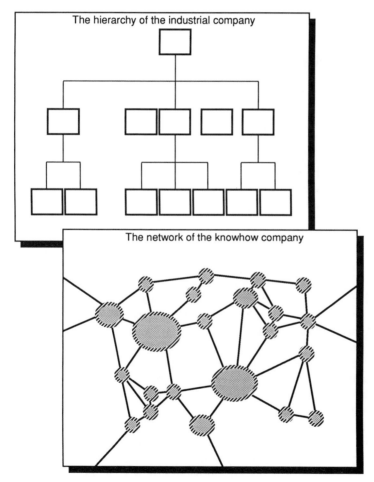

**Figure 8.3** Power network of the knowhow company

learn from. The informal power they possess can never be replaced by the formal hierarchy.

This informal network hierarchy exists in any organization—be it industrial or service or knowledge-intensive. The difference is that in the knowhow company the informal network is so much more powerful than in any other kind of organization. This is because the informal power is normally in the hands of the professionals, who have a lot more power than the workers in the factory or the white-collar workers in the office. The leader must thus understand the informal forces of the knowhow company to be able to manage it.

Which are the forces? They are more easily understood if we realize that they emanate from the group of professionals. So, if the professionals are not led by someone who is able to manage these forces, the organization forms itself around what is seen as important from the viewpoint of the professionals. The unmanaged knowledge-intensive organization thus:

- Seeks complex problems to solve—irrespective of their importance for clients
- Gives full freedom for the professionals to develop their skills—irrespective of the costs
- Invests heavily in R&D—irrespective of the market

In the knowhow company the professionals are the high-status people, the more skilled in the profession, the more influential. Unfortunately, the "guru" is generally not the best manager of the company. However, he or she may have the greatest power in the organization because the other professionals listen to him or her. The "guru" is also very often the person with the best contacts in the industry and the highest billing rate.

The knowhow company thus very often finds itself in the dilemma of having the most powerful person as an unable and unwilling leader. The knowhow company with the unwilling professional as the leader is most often not managed at all. The "leadership" consists of letting the professionals do what they want in terms of exciting new experiments or new programs.

I call this kind of unmanaged company an "agency".

This kind of leader is more common than one might believe, because so many of the knowhow companies are partnerships of lawyers or architects or accountants where nobody really wants the boring task of managing the company. "I did not study law/medicine/accounting in order to shuffle papers in a company" is a common phrase.

We thus very often find the poorest accounting systems in the auditing firm, the most pathetic management in the management consultancy firm—and the poorest marketing of the university itself in the university's marketing faculty!

Many knowhow companies, desperate to find a solution to their top management problems, look to the manufacturing industry for help. There they

Figure 8.4    The knowhow company. Four categories

have the experience! Unfortunately, that experience is not applicable to the knowhow companies. This revelation usually comes as an unexpected blow to everybody when the new manager starts to send out memos with orders regarding how to report meetings with clients, changes the accounting system, asks the professionals to clean their messy tables, questions them about where they spend their time, why they travel so much and should they not be able to reduce the number of employees? The industrial manager is then met with scorn whenever there is a discussion about the content of the business. The business idea is tied to the profession, and everybody relishes seeing the non-professional manager revealing his ignorance in these matters. A manager who is unable to lead the professionals creating the revenues is thus very easily reduced to a sour administrator of the costs, and the power rests with the experts.

The manager might then try to get rid of the most troublesome specialists and make the company more manageable by introducing standardized procedures, going towards the right in Figure 8.1. This kind of company might be called a "factory". (See Figure 8.4.)

# KEY TO SUCCESS—BALANCE THE DICHOTOMY

One key to success for leadership in a knowledge-intensive organization is to be able to balance the management of both the professionals and the organization strategy of the knowhow company. It is a very difficult task because the professionals rarely accept leadership by any one except a professional. Since the architects make up the majority of all employees in an architect firm and so have formed the whole culture, it is thus more or less impossible to manage the company if the top manager is not an architect himself.

But architects are poor managers! How does one solve this problem? The leader who knows everything is, of course, one solution, but rare. One clue is to be found in the fact that many successful knowhow companies are run not by one CEO but by two or even three. In some industries this has become the norm.

The newspaper is run by one editor (the manager of the professionals) and one managing director (the administrative manager). Sometimes their two tasks are combined in one, called publisher. The advertising agency often has one creative manager and one administrative, the film industry has the duo of producer/director, and the boxer has his promoter. The managing director thus has a much weaker position in the knowhow company than in the manufacturing company. Unless he can team up with the manager of the professionals his powers are reduced to mere administration.

The balance of power between the professional knowhow and the managerial knowhow is crucial to understanding the strategy of the knowhow company. The balance may shift abruptly when one of the top team is changed or is becoming more powerful. These shifts of power explain many of the otherwise incomprehensible strategic moves of some knowhow companies.

That the balance does affect the business idea can be seen very clearly in some cases. Just imagine for a moment that you are looking at a movie. Think of the text at the beginning (or the end) of the film saying who were the people responsible for making the production. The later the names appear, the more important they are. Who is usually the last name? Right. The director. It tells you as a viewer that the creative content of this movie is in the power seat of the production. The producer comes in as number two, counted from the end.

Now think of some of Stephen Spielberg's monster movies. He is called producer but still makes it as the last name of the list. It is because the film is based on its technical effects, which are so complex that the film-making has to be in the hands of the producer.

Now think of Dallas or any other soap opera. Who is the last name? You don't remember? Actually, the list is full of producers, executive producers, operating producers and assistant producers. The name of the episode's director appears very briefly in the middle. What that tells us about the creative content of Dallas is obvious, but it also tells us that the TV production of the soap opera is run like the conveyor belt in a factory.

The conveyor-belt organization is actually a very primitive form. No biological process is so crude. Still, it has proven its productivity for more than 50 years and is still the most efficient organization when the production is run by unskilled, disinterested labour who use their working hours for pondering about what to do during their spare time.

This is why the factory strategy functions so well with immigrants or illiterate youngsters, but try to put a team of Harvard graduates in there and count the hours they stay on the job!

In fact, McDonalds has a perfect match between personnel idea and business idea and this is probably one of the cornerstones of its success.

## BUSINESS IDEA—PERSONNEL IDEA

The concept of the personnel idea was first suggested by Richard Normann in his book *Service Management*. It is very useful in understanding any non-manufacturing industry, be it service company or knowledge-intensive organization.

The personnel idea is the comprehensive opinion among top management about what kind of employees they will recruit, how the employees will be developed, motivated, remunerated—and outplaced.

I suggest that a knowhow company must have a very close link between its business idea and personnel idea, otherwise it cannot function.

Many knowhow companies in the management consultant industry have, for instance, copied McKinsey, who has a very distinct personnel idea, sometimes shortened to "up or out". Young bright graduates are recruited and introduced to the McKinsey toolkit and then developed through a tough career program by which they either end up as a senior partner or outside—very often as an important buyer of McKinsey services.

Contrast that with a personnel idea by which a consultant company mainly recruits experienced line managers as consultants and expects to keep them for 5–7 years while they consult clients from their own experience.

Two very different strategies, businesses and concepts for solving clients' problems will be the result of two such different personnel ideas.

## SOME SUCCESS FACTORS

I have come across a vast number of knowledge-intensive organizations in the last few years, some as a consultant, some as a researcher, some as a board member. Here, in summary, are my findings as regards successful strategies.

### Focus

Focus is clearly a success factor. It is much easier to manage a narrowly focused knowhow company than a conglomerate. This is because (a) a leader from another profession will not have the automatic following from the professionals in the other; (b) it is more or less impossible for the conglomerates to achieve better quality than the focused companies. Saatchi & Saatchi, who tried to build an empire consisting of a portfolio between advertising, management consulting and finance, is the negative example. The biggest Swedish consultant firm, Indevo, tried to build the same kind of conglomerate and failed too. It will be very interesting to see whether the French computer consultant Cap Gemini, who recently acquired a minority interest in the French/Swedish management consultant Siar/Bossard, will succeed.

## Organic Growth

A fast acquisition-based growth strategy—like that of Saatchi & Saatchi—seems to create too dangerous a turbulence. Acquisition of a knowhow company is nothing more than recruiting a large bulk of new people—unseen. This normally creates disenchantment among the professionals in both camps and quality, motivation and consequently productivity are affected negatively.

## Quality Control

All professionals want to produce high quality. Clients want it too. The key is the follow-up of quality through rigid systematic client reviews.

## Developing the Core Knowhow

The knowhow is the most important asset and is regarded as a balance sheet item to preserve, improve, develop, acquire and guard. The professionals are given ample resources for research into the core areas.

## Keeping the Key People—Preserving the Knowhow

Various creative measures are found in order to keep the key people who possess the critical knowhow. The actions vary between beer on Friday afternoon and strict employment agreements and owner/partnership.

## Small is Beautiful

There seems to be no economy of scale in production; on the contrary, creative people like small organizations better than big ones. Efficiency measured as value added per employee is the same or even slightly better in small companies as compared to larger organizations according to the data I have gathered.

## Economy of Scope

There are some scale economies in PR and marketing. Big knowhow companies get more attention and larger accounts from big clients. Accounting firms also maintain that they need a certain volume in order to be able to keep specialist knowledge which their clients ask for, such as international tax.

## Strong Culture—Little Need for Formal Control

The successful knowhow companies see culture as a management tool and carefully maintain and develop it. This is because the stronger the culture, the lighter the formal control. If bright and knowledgeable people are well aware of what is allowed, how they are expected to behave and what ethics the company stands for, very little traditional top down management is needed.

## Leaders Come from the Profession

If the leader is a professional or ex-professional of the same industry as the company, he/she will find it easier to (a) get the professionals following, (b) truly understand the business. Very often this is impossible, so the leadership is divided between two or even more people. The traditional managing director, as we find him in the manufacturing company, takes on a different position in a knowledge-intensive organization.

# THE KNOWHOW COMPANIES—ORGANIZATIONS OF THE FUTURE!

All management theories up till now are based on the simple fact that the formal boss has an automatic advantage by being in control of the information flow, so he or she always knows a little more and has a better overview.

But suppose that this is not the case? Suppose that your subordinates are better informed than you are, have better relations with the key customers than you have, have closer networks within the organization than you do and—how awful—they are even more intelligent than you and they know how to show it.

Is it possible to be a manager under such circumstances? No, would be the classic answer—change the manager. Of course, a manager who is not accepted by his staff cannot function in any organization. However, in the industry the "grassroots" generally give in after a while, grinding their teeth.

They yield because the manager possesses an arsenal of instruments of power against which the individual subordinate is helpless.

However, many managers of knowledge-intensive organizations are precisely in this situation, and the most successful of them are able to handle the situation with great success. Our present theories of management are of little assistance in understanding the strategic implications of this, because they are based on the notion of the manufacturing company.

I therefore suggest that the strategists take a good look at the successful knowledge-intensive organizations, the knowhow companies. The knowhow companies might give some interesting clues as regards the organizations of the future because they have for decades been tackling the problems that the rest of the world is only now beginning to grasp.

The most successful knowhow companies have had to adapt to the needs of their clients, to tailormake their problem-solving. They have had to be very careful with how they organize in order to make room for creativity. They have had to learn to manage the difficult, highly skilled people that are now becoming numerous in the manufacturing industry also. The knowhow companies have had to invent individual remunerations tied to performance, they have had to maintain and develop the valuable knowledge of their employees as their prime assets. In order to survive, they have had to create a leadership based on mutual trust, respect for the individual, employee-driven, loose but still strong.

The managers of knowledge-intensive organizations have not created all these features because their managers are better than other managers. On the contrary, as I hope I have shown in this chapter, the strategy of the knowhow company is but one of several alternative strategies.

But, out of necessity, they have long ago had to find solutions to many of the problems that are now emerging in many other companies and organizations all over the world. This is because the companies in the knowledge-intensive industries are the first organizations since the beginning of the industrial era that are truly dependent on their staff.

## REFERENCES

EEC Commission (1990) *Business Services in the European Community*. Report to the Directors General for Industry, Brussels, July 1990.
Gummesson, E. (1977) Marketing and purchase of consultancy services. MTC University of Stockholm.
Karlöf, B. (1989) *Affärsstrategi*. Ledarskap, Stockholm.
Kelley, R. E. (1985) *The Gold-Collar Worker*. Addison Wesley, Reading, Mass.
Normann, R. (1983) *Service Management*. Liber, Malmö.
Sveiby, K. E. (1989) *The Invisible Balance Sheet*. Ledarskap, Stockholm.
Sveiby, K. E. (1990) *Kunskapsledning*. Ledarskap, Stockholm.
Sveiby, K. E. and Lloyd, T. (1987) *Managing Knowhow*. Bloomsbury, London.

Part Three

# OTHER TOPICS

# 9

# STRATEGIC MANAGEMENT OF JAPANESE STEEL MANUFACTURING IN THE CHANGING INTERNATIONAL ENVIRONMENT

**Atsuhiko Takeuchi**

*Professor, Nippon Institute of Technology*

## INTRODUCTION

Following the internationalization of the Japanese economy in the 1980s, together with other industries the steel industry has encouraged rationalization and intensified its competitive force. The value of the yen has escalated sharply since 1985, producing the greatest impact ever experienced by Japanese industry. Of these industries, the steel industry, which maintained large and obsolete equipment, was particularly subject to rises in cost resulting in a deteriorated international competitive position leading to a crisis of near collapse. Faced with this situation in 1986, Japan's major steel manufacturers were forced to change their strategy management and initiated a 10-year restructuring survival program which included the cutting back of 40 000 workers. Under this restructuring, steel production will remain the main activity in the future but each company will make positive efforts to enter into new fields, aiming finally at realizing half of their sales from these new ventures, or in a multibusiness policy. In pursuit of

International Review of Strategic Management.
Edited by D. E. Hussey. © 1992 John Wiley & Sons Ltd

these policies, dynamic investments are now being made. Unlike Europe and the USA, investment and personnel reduction are concentrated over a period of three to five years. The restructuring of the gigantic companies which make up the steel industry, one of Japan's basic industries, is the largest in Japan and is having a great influence on other industries.

This chapter describes first the strategy for the restructuring of steel manufacturing in Japan, referring mainly to the investment activities of the Nippon Steel Corporation; second the impacts upon the employment system and the regional economy of layoff, reemployment and transfer with restructuring; and third, changes in the regional system resulting from the restructuring of the steel and other industries.

## GENERAL VIEW OF JAPANESE STEEL INDUSTRY

Before the great changes resulting from a higher yen value are set out, the development of the steel industry up to the first half of the 1980s is briefly described.

Japan's steel industry was totally destroyed during the Second World War. However, as steel was indispensable for the nation's rehabilitation after the war, it recovered through governmental support and moved towards development, with the Korean War providing increasing demands. During the high growth period of the Japanese economy in the 1960s, the steel industry experienced remarkable expansion, and in the 1970s improved qualitatively. In Japan's steel industry the most outstanding enterprise is Nippon Steel, followed by NKK, Sumitomo Metals, Kawasaki Steel and Kobe Steel, these five dominating the iron and steel industry. Japan's major steel works before restructuring are shown in Figure 9.1. All of these works were distributed along the Pacific coast. Nippon Steel was established in 1901 as the government-operated Yawata Works in the present Kitakyushu City (Kyushu); the works developed in line with the government policy of industrialization and amalgamated with steel manufacturers in Kamaishi (Tohoku) and Muroran (Hokkaido) to become Nippon Steel in 1925. Nippon Steel held a monopolist position in Japan's iron and steel production, Yawata (Kitakyushu) being particularly dominant. Following the Second World War, by order of the occupation forces, Nippon Steel was divided into Yawata Steel (Kyushu) and Fuji Steel (Kamaishi, Muroran and Hirohata). In the 1960s, Yawata Steel constructed plants with large blast furnaces at Kitakyushu, Kimitsu (Tokyo) and Sakai (Osaka). Fuji Steel built similar plants at Oita (Kyushu) and Nagoya. Both companies grew through intensive competition with each other, and in 1970 were merged into Nippon Steel, the world's largest producer.

At present, Nippon Steel has large plants in the three metropolitan areas of Tokyo, Osaka and Nagoya, and also in Hokkaido, Tohoku, Setouchi and Kyushu,

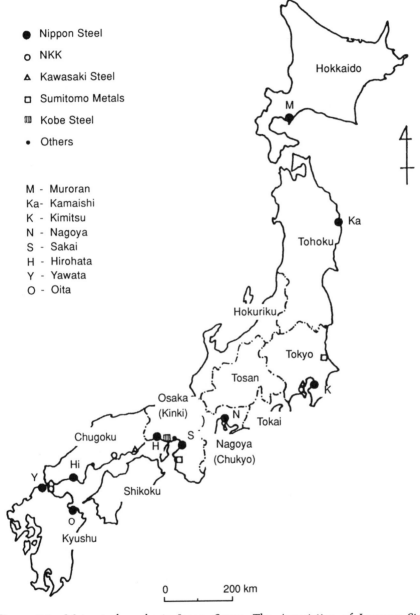

**Figure 9.1**   Main steel works in Japan. *Source:* The Association of Japanese Steel Industry

thus controlling the national market and overwhelming other manufacturers. Until the early 1950s, apart from NKK only Nippon Steel had large blast furnaces, and its plants were located in Kyushu, Hokkaido and Thohoku, remote from the three metropolitan areas, while in Tokyo and Osaka a number of plants produced steel materials and rolled steels, these manufacturers being the center of production in the large cities. After the Second World War and during the 1950s, the larger among these big city manufacturers constructed large plants with blast furnaces, experiencing a remarkable growth during the 1960s.

NKK started in 1912 as a manufacturer of steel pipes in Kawasaki (Tokyo), then updated its prewar blast furnaces in a plant renewal program while also constructing a large plant at Fukuyama (Hiroshima). In Osaka, Kawasaki Steel constructed new plants at Chiba in the Tokyo area and Mizushima in Okayama (Setouchi). Sumitomo Metals followed suit at Wakayama in Osaka and Kashima in Tokyo. These three companies then had two strategic points in both eastern and western Japan, but Kobe Steel had no plant in eastern Japan, although it relocated its main plant to the suburb of Kobe (Murakami, 1977).

## LOCATION CHANGE FOLLOWING THE CHANGE IN ECONOMIC CONDITIONS

Prior to the Second World War, the iron and steel manufacturers imported most of their material—coal and iron ore—from China and other Asian countries. Consequently, from the freight aspect, Yawata, Kitakyshu, was favorably located over other areas. Because of this, Yawata occupied an overwhelmingly high position. The location of Kamaishi and Muroran, adjacent to an iron mine or coalfield, was advantageous in Japan due to scarce resources. This situation was changed by a halt in imports from China due to the Korean War. The materials supply sources spread to the USA and Canada, and even further, to Australia and Brazil. The distances between Japan and its materials supply sources are the greatest in the world, and the country's import dependency and imports are the highest in the world (Yamaguchi, 1969). It was the aim of the steel industry not only to enhance its steel production capacity but also to improve the international competitive strength of industrial products made of steel. The steel manufacturers then attempted to reduce costs through importing large volumes of materials via ultra-large ships and by mass production at large-scale plants at high technological levels. Typically, the steel industry is located on a broad land area facing a port providing a water depth of 15 m or more. In Japan, however, such wide lands facing ports are limited to reclaimed lands. Dubbed the "seaside fire", Japanese steel works are located about 1–2 km from the former coastline (Yamaguchi, 1988).

The overwhelmingly favorable economic condition of Kyushu ceased, as the severe locational competition rules brought in a freight equalization scheme. This

**Table 9.1**    Main Nippon Steel works

|  | Muroran | Kamaishi | Kimitsu | Nagoya | Sakai | Hirohata | Yawata | Oita |
|---|---|---|---|---|---|---|---|---|
| No. of employees |  |  |  |  |  |  |  |  |
| 1975 | 6787 | 4173 | 7269 | 8654 | 3495 | 8173 | 21 570 | 3140 |
| 1990 | 3128 | 1410 | 6754 | 6746 | 1892 | 4664 | 10 676 | 3590 |
| Output of Crude | 1499 | 0 | 8711 | 4363 | 1708 | 1714 | 2738 | 7414 |
| steel in 1989 |  |  |  |  |  |  |  |  |
| (1000 t) |  |  |  |  |  |  |  |  |
| No. of furnaces | 1 | 1 | 2 | 2 | 2 | 2 | 2 | 2 |
| in 1987(*) | (−1) | (−) | (+1) |  | (−2) | (−2) | (−1) |  |

(*) Addition/reduction caused by restructuring.
*Source:* Nippon Steel Corporation, 1990.

also caused the prewar plants at Kamaishi, Muroran and Yawata to gradually decline during the 1960s to finally become a burden upon Nippon Steel. This was the case until the early 1970s, when there was an advancement of high-efficiency, large-scale plants to areas close to the three metropolitan areas—the centers of the market—along the Pacific Coast. However, after the oil crisis in 1973, no new localization of large plants occurred. The large enterprises reorganized their affiliated manufacturers of steel materials and simultaneously carried out rationalization of their own plants towards economy in energy, reduced costs and quality improvement. Thus, output was recovered but no appreciable subsequent growth took place. The domestic demand for steel hardly increased at all and exports remained stagnant.

In the 1980s, world steel production became depressed except in Asian NIES. Japan's steel manufacturers attempted rationalization through the closure of plants and a reduction in employees. In the case of Nippon Steel, 10 of its 23 blast furnaces were reduced and the former 64 000 employees were cut to 46 000. However, such rationalization remained in the realm of the steel manufacturer and was not accompanied by strategic change in the style of management or its regional systems. (See Table 9.1.)

# CHANGING ECONOMIC ENVIRONMENT AND CHANGE OF STRATEGIES OF STEEL MANUFACTURING

With the yen's rise triggered by the G-5 Plaza Accord of September 1985, the export environment of Japanese industry deteriorated rapidly and production was retarded. The value of the yen rose from 258 yen (to USD) in 1980 to 130 yen in 1987, resulting in costs doubling internationally. Japan's hourly wage, which was low at 9.04 dollars against 16.8 dollars in the USA in 1982, exceeded that of the USA in 1986. In the face of the yen's appreciation, the machine industries, such as the automotive and electronics industries, responded relatively quickly with high technologies and overseas advancement of plants and are now creating an international division of labour system. Conversely, the steel industry, burdened with huge facilities, was unable to remodel its plants, change its production items or relocate plants into other countries in a short period. In addition, as a result of expansion of the machinery industries, or users, into other countries, the increase in new materials and increasing imports from NIEs or, more particularly, Korea with its advantageously low costs, exports decreased and the impact was extremely serious. The production cost of crude steel of a Korean steel manufacturer dropped to about 30% lower than that of Japanese manufacturers. Steel consumption per unit GNP halved during the period 1973–1985. MITI forecast that steel production in 1990 would be 10% less than that of 1986. The steel industry was stunned by the rise in the yen and a crisis resulted.

Under these circumstances, the steel manufacturers disclosed a restructuring plan to be completed by 1995 or 2000. One of the major factors in these plans was the enhancement of the steel industry's international competitive position by thorough rationalization. It was intended that productivity be improved by 30% from 1987 to 1990 to create a structure providing profit against decreased production, for which a reduction of 40 000 workers overall was planned. A further plan is to remodel the structure currently depending solely on steel production and thus positively advance into new industrial fields; towards which it is intended to strengthen management by multibusiness policies. In the case of Nippon Steel, the intention is to reduce the share of steel, which accounts for 80% of the present total sales of 2200 billion yen, to 50% of the total sales of 4000 billion yen in 1995, the remaining sales to be accounted for by engineering, new materials, electronics, information, social development and living-related devel-

Table 9.2   Nippon Steel's multiple business program (100 million yen)

| | Production target in 1995 (%) | Production result in 1986 (%) |
|---|---|---|
| Iron and steel | 24 000(60) | 19 000(78) |
| New materials | | 50(—) |
| Chemicals | | 2300(9) |
| Engineering | 4000(10) | 2750(11) |
| Electronics | 8000(20) | — |
| Information and communication systems | | |
| Life and social services | 4000(10) | — |
| Biotechnology | × (X) | — |
| Total | 40 000(100) | 24 500(100) |

Source: Nippon Steel Corporation, 1989.

opment (Table 9.2). The other four companies also intend to reduce the role of steel and positively deploy into new fields.

Such restructuring will accompany changes in location including closure, redevelopment and installation of new plants, with the location of new ventures liable to have various impacts.

# NEW STRATEGY FOR STEEL PRODUCTION

Nippon Steel resolved to reduce its steel production by 100 million tons from the 1986 figure to 2400 million tons. During this period, five blast furnaces will be demolished and employees will be reduced by 19 000 from 46 000 to 27 000 in 1991. Of the employees to be reduced, a natural decrease of 11 000 due to retirement at the age limit, etc., is estimated plus the relocation of 4000 workers to other enterprises and the employment of 6000 in new fields. Large-scale reduction in employees poses serious social problems not only for Nippon Steel but also for other steel manufacturers. Also, through rationalization, the regional system of steel production is changing greatly.

First, steel manufacturers have landing operations overseas. However, steel production is a typical "flag" industry—it is very hard for Japanese steel companies to open their own factory as an overseas operation. They are therefore making inroads into the field of joint companies in the USA. Japanese automobile and electrical home appliance manufacturers have recently launched into North American production, increasing the demand for cold-rolled steel sheets. To meet this, Nippon Steel decided to begin production in the North American market as well and, as the first step, established I/N Tec, a joint venture in Indiana with Inland Steel Company with a capitalization of 40%. It began commercial operation in 1990. Nippon Steel next established I/N Koto, another joint venture with the same company for the production of coated sheet. Cold-rolled sheets' major applications are for automobiles, electric appliances and building materials. Nippon Steel consider that these products will help to achieve high-efficiency production by Japanese manufacturers who promote business development in North America, and also improve the efficiency of American industry, which is working towards its own revitalization through improvement in productivity. Total investment in these two joint ventures amounts to 100 million dollars. Two companies created new employment of 450 workers. Meanwhile, Nippon Steel purchased stock amounting to 185 dollars from Inland Steel in 1989 to strengthen the relationship between the two companies, thus becoming a minority stockholder with 14% of the voting right of Inland Steel.

As a result of Nippon Steel's restructuring plan, five low-efficiency blast furnaces at Muroran in Hokkaido, Kamaishi in Tohoku, Kitakyushu and Sakai and Himeji in the Osaka region have been closed, and other low-production facilities have been reorganized. On the other hand, in the Tokyo region, Kimitsu is to construct a new blast furnace to raise its total of furnaces to three. A new research institute for steel-making has been built in Futsu (near Kimitsu). This is the world's top institute and is staffed by 1000 researchers. The institute in Kitakyushu is to be closed.

In plants throughout the country, efforts are being made to enhance productivity, and thorough rationalization is being carried out at subcontractors and other auxiliary divisions. This rationalization and reorganization has a great influence on the regions where the plant concerned is located. The impact on Kamaishi, Muroran and Kitakyushu, which have a long history as cities with steel as their only industry, has been extremely serious.

Kamaishi is a single-industry city surrounding a plant which was established more than 100 years ago and is part of an iron mine. The plant facilities are obsolete and generally of low efficiency. Further, the port has a shallow water level. These factors made the plant a heavy burden upon Nippon Steel and it was completely rationalized. The Nagoya Works was started in 1958 with workers transferred from the Kamaishi Works. Through rationalization, the number of workers at the Kamaishi Works decreased from 8500 in 1963 to 1410 in 1990. During this period, the city's population decreased greatly from 92 000 to 56 000. The downswing of Nippon Steel, which generates 40% of the tax revenue of Kamaishi City, is having a serious impact on the city's economy. Under the present restructuring plan, the number of workers is reduced by 1400, of whom 190 have been transferred to Kimitsu in Tokyo and 100 to Muroran. Of the 700 remaining workers at the Kamaishi Works, 400 have been assigned to steel-making and the others to employment in new fields. The Muroran Works (Hokkaido), with a coal field and iron mine located nearby had one of the highest productivity levels in Japan until the 1960s. However, its level fell as a result of rationalization and international competition and the number of workers decreased from 9934 in 1962 to 3128 in 1990. By restructuring, the remaining workers will be further reduced to 1000 in the year 2000. As in the case of Kamaishi, the decline in the steel industry is having a serious impact on the regional economy. Kamaishi and Muroran are located in typical depression areas and now receive remedial assistance from the national government.

Kitakyushu (Yawata) is the largest single-industry city concerned with iron and steel in Japan. It was once not only Japan's leading steel producer but formed one of four big industrial regions together with the three metropolitan areas of Tokyo, Osaka and Nagoya in the prewar period. However, with the decline in the steel industry, its position in Japan's industry is rapidly falling (Takeuchi, 1966b). Accounting for only 1.9% in 1963 and 0.95% in 1986, Kitakyushu is now one of the local industrial areas. By 1990, the number of Nippon Steel workers had decreased from 44 000 in 1963 to 11 000. Concurrently, the proportion of Nippon Steel workers in the total industrial workers of the city decreased from 40% to 25%. Nippon Steel had an excellent engineering division in the works but the company made no effort to nurture the machinery industry in this region (Takeuchi, 1966a). Consequently, Kitakyushu had no large-scale complex of machinery industry available. In addition, following company policy, all daily consumables were purchased in large cities and resold at cheaper prices through the company's co-operative facility, obstructing the development of local light industry. Local commerce was also inactive and Kitakyushu did not grow into a large industrial region, although it had the potential. However, this situation worked favorably towards the independence of the engineering division under current restructuring.

This decline in the principal industry has damaged the regional economy in the same way as that of the previous two cities and those of the other heavy, chemical or other single-industry cities. However, Kitakyushu City is a one million population city born of the consolidation of Yawata and other municipalities and is located close to Fukuoka, which is the regional capital of Kyushu and active and prosperous, so the impact of the restructuring of Nippon Steel is not as serious as in the other two cities. And it is lucky for Nippon Steel that Toyota Motors made its decision to start the construction of a big new factory in Kitakyushu by 1992. Kitakyushu will be one of the centers of the motor industry and also a large market for steel in the near future.

In contrast to these three regions, where the steel industry is in the course of decline, Kimitsu, in the Tokyo region, has a newly constructed blast furnace as the champion factory. Rationalization is also in progress here, and it is planned to increase production by 40% and decrease the workforce by 30% between 1986 and 1995. In the field of related works, the number of workers engaged in the handling of materials has reduced from 171 to 59, those engaged in in-plant carriage from 240 to 147, and electrical engineers from 104 to 36. Kimitsu is to receive 900 workers from the other plants, but with the ongoing rationalization, it is difficult to create new jobs. The company's steelmaking research and development sector and its plant's engineering and technology sector will be consolidated into the research and engineering center to be completed in Futsu (Tokyo region) in 1991. This integrated and centrally located new center is expected to play a pivotal role in the company's overall R&D activities through its greater concentration of human and physical resources. It is linked to the closure of the research institute in Kitakyushu, Yawata. Here, the decline in the position of Kitakyushu and the rise of the position of Tokyo or, more particularly, the Kimitsu and Futsu district, as a nucleus of a nationwide system may be noted. Nippon Steel has also reduced administration expenses at its head office by 26%, as a result of which about 30% of the workforce—mostly top people—have been retained; it is planned to reassign them to new fields other than steel and largely in the Tokyo area.

# NEW BUSINESS AND ITS LOCATION

What characterizes the restructuring of Nippon Steel is its multibusiness management policy, which is intended first for the reemployment of those workers no longer required for steel-making. It's second objective is to utilize the knowledge and expertise accumulated during the company's long history in steelmaking, including peripheral fields such as production, systematization, instrumentation control, and energy and manpower savings. Nippon Steel plans to realize 50% of its total sales from new enterprise. The types of new enterprises and their locations are briefly set out in Table 9.3.

## Engineering

Nippon Steel had plants related to steelmaking and branches for the production and repair of machinery and parts. In the 1960s, the Yawata Works contained an engineering branch employing 6000 workers. This branch comprised divisions such as civil engineering, construction and steel fabrication, and it is planned to establish it as an independent venture which will include steel technology related fields (integrated steelworks construction, steel plant construction and operational guidance, chemical plant construction, industrial machinery supply, and drill string supply), natural resource development (platform and seaberth construction and pipeline construction), and construction fields (buildings, bridges and gas and water conduits). These are intended to extend the use of steel, enhance the added-value factor, and enable production of very high-level technology such as hot isostatic press (HIP) and low-pressure plasma spray (LPPS). Also being considered is a move into high-technology related machinery and microelectronics related machinery in the future. The plant is located in Kitakyushu, but the R&D is relocated to Tokyo.

**Table 9.3** Nippon Steel: distribution of new business (1987–1995)

|                           | Hokkaido | Tohoku | Tokyo | Nagoya | Osaka | Kyushu |
|---------------------------|----------|--------|-------|--------|-------|--------|
| Engineering               |          |        |       |        |       | 1      |
| Chemicals                 |          |        |       |        |       | 1      |
| New materials             |          | 1      | 3     |        | 1     |        |
| Electronics               |          |        | 3     |        |       |        |
| Information & communications | 1     |        | 6     |        |       |        |
| Life services             |          |        | 9     |        |       | 2      |
| Biotechnology             |          |        | 1     |        |       |        |
| Others                    |          | 1      | 9     |        |       |        |
| Total                     | 1        | 2      | 31    | 0      | 1     | 4      |

*Source:* Nippon Steel Corporation, 1989.

## Chemical and New Materials

Soon after the establishment of Nippon Steel, this division was instituted as an independent concern designed for the use of coal tar extracted from coke gas. This company will move into chemicals, pharmaceuticals, agricultural chemicals and biotechnology. The main plant is located in Kitakyushu, but a joint venture with Mitsubishi is located in Tokyo. The above two enterprises are to develop the company's business scope and fields currently in existence and use the plants in Kimitsu. The other four companies do not have chemical businesses. New material business will come from the development and production of high value-added materials in combination with the chemical enterprise, including fine ceramics, fine chemicals, chemicals and composite materials, magnetic materials and functional alloys. The business is located in Himeji (Osaka), Kamaishi and Kitakyushu, with the comprehensive development center located in the Tokyo region. The materials research center is located in Tokyo.

## Electronics and Information and Communication Systems

Nippon Steel places this field at the center of the multibusiness strategy. It mainly comprises the manufacture and sale of supercomputers. Specifically, it is designed for the docking of the hardware developed jointly through a venture enterprise, utilizing the unique software and abundant human resources developed by Nippon Steel. There are two joint venture companies working with American companies and both are located in the Tokyo region. Also in Tokyo, a research center for electronic appliances has been set up. Nippon Steel lacks precision machinery assembly and processing technologies, and by taking Sankyo Seiki located in the Suwa district, with its high-level technology in this field under the control of M&A, Nippon Steel plans the development and production of new products.

Nippon Steel established four information and communication systems companies (Table 9.4) and employed about 3000 electronic and information related engineers. Originally, there were 1900 systems engineers and 1100 electronics and information engineers in Nippon Steel, which was proud of this high level of technological sophistication. NSICS was established by a spinoff of this staff. This company will meet the needs of Nippon Steel Group-affiliated companies deployed at various sites. It has 10 branches throughout the country, but the greater part of the workers are in Tokyo, as is its R&D facility. Two of the companies are joint ventures with IBM and Hitachi, the world's leading computer manufacturers. One is set up to concentrate on overall systems services, including both hardware and software, with the primary focus on smaller computer systems. The other is set up to develop and market office automation systems linking multifunction workstations to mainframe host computers. NCI Systems Integration Inc. is engaged in systems integration and related businesses.

**Table 9.4** Information and communication systems companies established by Nippon Steel

| | Capital (100 million yen) | Investor (%) | Approximate no. of employees |
|---|---|---|---|
| NS Information & Communcation System Inc. | 22 | Nippon Steel(100) | 2100 |
| NS and I System Service Corp. | 20 | Nippon Steel (51) IBM Japan (44) Nittetsu Shoji (5) | 270 |
| Nittetsu Hitachi Systems Engineering Inc. | | Nippon Steel (51) Hitachi Ltd (49) | 110 |
| NCI Systems Integration Inc. | | Nippon Steel (51) C.Ito. Ltd (49) | 20 20 |

Source: Nippon Steel Corporation, 1989.

The four companies were established in Tokyo, which was the center for electronics and information systems; they are matched with local systems of related industries. Software companies were also established in Kamaishi and Muroran, but were of a lower level and offered low wages. Of interest relative to the industry is an aircraft repair company established in cooperation with JAL and an American venture business in Tokyo. This company uses the new materials developed by the Nippon Steel Group. Electronics and information is also the main field of new business in other companies. The chief example of this is Kawasaki Steel, who set up a joint venture with LSI Logic (USA) for the establishment of a new factory in the Tokyo region. The inroads on the electronics industry made by steel manufacturers have a considerable impact on the management of existing companies.

## Life Service

Nippon Steel has placed special emphasis on the park complex "Space World", one of the full-scale service businesses, opened in April 1990 with great success. Space World is an education-oriented park complex developed under license from a US firm. It is located at the site of the plant in Kitakyushu city. Of the 20 billion yen capital, 50% is being borne by Nippon Steel and the remainder by the city. The drastic industrial change in this once single-industry city will completely change its character. Other ventures include a convention center, catering, and silverware. Most of these enterprises are deployed around the Tokyo area. Noting the new ventures in regions other than Kitakyushu where the blast furnaces were decommissioned, PNS (ceramic capacitors) was established in Kamaishi, and today employs 110 people. However, only five workers were transferred from Nippon Steel. Also, soybean protein and iron dust products have been established, but only 250 of the 500 intended jobs were created. Further, as the new plants are generally dependent on female workers, the employment problem of older male workers remains, therefore, unresolved. Other proposals are: first, that it is designated as a maritime entrance to the Tohoku region and receives governmental investment on a large scale (the construction of a grain center by Nippon Steel at the site of the loading yard and an exclusive wharf by Toyota Motor is now being discussed); secondly, the construction of a biotechnology-related plant undertaking R&D for MITI and the Ministry of Agriculture, Forestry and Fisheries; and third, developments for the promotion of tourist services.

In Muroran, new plants for software (300 workers), work clothing (200 workers), etc., are established, but conditions there are not as good as those in Kamaishi and there are no bright prospects for the future.

The new business, which is expected to account for 50% of Nippon Steel's total sales in the future as previously described, intends to use the existing plants. However, reflecting the structural changes in Japan's industry, it is deployed in and around Tokyo, and is sucking up the human and technological resources of the plants in provincial areas. This is inevitable as long as Nippon Steel is going to restructure along with the high technology and R&D centered in Tokyo. The style of management is the same as that of other steel manufacturers. Nippon Steel has vast land holdings of 12 000 m² near Kimitsu and Futsu. Through the effective use of this land, Nippon Steel's business system centred on Tokyo will be further intensified.

# IMPACTS OF RESTRUCTURING

Nippon Steel has an improved steel productivity of 60% over the period 1986–1990, and 19 000 workers will no longer be needed. On the other hand, although business is actively deployed, the type of business does not generally match the quality and desires of redundant workers, and the number of workers required for the new business does not match those made redundant. Further, the components of the restructuring vary from region to region. Therefore, the restructuring of Nippon Steel, along with that of the other steel manufacturers is having a great impact on the employment system and the company is, therefore, taking various remedial measures. The first measure is to secure employment. Of the 6000 workers employed in the new business, 2000 are employed only to maintain the livelihood of the redundant workers. A company called Nippon Steel Business Promotion was established and is carrying out various projects at different sites. These projects represent fields wherein no specific training is required. Other than these, transfer to other plants, assignment to other divisions or enterprises and temporary transfer to the new business are being extensively carried out by Nippon Steel. Technological changes are also noticeable in steelmaking. In these cases, types of work carried out over a long period of time do not always fit the new jobs. Thus, using its own and other professional schools, Nippon Steel promotes education on a large scale, related mainly to computers. Education is available at all plants, and up to 500 workers attend the lectures provided. For older workers who are not suitable for job conversion, measures to ensure a "happy retirement" are taken and a special allowance given.

Those most affected by the changing employment system resulting from restructuring are the blue-collar workers, for whom the above measures are taken. In the case of white-collar workers, 5300 of a total 21 000 have been transferred to new companies. White-collar workers have generally experienced temporary transfers, and as they provide the top-level ability in Japan, they require no additional training. Also, interregional transfers are always achieved through managed personnel transfer, and here no problem is involved. Many white-collar workers now work at the head office and in research institutes remote from the steel factories. They work for Nippon Steel but are not always attached to steelmaking. The establishment of new companies will highlight their jobs and is thus welcomed by the white-collar employee.

In Japan, a long company history does not mean antiquated management. Long-established companies are often more youthful and innovative in a changing international environment than new companies. Nippon Steel is a typical example of this. It responds quickly to changing economic conditions and dynamically deploys relocation before other companies. Nippon Steel introduced the computer before other companies in Japan and established production and management control systems. It also constructed a strip mill for the production of thin sheet for automobiles and beer cans, and in this way leads other companies in business activities. The restructuring of Nippon Steel, at the forefront of Japan's steel industry, may, therefore, be counted a flexible and innovative business activity.

# CONCLUSION

Nippon Steel, together with the other Japanese steel manufacturers, having had its international competitive force eroded and its management degraded due to the sharp appreciation in the value of the yen since 1985, is striving towards restructuring on a large scale.

The principal thrust of such restructuring is to establish a new regional production system through the rationalization of steel production. In this way, the steel manufacturers continue to maintain their character as steel manufacturers and to realize more than 50% of their sales from steelmaking. This may be described as the focus of the restructuring strategy of Japan's steel industry. At the same time, efforts are being made towards the development of new forms of business for the reemployment of redundant workers arising from rationalization and for the utilization of human resources and technological expertise related to engineering, electronics and information. This is a multibusiness policy, with steelmaking playing the central role. The restructuring of Nippon Steel is producing great changes in the employment system and regional economies. For the workers, various measures are taken to ease job conversion. Presently, large-scale restructuring is in progress, not only in the steel industry but in many other industries; at the same time, the wage system under the seniority rule and the lifelong employment system are also experiencing change. However, in most cases it does not result in the workers losing their respect for their companies.

Also, as the new businesses of the steel manufacturers are generally developed through linkage with high technology, the position of the Tokyo region, which is the core of the high-tech industry in the regional system of the respective companies, continues to increase in importance.

Here, it should be noted that domestic demand for steel has continued to increase since 1987 against the prediction of the steel manufacturers. Japanese steel manufacturers made a loss in 1986 of 41 billion yen. The situation has turned round and profits in 1990 were 577 billion yen. However, the manufacturers have not changed their basic strategy of restructuring, realizing that this increase in demand for steel is a temporary phenomenon only. They have solved the situation by the use of temporary measures such as the closing of iron works. By investing the large profits they were fortunate enough to realize from the increased demand, the restructuring strategy of the steel manufacturers will proceed steadily.

# REFERENCES

Murakami, M. (1977) Iron and Steel Industry, Regional Structure of Japanese Industry, ed. Y. Kitamura and T. Yada. Taimeido, Tokyo, pp. 48–62.

Takeuchi, A. (1966a) The decline of industry in Kitakyushu area. Geographical Review of Japan, 19. 1–14.

Takeuchi, A. (1966b) The formation of Kitakyushu industrial region. Annals of Association of Historical Geographers in Japan, 8. 77–90.

Yamaguchi, S. (1969) The development and its improvement of the locational factors along the seaside of Japanese iron and steel works. Report of Researches of Tokyo, Gakugei University, 21. 58–77.

Yamaguchi, S. (1975) The location change of iron and steel industry. Proceedings of IGU Regional Congress, 24. 30.

Yamaguchi, S. (1988) The Location and Its Change of Blast Furnace in Japan. Taimeido, Tokyo.

# 10

# WORKFORCE 2000: THE NEW MANAGEMENT CHALLENGE

Wolfgang Pindur
Kathleen Donoghue
Loretta Cornelius

*Old Dominion University*

and C. Donald Combs

*Medical College of Hampton Roads*

This chapter focuses on management in the twenty-first century by discussing future management from the perspective of motivation. This is clearly the essence of future management, since organizational success will depend in large measure on how managers manage the human resources of their organizations.

The systems of management are becoming obsolete and no longer responsive to either the workers employed in the various organizations or the constituencies they are designed to serve. Management systems have led to an overemphasis on formal rules, regulation and hierarchy. They have stifled the desire and the ability of managers to innovate. The various management systems have emphasized regulation instead of flexibility and have led to the creation of individual power centers that are often not related to the overall purpose of the organization. These systems have caused managers to lose the ability to respond to environmental changes. New product development is often hampered both by the risk of doing something new and by the many channels of review required for any new idea. Individual enthusiasm, creativity and initiative are stifled by the focus of the various management systems on control, particularly control at the central level.

International Review of Strategic Management.
Edited by D. E. Hussey. © 1992 John Wiley & Sons Ltd

These current management system problems are documented in a report prepared by the National Academy of Public Administration published in 1983 (NAPA, 1983). The report concluded that the crucial elements of leadership in management suffer due to a preoccupation with process. Management increasingly focuses on perfecting the tools of control and fails to recognize the human resources requirements of the fast-changing environment.

Cultural diversity will represent new challenges and opportunities for managers. The challenges facing the United States in the area of cultural diversity are documented in a recent report by the Hudson Institute entitled *Workforce 2000: Competing in a Seller's Market* (Johnson and Packer, 1987) which cited major workforce changes and the failure of organizations to respond to these. Despite the report's finding that the workforce will become increasingly diverse, few companies are offering workers training in English as a second language or in techniques for managing cultural diversity. Few companies have responded to the changing structure of the family, and have failed to create programs that recognize the growing phenomenon of the two-income family unit. Training programs have not been adjusted to meet the challenge of educating workers for the rapidly changing technology. This is true despite the feeling among the authors of the report that education and training are the primary ways of preserving and building a nation's human capital and that human capital formation plays a critical role in the growth of any nation's economy.

The focus on human capital is consistent with the views expressed by Alvin Toffler in *Powershift* (Toffler, 1990). Toffler declares that the "inner life of the corporation" must change to accommodate the new realities of organizational survival. He declares the "smokestack" era and its notions of productivity and efficiency to be a thing of the past and calls for "de-massified" organizations that are able to respond quickly to changing internal and external environments.

Managers must increasingly cope with the rapid pace of change. The explosion of technology, new workers with new values, and changing loyalties all affect the survival of organizations in the present and the future. In order to survive managers will have to adopt an anticipatory style of management to provide the leadership for effective organizational responsiveness. Managers who view the changing social, technological and economic environment as an opportunity for renewal will thrive and profit from the new order. Those who resist and those who are unable to see the reality of the new workplace will be unable to function.

The issues cited above will become more serious in the future and will have to be addressed if organizations are to function effectively. The key to changing the outmoded systems of management lies in adopting a people-oriented management approach that builds the capacity of organizations to respond effectively in a changing environment.

A recent study by the Auditor General of Canada asked the questions "Why do some organizations perform significantly better than others and what can be done to encourage and assist others to do likewise?". The study concluded that the single most important attribute of high-performing organizations is a "mindset that seeks optimum performance" (US Office of Personnel Management, 1990). People hold values that drive them to always seek higher levels of performance. The members of the organization are adaptable and change their methods of doing things without changing their values related to high performance. The key to this is "adaptability", the ability of the organization to perform well even in a changing environment.

The Canadian report also offered other suggestions relating to organizations of the future. Effective organizations will have an environment that challenges, encourages and develops people by giving them the power to act and use their judgement. This is done in the belief that high performance is a product of people who care and can only be achieved in an environment that reduces the fear of failure and the fear of taking risks.

These organizations must have a leadership style that is participative and not coercive or authoritarian. Leaders will have to articulate, in concert with the workers, clear purposes and goals. These goals will then become the driving force of the organization and will form the basis of interactions among the organization's members.

Clearly articulated goals will affect the work styles of members of the organization. Creative problem-solving is the norm in the effective organization. Rules are questioned and removed when they hinder the accomplishment of the organization's purpose. Internal monitoring systems will be used to replace the exercise of authority by those external to the organization.

Finally, the effective organization is characterized by a strong client/customer orientation. The bottom line will be clear to all members of the organization. In government the organization will emphasize citizen satisfaction, while in the private sector it will emphasize customer satisfaction.

The need for organizations to emphasize optimum performance, clients/ customers, innovative work styles, participative leadership and people will become even more important in the future since it is clear that managers must increasingly cope with the rapidly changing environment. The explosion of technology, new workers with new values, and changing loyalties that affect the survival of organizations in the present will become even more important in the future. In order to survive, managers should adopt an anticipatory style of management to provide the leadership for effective organizational responsiveness. Managers who view the changing social, technological and economic environment as an opportunity for renewal will thrive and profit from the new order. Those who resist and those who are unable to see the reality of the new workplace will be unable to function.

## MOTIVATION AND PRODUCTIVITY TODAY

Organizations are preoccupied with productivity. Recent competition, especially that provided by the expansion into international markets and global economies, has caused organizations to reassess their strategies relating to productivity and innovation. Organizations around the world are engaging in critical evaluations of their organizational self-worth. These self-evaluations have not necessarily induced an epidemic of effective new efforts, innovations or ideas in today's workplace. Instead, these assessments are often responded to with individual worker feelings of powerlessness, loss of focus, and employee awareness that there is something just not right within the organization and the daily course of operations. This seemingly invisible trouble begins to weave its way through the organization until it is finally recognized in the boardroom of the organization's leadership as a general overall stall or slowdown in the organization that is reflected in declining efficiency and effectiveness.

In these attempts at organizational change, we fail to fully reexamine the nature of work and what basically and intrinsically motivates individual employees. Employees are, essentially, the smallest unit of what comprises organizations, and it is with these smaller units of organization that there lies the answer to the larger question of what makes or does not make organizations succeed. It is the work effort and performance of each individual employee that results in real productivity. Motivation is the key ingredient that provides incentive for the individual employee to perform, and employee performance yields the productivity organizations want. A better motivation of employees typically means better employee and organizational performance. Clearly, closer attention by organizations and managers to essentially what individual employees want and need, and what really motivates today's employees and what we think will motivate them tomorrow, will result also in what businesses, industries and governments fundamentally want for the future, that is, to grow and further achieve corporate and organizational goals.

## TODAY'S TECHNOLOGY AND CHANGE

A predominant factor influencing motivation in today's workplace particularly worth noting is that the organization is surrounded by an environment characterized by significant and unprecedented change which affects both managers and employees alike. According to Nightingale, the technology we work with today was invented in the past 35 years and most of today's senior managers, persons who steer the company ship, are out of touch with the technology driving their organizations since much of it was introduced after they passed their peak learning years (Nightingale, 1990).

While one may want to dispute this categorical assumption of learning and ageing, we can easily look around and see that many organizations today are central, hierarchical, and directed by managers who represent older generations, while the functional work of production and services is frequently managed and supported by other generations in the organization consisting of younger employees. Yet it is older managers, by their strategic position within the organization, who are responsible for leading organizational planning and development efforts and are charged with facilitating and motivating tomorrow's organizational leaders and followers.

Nightingale also describes today's top managers as spending too much time trying to figure out how best to ride out whatever storm happens to be underway at a given time, with the manager's primary focus on the organization's survival. For example, the 1970s and 1980s were periods of constant and accelerating change which left managers and workers alike staggering. Today, with the convergence of social, political, economic and technological change, the average person, according to Nightingale, is assaulted by continuous turmoil. In the workplace, this assault leaves workers with little to believe in, with feelings of discontent.

As a result of these technological and environmental change forces acting on organizations, the ability to motivate and improve employee performance under these circumstances is essential. Marvin R. Weisbord suggested that management's success in creating productive workplaces of the future will depend on the ability to focus on purposes, relationships, and structure (Weisbord, 1987).

Purposes or mission are actually what business an organization is in. They embody future visions on which organizational security and meaning depend. By conducting futures search programs at work which involve all employees at various organizational levels, workers contribute to determining organizational missions and purposes, develop a better sense of ownership of organizational objectives and goals, and are energized at a personal level to achieve them (Weisbord, 1987). Furthermore, under these circumstances change is incorporated as an acceptable transition process and not a threatening attack.

Relationships are connections with coworkers that enable people to feel whole as persons. Relationships require cooperation across lines of hierarchy, function, class, race, and gender (Weisbord, 1987). By developing work teams and conducting meaningful team-building interventions encouraging ongoing associations among workers, a sense of community develops as part of a larger corporate culture.

Finally, structure provides for who gets to do what and how in an organization which affects the self-esteem, dignity, and learning abilities of individual workers. By incorporating the techniques of self-management and work redesign, individual workers are empowered to create a personal environment of creativity and productivity (Weisbord, 1987).

According to Weisbord, these three modes of operation mutually reinforce one another and are part of an overall strategy for growth and ongoing development of organizations faced with rapid change. A clear focus on purposes, relationship and structure will help meet each individual employee's personal need for dignity, meaning and a sense of community. By focusing on these personal needs individual employee motivation is supported, a group morale is formulated and the organization realizes more productive output by its workers (Weisbord, 1987).

# DEMOCRACY IN TODAY'S WORKPLACE

It is somewhat ironic to look at the history of work and the still present hierarchical and authoritarian nature of corporations and government compared to the increased freedom and democracy in today's world evidenced by events in Europe and the Soviet Union. Workers to a certain degree live conflicting lives of flexibility, freedom, and personal choice in their lifestyles away from work, while at work the basis of organization manager–employee relations is rigid and autocratic. As a result, workers can be made to feel demoralized, which can result in withdrawal, resentment, low performance, and dissatisfaction.

Much of today's authoritarian style of management is a holdover from business and government traditions rooted in the scientific management movement of the early part of the twentieth century. These early organizational designers toiled at defining work by breaking down jobs into tasks and tasks into detailed steps in order to perform particular jobs as efficiently as possible. There was little concern for particular talents or attributes brought to the job by individual workers.

This early scientific and quantitative approach to worker performance later helped spur mid-century efforts to organize labor and form unions to represent workers collectively. Interestingly, many of today's workers now demonstrate a desire to refocus from a collective perspective of workers to a new recognition of the very specific knowledge, skills and personal abilities individuals bring to their jobs. In return, workers today and in the future will look to employers for variety in methods used to meet the needs of individual workers and discretion in the ways in which workers are applied.

Finally, during the 1970s and 1980s, the Government's intervening through public policies of equal employment, wage and labor laws and protective rights dramatically imposed individual protection and empowered employees in the workplace, establishing what we know today as democracy on the job. It is anticipated that workers in the future will expect and demand further recognition of their individual democratic rights which will call for change and restructuring of employer–employee relations in the twenty-first century. This empowerment of workers will likely be felt throughout the organization down to the lowest ranks.

# INDIVIDUALS IN TODAY'S WORKPLACE

Organizations today are also increasingly recognizing that the demographics of their work forces have important implications for the motivation and productivity of workers. Over the past two decades the ageing of society and the dramatic influx of immigrants, women and minorities in the workforce have required employers and managers to incorporate these members into their workforces in a relatively short time span. Also, the average education level of workers in the labor force has increased and is expected to continue to increase. The average level of income of workers has also been on the rise, bringing with it greater instances of personal economic well-being.

Accompanying the socioeconomic and cultural diversification of this new workforce has been the bringing of different attitudes, values and expectations to the workplace. For example, more than ever before, employers are having to recognize the needs of the family behind the worker. Both men and women are bringing to the workplace special family responsibilities for childrearing and elder parental care, and are requesting health care, leave options, and other individualized benefits from their employers. The needs of these new generations of workers must be recognized by organizational leaders and with them comes the need for managers to acknowledge demographic differences and respond to specific employee preferences.

An important concept that employee motivation theorists often overlook is the phases of adult life and how these affect employees and groups of employees today. A 21-year-old recently hired college graduate has a considerably different view of a new job from the 45-year-old department supervisor, and the 58-year-old senior employee may have a distinctively different set of motives to continue working even though his employer offers an impressive early retirement package. Each is at a different stage of adult life with different aspirations and motivations.

Looking ahead to the first decades of the twenty-first century, the majority of workers will be age 40 or above and in the mid and later cycles of their working careers. This increase in prime-age workers will be coupled with an anticipated shortage of younger workers in the labor market, an expected result of the drop in birth rates in the seventies and eighties. Invariably the mature workers of the next century will also hold different objectives and expectations of work from those which they hold today as younger employees.

Without exception, today's workers form a social and economic heterogeneous group and their needs, and expectations, are wide-ranging. This is a far cry from just 25 years ago, when the workplace was dominated by white men who typically were sole household income providers. The new diversity in the workplace has brought with it changes in attitudes, values and expectations. As a result, the organizational work culture of the future can be expected to be one of contrast and differences. Instead of trying to treat all workers alike, with equal policies and compensation methods, employers will need to take time to learn the new values of workers in order to provide meaningful alternative programs that foster job satisfaction for the modern employee.

## EMPLOYEE PERSPECTIVES ON THE MEANING OF WORK

In order to motivate the workforce of the future managers will need to know and understand how employees think and feel. While hard data on worker attitudes and values are limited, research does show a correlation between education and income levels and worker values towards the rewards of working. White-collar, better educated job-holders are typically depicted as valuing intrinsic factors of working such as holding an interesting job or developing one's abilities, whereas blue-collar skilled workers are portrayed as working more for the extrinsic material rewards of work, for income and purchasing power. If this portrayal is accurate and the gap between such groups widens to further class distinctions, this could provide particular challenges to managers and employers of the future dealing with divergent reasons and motivations of workers from different social strata.

And while some believe the work ethic of hard work is waning and that workers today are not concerned with efficiency and production, others would agree that current trends toward equality, social responsibility, and personal fulfillment through work will lead to a higher order of work life in the future.

Unquestionably, attitudes, ideals and goals of employees are shifting. In order to motivate new value workers, organization managers will be called upon not just to improve human relations skills but to engage in more dynamic interpersonal relations with their workforces. This will have to be done by developing an orientation towards the individual person and one's self-fulfillment through work.

## THE INDIVIDUAL AND SELF-FULFILLMENT

As we look ahead to the next century, by the year 2000 persons between the ages of 40 and 50 will comprise the majority of the workforce. This is essentially a result of the baby boomer generation coming to middle age. As youth and young adults, and a growing population majority, this generation has in the past always captured society's attention. Today its beliefs, orientations and perspectives on the meaning and value of work are dramatically influencing the workplace.

Daniel Yankelovich, writing on this subject, refers to these members as a new breed of workers struggling with a shift in relationship between success and self-fulfillment as these terms take on new forms of cultural definition (Yankelovich, 1981).

According to Yankelovich, for earlier generations success was clear, unambiguous and tangible. People found self-fulfillment in their pursuit of success and success was to a great degree measured in terms of increased family income, consumption of goods, better homes in good neighborhoods, automobiles, and their children's education (Yankelovich, 1981).

Yankelovich finds the new breed of workers no less interested in these items, yet they have come to feel that this kind of success is not enough to satisfy yearnings for self-fulfillment. They are reaching out for something more and for something different (Yankelovich, 1981).

Today's new breed has interests and motives that are in great contrast to the earlier generation's traditional values. Previous generations seemed to be clear about their goals. Many people today do not know whether or not they are being self-fulfilled and often feel disoriented, confused and disengaged. People are asking themselves "Am I happy?", "Am I being self-fulfilled?", and "Am I doing what I really want to do?" (Yankelovich, 1981)

In the pursuit of this elusive goal of self-fulfillment, workers of today move from one place to another, leave one job for another, and change careers. This new breed brings the need for self-fulfillment to its expectations of work. As employees, the new breed wants to know how work can help in this search for Maslow's higher-stage needs of self-esteem and self-actualization. And for many women of this generation who compare themselves to previous generations of housewives, the symbol of self-esteem through a paid job has reached equal if not more importance than motherhood.

This new preoccupation with self has particular implications when contrasted with the traditional incentive and reward systems of work. Whereas in the past employers relied on the carrot-and-stick approach with money and success being the carrot and fear of unemployment the stick, with this new breed of workers the elements of motivation to work have changed and are more complex and diverse. Larger society views this "me" generation as giving less and demanding more—more pay, more benefits, and more time off to do other things.

An attempt to predict what will motivate these new workers in the future is not easy considering continuing rapid change, evolving socioeconomic and cultural forces, and the myriad of theories and techniques for motivating employees about which there is little consensus. Nevertheless, a look at the various techniques and strategies demonstrated in the most recent decades provides a perspective on what may motivate these workers in the decade and century ahead.

## TODAY'S STRATEGIES AND TECHNIQUES

The recent changes in technology and the reshaping of value systems are requiring traditional managers to employ new methods in order to affect the behavior of workers. Yet throughout the literature on workplace experiences, motivating the modern work force still remains one of the more serious and critical challenges for organizational leaders. The future success of business and government organizations rests with the ability to motivate workers, and motivating workers remains very much dependent on aligning organizational goals and objectives with the individual and personal interests of employees. Organizational interests must in some way be transformed to the operational level and be assimilated and incorporated into the unique personal interests and motives of each worker.

### Job Design

In recent years there has been concern for situations in which the job itself provides minimal satisfaction for workers. In these cases, job tasks are repetitive and require little thinking and few choices. Many organizations try redesigning jobs to make them more varied or complex, or give the employee more control over the job and more responsibility. In other cases, where the jobs themselves remain the same, employees have been rotated from job to job.

Job enrichment programs are a response to repetition and employees having to do the same tasks over and over again. Job enrichment on the assembly line makes workers responsible for production and inspection of their own work, and in many cases workers assembled entire products rather than several employees each handling a portion of the job. This alternative to specialization of employees was responded to favorably and the company experienced improved productivity. Job enrichment also makes workers' tasks more interesting and intellectually more challenging, which gives them a sense of autonomy and responsibility. Job enrichment can be combined with strategies encouraging employees to set daily quality and quantity goals. In this sense, workers are delegated responsibilities for planning, organizing, and controlling their work tasks, a responsibility usually reserved for management.

Finally, job rotation has been tried in instances where it was felt job tasks could be best handled as assigned to a position but the job-holder would be rotated from time to time. Job rotation can stimulate the interests of workers in other organizational jobs, departments or functions. It can also provide insurance for employers as they have multiple workers to perform functions as needed.

Another aspect of the workplace which can improve employee motivation, yet which may not have been credited enough for impact, is recent improvements in the physical work environment. As a result of applied architecture, design, and ergonomics, it has been shown that the physical surroundings of work settings, use of space and color, and office arrangements can greatly contribute to job satisfaction. The ability of an organization to satisfy workers' needs in this way should not be underestimated.

## Structures

Changes of the past decade have also required organizations to reconsider their structures. Traditional growth and expansion of organizations typically has meant becoming bigger. Bigger also meant better, yet this too is changing.

Old theories of management and organizational structure based on an authoritarian hierarchy are changing. Organisations are "flattening out" and unnecessary levels of supervision are being eliminated.

According to Robert H. Guest, the United States is the most oversupervised country in the world, with, for example, an average of 12 management levels between the president of a private firm and those who deal directly with workers and customers. Guest argues that organizational authority patterns of the future will increasingly shift from hierarchical to participatory patterns with increased opportunity for workers to have input into decision making . Management will be carried out by delegation or through networking rather than through dictatorial relationships (Guest, 1986).

## Compensation Systems

The restrictive economy of the past decade and the changing environment have also made it increasingly difficult for many large and small organizations to provide employees with increased monetary compensation in terms of significant raises in pay. Organizations that have experienced these structural changes are finding the need to revise traditional reward systems. Instead, greater attention has had to be directed towards other types of reward incentives to motivate workers towards meeting new organizational objectives.

For example, traditional management typically has provided more salary or pay to managers with larger work centers that require supervision of more employees or a larger departmental budget. In essence, organizations have rewarded building bigger bureaucracies. Perhaps it might be better to reward managers in relation to work center production levels, in relation to keeping personnel costs down, and in line with what their subordinate employees receive for productivity. Changes in organization hierarchies of the future will require significant changes in compensation practices of managers and workers alike.

## Work Schedules

Though there have been a number of experiments in alternative work schedules, the five-day, 40-hour work week has remained the norm despite the feeling that workers derive much satisfaction from an increase in flexibility and leisure time. Expanding the work day, flexitime, staggered hours, and the four-day work week have all been experimented with in the 1980s with mixed results. Each of these has challenged traditional organizational structure and work patterns and requires different degrees of change and flexibility.

Work-at-home jobs tying workers to the office by use of computer terminals are in vogue and very popular, especially with dual-career workers such as women who are also at home serving as the primary daytime caregiver for young children. Yet there remain degrees of unacceptability to these jobs, with a sense that these employees are "not on the organizational premises" and, therefore, perhaps less valuable employees. This adds to the notion that these workers are not full-status organizational members and are considered on the periphery of organizational life, removed from the rights and responsibility to determine organizational priorities. As exceptions to the rule, these employees may be treated differently in ways that in the long run may not support their increased personal value and worth to the organization.

Work-at-home jobs may also breach the traditional sanctity of separation of work from home life, an underlying social value which may or may not continue into the twenty-first century. As workers tend to expect more recognition from their employers of the needs of their family and personal lives, we may see an increased family involvement in the workplace beyond the traditional offering of health and retirement benefits to family members and the annual company family picnic or social gathering. Until this subgroup of employees working out of the home are perceived and treated as vital to the success of the organization, the concept of work-at-home jobs for the future will continue perhaps not to be fully appreciated.

The increase of part-time employment opportunities in the 1980s brought probably the greatest new dimensions of flexibility to the workplace and job design. Partly as a result of changing demographics, with more women, immigrants, young adults and older workers in the workforce, part-time employment provided an economic alternative for retail trade and service industries as well as growing public services during the 1980s. Investigations of the attitudes and work results of part-time workers find these positions to lend a high degree of job satisfaction and a high productivity level.

It is anticipated that the part-time job will offer more in the future as young people, women and older workers comprise greater shares of the labor force.

## Participatory Management

It is unclear as to whom or what we can attribute with any certainty the invention of participatory management, also commonly referred to as employee involvement. Perhaps participatory management evolved only after management exhausted its own ideas for change, innovation, or improved productivity.

Perhaps, too, participation of employees in decision-making processes at work is yet another important change in work values and another product of the growing democracy and rights demanded by workers. Nonetheless, employee involvement has become a growing expectancy among employees and can be assumed to play a greater role in future job design.

Results management has emerged as a way of organizing work that has, to a certain degree, deemphasized traditional management by authority approaches of hierarchical business and government organizations and directed more attention towards the perspectives and experiences of employees. Using various participant techniques of management by objectives to involve superiors and subordinates more in planning work, teambuilding to help work groups become more effective in accomplishing shared tasks, and quality circles as a method for group problem-solving, workers began to achieve a greater role in decision-making and design of their work methods.

While clearly the evolution of employee participation and participatory management preceded the 1970s, it was not until then and during the following decade that contemporary employee participation became an organizational mission. About this same time a new process of managing human resources, which has now come to be known as organizational development, was evolving as a field within management, with roots in the disciplines of psychology and sociology. Organizational development brought to the organization methods by which individual needs could be integrated with organizational goals.

The key unifying element of organization development is the concept of planned change. Planned change is an alternative way of systematically managing against the haphazard waves of today's uncertain organizational environment and a method of using the human resources of employees to their maximum potential in such settings. Organization development, according to Varney, attempts to improve organizational processes so that both organizational and individual goals are readily attainable.

Increased employee participation in management decisions and employee-involvement workplace experiments in the 1970s and 1980s have largely been considered a success. Quality and innovation in design, better customer service, and competitive productivity performance improved when the workplace was redesigned and employees were given greater charge.

Employee involvement led to improved trust between management and workers, and as a result better organization procedures and processes were suggested which led to improved decision-making. In response, management found less resistance from workers to the introduction of new technology.

Quality-of-work-life projects developed in the United States in the 1950s were an outgrowth of similar programs begun a decade earlier in Europe. The US approach to quality-of-work encompassed a variety of techniques which have evolved to include job redesign, greater employee participation opportunities and new methods of compensating workers for improved productivity.

The effectiveness of employee involvement and quality-of-life approaches can largely be attributed to improving the alignment between employee needs and workplace results. When employee involvement and teamwork approaches and team systems were implemented, a significant outcome was the increased communication between management and employees and a genuine sharing of ideas and methods to improve production and performance. The further evolution and application in the future of team systems by business, industry and government will offer probably the most promising change for organizations headed into the twenty-first century.

## Work and Health

Greater society has shown increasing concern for the rights of workers to a healthy working environment through the passage of government policies and regulations. Going a step further, the concept of the employer serving as provider of health care has evolved and there is growing expectations from workers that this role be expanded. In more recent years, wellness programs and fitness programs have been initiated in the workplace as a preventive measure and as more than just a response after problems have occurred within the workforce.

Inasmuch as today's employees are better educated and enjoying a more active and healthier lifestyle, many are also not interested in compromising health and well-being for the sake of the job. Reassessed in particular have been the results of workaholism in the seventies and eighties and worker pursuits of the goal to get ahead. These priorities are now in great competition with a person's need for personal and leisure time to pursue other interests. Current-day employees are now essentially looking for more balance between their work and leisure lives.

Further, in response to the increased incidence and awareness of employee health-related problems such as alcoholism, drug use, hypertension, heart disease, emotional distress, and personal and financial problems, organizations have had to provide responsive measures. Training in such topics as stress management, time management, and dealing with difficult people have all become popular topics as part of employee assistance programs.

Table 10.1 summarizes the experiences of recent decades and the introduction of new strategies and approaches that have set the stage for what will motivate employees in the future. It has been an evolution of increasing individual freedoms and worker involvement in work design and workplace decision-making.

**Table 10.1**    Managerial changes and employee impact

*1970s*

Questioning of previous generation's postwar traditional work ethics and values

Antiestablishment protests against conformities of work, money, and extrinsic needs

Accompanied by growth in fields of self-awareness and interpersonal relations

Traditional top-down management dictates organizational change by introducing procedures and work methods to improve efficiencies

   *Impact on employee motivation:*

Hierarchical, authoritarian, bureaucratic organizations emphasize directing, organizing, planning and controlling of workers

Employee treatment by management is impersonal, workers viewed as adversaries of management. Interests of workers represented by employee groups, unions and collective bargaining

Beginning of participatory management through employee representatives, *ad hoc* task forces, feedback meetings, teamwork sessions and proactive groups

*1980s*

Demographic changes impact the work force with women, minorities and older workers bringing diversity and equality to work environment

Changing family structures and roles (two-income households, divorced single parents, women's issues) bring stress and personal needs to workplace

Technological change, growth in size of corporations and the globalization of markets spur international competition

   *Impact on employee motivation:*

Rights of workers come into focus with some gains in workplace democracy, employee participation and job satisfaction

Changing personal value systems of individuals within large organizations impart feelings of powerlessness, loss of focus, mission and purpose for workers

Personality-driven leadership styles attempt to bring humanism to the work setting and to managing organization's employees impacted by rapid change

*1990s*

Economics necessitate structural changes, flattening of organizations, decentralization, eliminating middle managers and levels of supervision

Cutback management results in reduction in wage increases and benefits, and the downsizing of workforces

*Continued*

**Table 10.1** _continued_

---

Creation of smaller, more diverse centers of productivity within the organization designed as self-managing work units

Shifting of organization interests from material and technological to human resources interests

_Impact on employee motivation:_

Closer communication between levels of management brings greater employee involvement in decision-making and increased management concerns for the worker

Team building and team leadership are driving forces for quality and results-oriented performance improvements

Employers will reward employees who are flexible, autonomous, and self-motivating, based on individual skills and attributes

New rewards and methods of compensating employees include pay-for-knowledge (skill-based pay), profit-sharing, gain-sharing, support for continuing education and training

_2000s_
Expectation for the workplace to provide opportunities for growth, creativity and continuing life-long learning

Expectation for work to provide employees with better quality of life and support of personal interests outside workplace

Employee expectations for greater interpersonal dynamics from work with more meaningful relationships among organizational members

_Impact on employee motivation:_

Positions providing independence, autonomy and flexibility that are self-directing and self-managing will be premium jobs

Open communications between organizational members and greater equality among workers bring shared ownership of organizational mission and purposes

Employees will be provided with a greater sense of dignity, self-worth and personal meaning through work

---

# THE TWENTY-FIRST CENTURY

Managers and supervisors today must be facilitators first, and unlike past managerial approaches based on management as a system of authority, present and future managerial styles will need to be based on management as a resource devoted to customer/client satisfaction and in this process provide worker satisfaction.

Probably no other organization function will play a more key role in an organization's ability to motivate employees than will the human resource function in the future. Employee services and benefits as a human resource support will be a more significant leverage in motivating workers.

Twenty-first century employers will more than ever be called upon to make structural changes to their organizations. Management will not only continue to adjust and fine-tune the hierarchies and ratios of supervisors to workers as in recent years, but personnel policies and compensation methods will also change. Knowledge-based pay systems will take on a greater importance over traditional seniority and tenure entitlements. Pay-for-knowledge systems will encourage diversification in workers and will provide incentives for them to continue their education and receive on-the-job skill enhancements.

The future workplace, though, will not be ruled by the authoritarian supervisor or executive. Instead, organization justice and punishment will be dealt out by peer workers and members of the work team.

Traditional organization will not disappear but the structure will be systems-based. Systems will be designed to support systems. As an example, administrative and personnel systems will be considered equal with those of manufacturing or sales and networks of work team relationships will support equality and system interdependence. One organization system will be expected to lend support to another.

Most managers today fail to recognize and respond to the fact that the twenty-first century is less than a decade away and if like degrees of change experienced in decades preceding the year 2000 should continue, and they more than likely will, it is imperative that managers get ahead of the curve, prepare and be ready for the "wave" of change.

As we look ahead to the future, the twenty-first century employee will, as in other generations, be significantly shaped by the immediate previous decades. In this case, the employee will have witnessed the flattening of organization hierarchies, the downsizing of workforces, the increased involvement and participation of employees in organizational decision-making, and changes in compensation methodology set in motion during the 1990s. As a result of these experiences, we anticipate that workers of the future will expect longer and more significant commitments from employers. In exchange, the employee will be willing to provide a similar long-term commitment to the employer. This lengthening and perhaps deepening of commitment and seeking of stability and loyalty between employer and employee will be a probable outcome of more effective communications and the building of better understandings between managers and workers afforded in the 1990s through participatory management. Yet, while the employee will be prepared to make a longer commitment than that which was typical in the eighties and nineties, the worker will not compromise and give up individual empowerment and what has been learned through the democratization at work.

As a result of curtailments of significant increases in wages and monetary benefits, we can anticipate that the future worker will look to work for support of other individual and more personal objectives provided outside the workplace, with such elements as flexitime, leaves of absence, work study, and personal leave policies taking on a greater significance to a larger working population and not reserved for select instances where it is convenient for the employer or peculiar to a job. The gaining of more personal time will be as significant a compensatory and motivator for the future as pay increases and perks have been to workers in the past.

Having experienced both positive and negative outcomes of change, future workers will be more comfortable with change *per se*, and will be inclined to look for favorable change situations and diversity in their work as opportunities to grow personally on the job. The twenty-first century worker will be also be aware that a longer commitment to an employer or within a single industry has experiential limits and therefore the employee will look for a workplace that can afford variety and multiple opportunities that result in personal growth and satisfaction on the job.

With further developments in participatory management and employee involvement, a greater democratization of the workplace can be assumed. We will see increased principles of worker representation by election, perhaps promotions by election or to represent workers, and the determining of worker pay increases made by peer team member recommendations.

Accompanying future workers' desire for a longer association with a single employer or industry, workers will expect more in terms of training and employee assistance from employers in this regard. While lifelong learning will become even more of a past-time of persons, the employer will be expected to provide regular and frequent on-the-job training to keep pace with changing technology integral to the success of organizations. Twenty-first century workers will expect training and development to expose them to new information and skills that they can apply directly to their work.

## SUMMARY

It is clear that the only constant is change. The escalating forces of change today often clash with the traditional approaches to management and leadership within organizational structures that are outmoded. Managers must implement new policies, new approaches and new organizational structures to manage and benefit from the process of change. The process of implementation will have to be carefully thought out. Instant solutions, gimmicks, and "quick fixes" will not work. Change will have to come about by using a managerial model that recognizes that organizations are functioning as systems that must work with both the internal and the external environment.

# REFERENCES

Guest, R. H. (1986) Management imperatives for the year 2000. *California Management Review*, Summer, 28.

Johnson, W. B. and Packer, A. H. (1987) *Workforce 2000*. Hudson Institute.

Kerr, C. and Roscow, J. M. (1979) *Work in America*. Litton Educational Publishing.

National Academy of Public Administration (NAPA) (1983) *Revitalizing Federal Management: Managers and Their Overburdened Systems*. DOT Contract No. 559-82C-00057.

Nightingale, G. J. (1990) Effective organizations. *Future's Research Quarterly*, Fall.

Timpe, A. D. (1986) *Motivation of Personnel*. KEND.

Toffler, A. (1990) *Powershift*. Bantam Books, New York.

US Office of Personnel Management (1990) *Personnel Research Highlights*. USOPM.

Weisbord, M. R. (1987) *Productive Workplaces*. Jossey-Bass, San Francisco, CA.

Yankelovich, D. (1981) *New Rules: Searching for Self-Fulfillment in a World Turned Upside Down*. Random.

# 11

# STRATEGY AND ORGANIZATIONAL DEVELOPMENT

**Ralph Lewis**

*Associate Director, Harbridge Consulting Group*

## INTRODUCTION

Organizational development is a term that has somewhat fallen out of favour with current thinking in management. There are several reasons for this. The first is that, as practised, OD came to be seen as synonymous with a certain orientation towards people and feelings that left little room for discussion of "hard" business concerns. In other words, some OD practitioners focused on the individual and their concerns and assumed that this would automatically lead to changes in the organization. Other reasons for the downplaying of OD were the recognition of the complexities of what real OD involved and the need for a complete integrated approach to the whole issue of organizational development in all its facets. This had to involve senior managers, those with the real power to change things in the organization, and of course this did not happen. Of course, because what was being asked of them was to give their power to the OD practitioners and adopt OD values which were not necessarily congruent with their own perceived patterns of looking at the world. Thus much OD overlooked the realities of power and politics. Finally, as already mentioned, the links with real business issues—summed up by business strategy—were usually missing.

So why look at strategy and its links with OD at this time? First, there are now some terms which over the last decade have come into managerial thinking that

International Review of Strategic Management.
Edited by D. E. Hussey. © 1992 John Wiley & Sons Ltd

act as a bridge between OD and strategy. The key concept is that of "culture". This we will return to later. Much of the pioneering work in terms of raising awareness was done by Peters and Waterman (1983). The impact of the Japanese managerial style and the debates and discussions about their business success in the light of their organizational cultures have also brought out much thought on strategy and links to culture (and hence to OD). The realities of political life in organizations have been recognized. Also and crucial to the discussion is the recognition of the importance of "vision" in terms of company success. Developing vision that is compatible with the organization and gaining employees' commitment to that vision is increasingly being seen as one of the key tasks of the senior management of any organization. Supplying vision, lest the people perish, is a key task underlying the role of the chief executive. In order to gain commitment to vision individual motivations of employees and their own meaning systems must be understood—hence the link back to culture and OD.

Basically, the recognition of most senior managers (and management thinkers) now is that strategy and the achievement of that strategy is bound up with the culture of an organization, individual perceptions of the strategy or vision and the behaviours that follow from this. This essential truth leads to a need to use the techniques of OD but within this far more comprehensive framework. It has been suggested that this combination of strategy linked to culture/organizational development is the whole essence of senior managers' roles.

What this chapter will do is describe a common framework that links strategy and organization development, the quadrant model of organization. The links between this and strategic thinking will be examined and then the interrelationship of strategy and organization development. For this last aspect, the organizational values, purposes and structures that form each of the four quadrants will be described in more detail. Finally, the process of strategy-setting leading to organization development will be described.

## THE QUADRANT MODEL OF ORGANIZATIONAL FUNCTIONS

Whenever any group of people get together for a common purpose we can talk of an organization. This is about the only definition of an organization that is universally accepted—that of people united for a common purpose. Hence the family is an organization, as are society, school systems, charitable foundations and, of course, commercial organizations. All these organizations, of whatever shape or size or form, industrial or social, have to carry out four functions if they are to achieve a common goal. These functions, in no priority order, are:

- Fitting in with others not in the organization, i.e. following society's conventions, laws, satisfying external stakeholders

- Managing the environment, getting resources, trading outputs
- Doing practical tasks to accomplish their goal
- Keeping those in the organization motivated and interacting effectively

The first and last functions can be classified as being concerned with "people", the middle two with the "task" aspects of the organization. Similarly, the first two functions can be thought of as looking at aspects "external" to the organization and the last two as looking at "internal" aspects. The four functions for the sake of simplicity can be shown diagramatically as in Figure 11.1.

Using this classification, the purpose, structure and effectiveness of different organizations can be examined. The first point to make is that all organizations need to ensure that all four quadrant functions are being carried out to certain minimum standards. If this is not done then the organization will collapse. For example, taking quadrant 1, that of external people, organizations of whatever kind if they do not adhere to the laws of their society will be stopped operating. This is as true of a commercial organization as it is for a social club. In the case of commercial organizations it is debatable whether shareholders can be classified as external or internal to the organization. However, for large commercial organizations, even though managers may mutter about them being run for the benefit of their shareholders, in practice shareholders are usually treated as outsiders who have to be mollified in order to let the managers continue to run the organization.

**Figure 11.1** Organizational functions

Hence the reaction of management teams to hostile takeovers, which, when looked at objectively, may in fact be beneficial to the shareholders but which the managers treat negatively because of their own needs. None the less, if shareholders are unhappy about the way they are being treated then they will sell, stocks will plummet and the organization may well go out of business or be merged.

The same logic applies to quadrant 2, the external environment, or, in commercial terms, the market. Not being able to get resources, financial or material or, increasingly, information, will lead to the organization not being able to function. This again is true for all organizations. The family cannot exist if there is no money or supplies coming in from the environment or if those in the family have no skills or services that others in the marketplace wish to purchase. In commercial organizations the equivalent would be manufacturing goods that no-one wishes to buy.

In quadrant 3, internal task, the function is that of doing key tasks efficiently. Again these have to be done to a minimum standard. Obviously production in an efficient way is the *raison d'etre* of many commercial organizations, but the same need for efficient production applies to all organizations. In the family, certain tasks like cooking and cleaning need to be done. If they are not, then the family will be split up by the state. Similarly, if Ford fails to be as efficient in its manufacture of mass-produced cars as the Japanese, then its prices will rise with negative consequences for its survival. The same reasoning applies, of course, to organizations in health care; they too need to be efficient and cost-effective, and here lie the seeds of the debate about emphasis on cost-saving being detrimental to the needs of the patient. This is an area to which we shall return.

Finally, the fourth quadrant is that of internal people, looking after employees' welfare, not necessarily in monetary terms alone, and organizing their interaction effectively through communication systems, status and power differentiation. Again there are minimum standards required in all organizations. If there is ineffective communication between employees the organization will not function effectively. If employees' needs are not being met they will go elsewhere and again the organization will collapse.

If we split management into functional specialisms and general management, by which is meant those with the role of directing the whole of the organization, it can be seen that the functional specialists will be oriented towards each quadrant. Production specialists fit into the internal task quadrant, marketing into the external task, personnel theoretically into the internal people quadrant and sales into the external people quadrant. Personnel is only put into the internal people quadrant theoretically because in practice many personnel managers tend to be task-oriented with the consequence that in commercial organizations there is no-one at management level representing the needs and priorities of the workforce. Finance as a function is slightly harder to define. It should, of course, be a tool of general management in running a business; more often than not, however, it is a historic measure of efficiency rather than a proactive business tool, and as such fits into the internal task quadrant.

General managers, by whom I mean those concerned with directing and developing the strategy of an organization, should be immune from bias towards any particular quadrant. They should sit squarely in the middle of the quadrants choosing between them as the situation dictates. In practice, of course, few mortals are capable of such even-handedness, hence the errors in directing organizations that creep in. A good general manager will be balancing the needs of the market with that of their capacity to produce goods or services, the needs of shareholders against those of the employees, changes in legal requirements and society's needs against efficiency, ecological requirements against costs in a competitive market, and the many other choices that have to be made. If this sounds familiar it should be, because by using the quadrant model of organizations as a basis the strategy-making process can be thrown into sharp relief.

# STRATEGIC THINKING AND THE QUADRANT MODEL

Strategic thinking is in essence very simple. It is the definition of the means by which the mission of an organization is to be achieved. Strategy formulation is the primary responsibility of the senior managers. It involves matching the values, skills and resources that people within the organization possess to the needs and expectations of people outside the organization. It involves being aware of all that may affect the organization both from external and internal sources and from technological advances and developments in people's thinking. Furthermore the multiple and sometimes conflicting objectives of all those involved have to be brought together. The factors analysed can be grouped very conveniently into the four quadrants outlined above.

|  | Quadrant 1 Sales/PR | Quadrant 2 Market | Quadrant 3 Production | Quadrant 4 People |
|---|---|---|---|---|
| Strengths | * | * | * | * |
| Weaknesses | * | * | * | * |
| Opportunities | * | * | * | * |
| Threats | * | * | * | * |
| Key success factors | Image Advertising Customer service | Market share Price Distribution Range | Productivity Product quality Facilities | Personnel Skills Loyalty Knowledge |

Figure 11.2  Using the quadrants in a SWOT analysis

Depending on the type of organization, each of these quadrants will have different importance. In business emphasis is usually on the task, more especially on the marketing quadrant. This can lead to confusion if the strategy just concentrates on this aspect and ignores all the other factors. All quadrants have to be taken into account in formulating strategy. The four quadrants provide a useful framework for strengths, weaknesses, opportunities and threats analysis (SWOT see Figure 11.2). In deciding which strategic option to pursue, managers need to look at their organization in the light of each quadrant's strengths and weaknesses and consider these factors before going for various options.


## THE LINKAGES BETWEEN STRATEGY AND ORGANIZATIONAL DEVELOPMENT

What is the purpose of a strategy? Basically it provides a means of:

- Setting the context of values and purpose of an organization
- Clarifying and defining specific organizational goals
- Providing guidelines for allocating resources in the most appropriate way to achieve the purpose and goals
- Guiding behaviours and activities as part of an integrative whole

What is the purpose of organizational development? It is to help an organization achieve its purpose through a process of discussion and clarification of purpose, of examining structures and processes and developing those that are most appropriate for the organization.

Wherein lies the difference between strategy and OD as it should be? There is basically no difference. As stated in the Introduction, OD had to a large extent been hijacked by those whose main concerns lay in quadrant 4, the internal people aspect of the quadrant model. In many ways this was inevitable. If there are no managers concerned with this quadrant then some mechanism has to arise which deals with employees' feelings and interests. Many managers lacking the interest or interpersonal skills simply could not cope with this area; hence they abdicated it to OD consultants. However, if OD is thought of in its true sense—a balanced development taking into account all the quadrants—then it has to be guided by those responsible for developing and directing strategy, and it is, in fact, synonymous with strategy. Both have to start with a profound sense of the purpose of the organization, its values and goals. Both then need to construct appropriate means of turning the "vision" into reality. We will look at how this process can be done using the quadrants.

## ORGANIZATIONAL VALUES, PURPOSES AND STRUCTURES

The underlying organizational values are a key determinant in any development of strategy—the key values, that is, of those with power in the organization. Of course, if these are incongruent with the mass of values of those in the rest of the organization, then any strategy developed by those in power will not be fully implemented. Hence the problems that senior management face in implementation—more often than not stemming from their inability to judge with accuracy the underlying values that shape the culture and behaviours of individuals in their organization. Let us take each of the quadrants in turn and examine the characteristics that make these up. The resultant descriptions will have parallels to Handy and Harrison's cultures of role, task, power and individualistic, but without the negative connotations (Harrison, 1987).

### Quadrant 1—Service Orientated, Clients as Individuals, Society's Concerns

The key values of those in an organization which fits predominantly into this category are service and caring for others in their own rights as individuals. There are usually moral or ethical concerns guiding these values. The prime purpose of organizations in Quadrant 1 is thus to serve their clients in the way that the clients themselves find most helpful that recognizes each client's individuality. Anything else is seen as a betrayal of moral positions. Subjective feelings are what count; therefore the key criterion for judging success in organizations of this type is the satisfaction of the client. The ideal structure for this type of organization is loose and flexible with the very minimum of authority. The reasons for this type of structure are twofold. First and foremost, it is only possible to respond to clients' individual needs if the respondees have room for using their individual initiative rather than having to follow guidelines laid down by others in authority. Secondly, of course, by the very nature of their value systems, individuals working in organizations of this type will tend to be anti-authority.

Examples of these types of organizations would be the health service, the educational system, churches, charitable organizations, universities, etc. They all exist to provide a service as their prime purpose. They do not exist primarily to expand their market share, to be very efficient in the way they carry out tasks or for the benefit of those in them, although, as discussed earlier, they have to do all these things to certain minimum standards. To return to health care as mentioned earlier, there is always a debate between those who see the need for more efficient means of operating services, presumably because they then see this as being of benefit to their clients, and on the other side those who see any emphasis on task efficiency as taking away concentration on the well-being of their patients. There is no easy way out of this dilemma; all we can do is return to the idea of the balanced general manager who, in setting strategy and priorities for their unit within the health service, will take both positions into account and deliver health care that ensures that patients feel better without neglecting the task or cost side, and vice versa.

It is difficult in industry to think of many examples where organizations exist with this orientation—perhaps PR agencies, where there may be a tendency to overservice clients and neglect costs. However, what is certain is that this type of organization is being demanded more and more by consumers and this is one of the main trends that Tom Peters is promoting to his audiences.

## Quadrant 2—Marketing Orientation, Control of Environment, Interaction

The values of those in organizations with the external task marketing orientation of those in quadrant 2 are to do with growth and expansion, competitiveness within the marketplace, both for raw materials and resources and for customers and buyers of their products or services. Unlike those in quadrant 1, people here do not see the customer as an individual, rather as a consumer of whatever the organization can sell to them. The prime purpose of the organization is to manage its environment—external people, finance, competitors, government all counting as different factors to be taken into account in the ways of doing this, but people as no more important than any of the other factors. Hence the propensity of those with this orientation to develop elaborate means of classifying the market, socioeconomic groups, etc. The key criteria for judging success is how well the external environment is being controlled by the organization. The need for growth and expansion makes sense in this context because the more market share, for example, the more control the organization has over the environment. Products or services are usually seen as a means to the end of attaining this goal rather than intrinsically of quality in themselves.

The ideal type of structure for this organization is one that can react to the marketplace and deliver products/goods according to the generally identified trends that the particular market or environment has. Usually matrix organizational structures are found. The matrix has several benefits in helping the organization attain its prime purpose of control—it provides a good means of collecting data from a variety of sources, usually geographical and product-differentiated, and collating the information in clearly defined ways. There is flexibility, but within these a defined *modus operandi* which allows the organization to plan and coordinate its strategy most effectively. Strategies of these organizations are usually couched in terms of growth, of market share, of being better and bigger, for the reasons already stated.

Examples of organizations such as these are Xerox, Unilever, General Electric now that Jack Welch has redefined its aims, and many other marketing organizations. A key indicator of their orientation is to look at their business decisions; if these seem mainly to do with growth for the sake of growth, rather than for clearly defined business reasons, then the organization is probably operating within a quadrant 2 framework. Examples of such decisions abound, with usually very negative consequences for those shareholders and employees of the original organization, the advertising industry and the merger of so many accounting firms for example.

Again the suggestion is not that growth in itself is right or wrong—simply that the well-tempered strategist recognizes this arena as one, just one, of the very many vital components that go towards a complete strategy. When this does not happen, the business plan ends up looking like a marketing plan and nothing else.

There are many other examples of non-commercial organizations which fit into this quadrant. The armed services of whatever country have, as their prime purpose, the duty to control their country's external environment and make it safe. This then turns quite readily sometimes into a policy of expansion. It may be argued that the army, for example, has a very hierarchical organization, but this is true only of the actual fighting elements. When staff advisors are brought in, intelligence-gathering arms, and the whole interrelationship of the different functions of the modern army is looked at, it becomes extremely complex and in fact very similar to a matrix organization.

## Quadrant 3—Production, Quality, Efficiency

The values that people have in organizations with this orientation will be concerned with efficiency and quality of products in themselves. People with these values concentrate on and enjoy producing things that are well-made, according to their own internal standards. In other words, a better mousetrap will be made because ultimately the organization wants to make better mousetraps, regardless of whether there is the market or individual customers to buy them. The prime purpose of organizations with this orientation is therefore efficient and better production. Success is judged on how well this is done. Within this there will usually be a dilemma between cost and quality considerations but these are usually seen within the context of internal clashes of values without reference to the external world.

The most appropriate type of structure for this organization will be a clearly defined hierarchy. The reasons for this are that only with this clarity can people know exactly what needs to be done, continue doing it more and more efficiently, become more skilled at it, and be able to understand how the components of the organization fit together in the most efficient manner. To have matrix organization such as those organizations in quadrant 2 would lead to duplication of effort, which is unthinkable, and much confusion as there would be no one boss. The total flexible organization of quadrant 1 would be even further removed from this ideal. So control and definition are essential for efficient production. Typically this applies to most manufacturing organizations, but it also applies to some retailers whose aim is to standardize every store regardless of location or local customer wishes.

The usual strategy for these organizations is to be product-led rather than customer- or market-driven. As stated earlier, the product orientation can be quality-driven or that of cost and price. If it is the latter, then strategies will concentrate on economies of scale; if the former, then value-added premium features. In both cases, however, as already mentioned, strategy is seen in terms of the product.

## Quadrant 4—Organizational Members, Caring and Respect

The main values of people with this orientation are to do with the relationships between those in the organization. The organization is run for the benefit of those in it and it is their concerns that are paramount. Fairness and concern for each other are overriding concerns within a clear social set of behaviour codes. Conflict will be frowned upon, as harmony is the key measure of success. Outsiders may be dangerous, especially if they hold different sets of values which might threaten the well-being and consensus of the group. Work is seen as a shared experience.

The types of structures that are most suited for these organizations are ones where there are maximum opportunities for social interaction and communication. They are not necessarily democratic; often, in fact, status is seen as very important. What is also essential is that everyone understands and follows the social conventions, so the structure must emphasize this. There are certain elements of this in Japanese organizations, with loyalty to the firm, i.e. other members, being absolutely key and above all this loyalty to the Japanese nation. The organization then provides identity and meaning for those in it and often becomes the focus of their whole life. Decision-making is a function of discussion and emerges from the group (Waterman, 1987).

The type of strategies adopted by these organizations is based on the needs of its members and satisfying these. Usually once this is done the organization can count upon the total commitment of its members. Those competing organizations will be seen as the enemy; whatever is done is done to defeat them as in a war.

## THE PROCESS OF STRATEGY AND ORGANIZATION DEVELOPMENT

The starting point of any strategy is to identify clearly the prime purpose of the organization and how it is to achieve this purpose taking into account all necessary external and internal factors. From the previous section it can be seen that a convenient classification for purposes is the quadrant model. Hence the purpose could be:

- To provide individual service to stakeholders (of whatever kind)
- To deal effectively with the environment (market, financial, physical, etc)
- To produce goods efficiently in terms of either cost or quality
- To provide rewards to those in the organization (in whatever form they desire)

It has already been shown that once the prime purpose is established there will then need to be certain minimum standards of performance laid down in the other quadrants if the organization is to survive. But these are secondary to the one main purpose. Often profit-making organizations lose sight of this and start to define themselves in financial terms. This ignores the fact that profit or return on capital are measures of efficiency but not ends in themselves. Many managers, for example, talk about the main objective of a commercial organization as being that of maximizing returns to the shareholders. They then by their actions negate this, by fighting hostile takeovers because they themselves may lose power instead of considering the best interests of their shareholders.

Having established the purpose then the next stage is to develop the most appropriate strategy for achieving this purpose. This must take into account a number of factors discussed earlier but essentially can also be related to the quadrants, i.e. if the organization has as its prime purpose that of producing goods efficiently, then its strategy must as a necessity involve cost-reduction methods and focus on internal methods of production. This does not mean that the organization will focus on this to the exclusion of the marketplace or employees, rather simply that this is its starting place. The different types of strategy are shown in Figure 11.3.

The tactics for achieving these strategies can again be classified by the quadrants given earlier. Tactics could include price changes, sales mix changes, product pruning, investment in more efficient production systems, training of more skilled staff, promotion and change in the image of the organization, lobbying for change in taxation, acquisitions, and whatever else seems appropriate.

The structure of the organization then follows naturally on from the purpose and strategy, as it should do. Here is where the process of organization development takes over in ensuring that the structure and processes that are happening within the organization are in line with the purpose and strategy already decided. The tools of those involved in this next step need to be both analytical and people-focused. The analytical techniques involve working with strategic concepts and designing the structure of the organization to fit the strategy as discussed above within the framework of the quadrants. The people side involves communication and building commitment. The last aspect is not easy as there will be political issues and different points of view to reconcile.

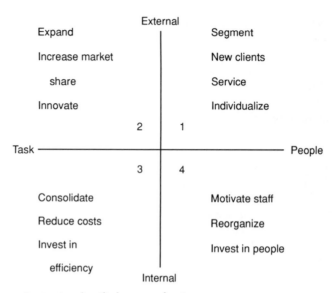

**Figure 11.3**   Strategies classified per quadrant

One of the key ways in which people can be brought on board in terms of commitment is through training and development. This is also essential in developing the necessary competences in individuals in order to meet the strategic purposes. This is absolutely vital as a tool in the armoury of the organization development process. Unfortunately, although the situation has much improved, a great deal of training is still based on the needs of the individual without reference to the strategic purpose (Hussey, 1990). This is not the case with Japanese management for example (Ellison, 1990), where strategy implementation is very much seen as resulting from the involvement and commitment of all employees. This is where the more traditional techniques of organization development can come into their own, i.e. participation and team-building.

However, if it is remembered that different organizations have different value systems as discussed earlier and classified according to the quadrant model, then it can be seen that there are some strategies which will be doomed to failure without drastic blood-letting and organizational change. The reasons for this are simple. People adopt the values of the organizations that they are in or are attracted to those organizations which already have values compatible with theirs. Attempts to implement strategies which require a shift from these values will meet with enormous resistance. Individuals' value orientations can be typed in the same way as that of organizations (Kilmann, Lyles and Mitroff, 1977). Sometimes it may be easier to replace key people in order to implement a new strategy than attempt to retrain them or change their values.

Examples where failure to recognize the essential nature of the organization and its values and those of the individuals in it has led to failure of implementation of desired strategy are numerous. One of the main issues of chief executives in the 1990s is their failure to implement change as they wish it to occur. But this has always been the case. It is just that now the problem is thrown into sharp relief because of the more turbulent requirements of the environment, which keep demanding radical new strategies. Rolls-Royce, for example, had been very much oriented to excellence of product and high quality—a trait that is admirable but which led to its downfall because it lost sight of the need to deliver these products to a market in cost-effective ways. Rolls-Royce changed, but only after the trauma of bankruptcy. Similarly, many new privatized companies have to change their business strategies to compete commercially. This involves having to change the whole structure of their organization and, even more importantly, the values of their employees. Usually this shift of values involves moving from a bureaucratic internal orientation of quadrants 4 (and possibly 3) to a more externally focused set of values, i.e. quadrants 1 and 2, marketing and customer-focused. Here is where organization development in its fullest sense can build and help implementation of strategy by understanding all the types of values as defined by the quadrants and developing appropriate structures and training in line with the strategy.

# CONCLUSIONS

In this chapter the conclusion has been reached that strategy and organization development are in essence concerned with the same thing: namely, helping the organization to achieve its purpose. However, organization development has become identified with a certain orientation towards people and as a consequence lost that link to organizational purpose.

By using the classification of organizations into four quadrants, each representing a particular function that all organizations have to carry out, it was shown that organizational values, purposes and structures formed a natural link. These characteristics were discussed. It was suggested that the task of the general manager or strategist was to allocate resources and priorities between these four quadrants. Organization development in its truest sense is about orienting the organization to deliver in terms of this strategy. However, in the cases of fundamental shifts of purpose or of strategy, the task of orienting individuals, i.e. changing their value systems, may prove too difficult and necessitate replacement or traumatic change.

Fundamentally, however, values, purposes, strategy and organization development should flow from one another in any organization if that organization is to be fully effective. The task of making this happen involves all, whether strategist or trainer or OD practitioner.

# REFERENCES

Ellison, F. (1990) Meeting the challenges of the 1990's. *MBA Review*, December, 33–39.

Harrison, R. (1987) *Organisation Culture and Quality of Service: A Strategy for Releasing Love in the Workplace*. Association of Management Education and Development.

Hussey, D. E. (1990) Developments in strategic management. In *International Review of Strategic Management*, Ed. D. E. Hussey. Wiley, Chichester, pp. 3–25.

Kilmann, R. H., Lyles, M. A. and Mitroff, I. I. (1977) Designing an effective problem-solving organisation with the MAPS design technology. *Journal of Management* 2 (2). 1–10.

Peters, T. J. and Waterman, R. (1983) *In Search of Excellence*. Harper & Row, New York.

Waterman, R. H. (1987) *The Renewal Factor*. Bantam, New York.

# 12

# A CASE HISTORY: SETTING UP A JOINT VENTURE IN HUNGARY

## Kay M. Fischer* and Imre Somody†

*Marketing Manager, †Managing Director, Pharmavit, Budapest

## INTRODUCTION

This chapter provides a case history of the setting up of an enterprise through direct investment in a Hungarian business. A closer examination of the rationale for engagement in Hungary and an attempt to form a comprehensive list of the alternative possibilities of operating an enterprise there fall beyond the scope of this work. It is merely a contribution to the discussion about direct investments from a practical point of view, based on actual experience.

The starting point of this reflection is Pharmavit Limited, an enterprise in the pharmaceutical and food industry, formed as a Swiss–Hungarian joint venture in 1988. The new production plants near Budapest were put into service in August 1989. Since that time, Pharmavit has been active in the Hungarian market with an increasing number of products. The scope of activity of Pharmavit includes the production and marketing of pharmaceutical products and food. The analysis given below may not be of general validity, especially as far as specific problems such as market situation or taxation are concerned. Investors in other industrial sectors may come up against very different environmental conditions.

The discussion of sector-specific details is therefore reduced to a minimum, while experiences that in the author's view can be generalized are discussed in detail.

International Review of Strategic Management.
Edited by D. E. Hussey. © 1992 John Wiley & Sons Ltd

A discussion of how we came to a decision on investing in Hungary is excluded here. It was an individual strategic decision, clearly understandable only in the light of the long-term dispositions of all the enterprises concerned and thus falling beyond the scope of this report. The basis of the actual discussion about the investment was a go–no-go analysis within the framework of a feasibility study. This study was the result of a three-month effort by a team of Hungarian and foreign economists in Hungary.

## ISSUING FEASIBILITY STUDIES THAT WORK

The requirements of the feasibility study were defined in accordance with the political and economic conditions prevailing in Hungary:

- The study had to use and analyze political and economic facts and developments. This task could only be carried out with the cooperation of those working *in situ*. The required results could never have been achieved from desk research of the relevant literature and available publications because of the lack of realism and superficiality that this approach would involve.
- The special conditions of the Hungarian market and the specific usage in Hungary had to be taken into consideration and their effects on the investment examined.
- Macroeconomic estimates such as the inflation situation, rate of exchange, capital market and competition had to be subjected to a sensitivity analysis. Here the control variable was the return on investment (ROI), the payback of which was not to exceed four years as a maximum in any realistically assumed environmental situation. The results so obtained were repeatedly reworked and corrected by the planning team.
- The study had to determine the phasing of the investment, based on network analysis where the different phases of the project such as (1) construction, (2) commissioning and registration of the products and (3) market entry were included in an integrated program so that bottlenecks became visible.

### Avoiding Time Lags

Execution of the investment according to schedule was a primary condition of the overall concept and, in particular, of returns on capital investment. In the team's view, a timely and smooth installation of industrial plant is an important factor in controlling the risks of an investment. Time lags in the construction phase would certainly have affected the returns of the enterprise unfavourably, since the opportunity to find new markets seemed to reduce with time. Since the

Pharmavit products were unknown in Hungary, the relatively small enterprise (with a registered capital of DM 1.2 million) had a fair chance of achieving a leading position in the market provided it was not preempted by others. Such an investment to achieve a competitive advantage had to avoid being put at risk by time delays. In this way, we acquired pioneer advantages in our field, building a significant entry barrier against even the biggest newcomers.

The bottleneck phases of construction detected by the network analysis (e.g. fitting large plants into buildings, registration of the products) could be overcome by means of checklists. In this way, it was possible to provide an appropriate margin for the management of unforeseen bottlenecks like, for example, unexpected shortages in building materials, coordination problems with foreign suppliers and problems relating to the development of the infrastructure.

Time limit monitoring became possible in this way which, in combination with a premium bonus system for the construction managers, resulted in a reduction of the actual construction time to eight months.

## Self-Fulfilling Prophecies

As shown by the above example, optimum planning and control can be a decisive factor in an investment project under the uncertain and unstable environmental conditions prevailing in Hungary. Division of the process into small projects and supervision to enforce total compliance with the time limits stimulated the contractors to demonstrate their capabilities and efficiency.

From the start, we made an attempt both to anticipate future environmental situations and to show the limits of what was possible, enabling us to envisage what was feasible.

In this sense, our plans have been self-fulfilling prophecies in that the vision of what was feasible was a challenge and a stimulus to maximum effort from all involved.

The experience and attitudes of pioneer enterprises may influence the economic restructuring process. When established, profit-oriented enterprises meet with many issues regarding rules and regulations. A leader investor is in a position to influence relevant legislation affecting its future environment.

## Information Management

A special demand is imposed upon the information management of an investment under the unstable environmental conditions in Hungary.

### Acquisition of relevant data from available sources of testing for reliability

The problem arises from the fundamental differences between centrally controlled and market economies. There is certainly not a torrent of information in

Hungary. The required information is usually available only from a state office, often from a Ministry, and frequently inaccessible to outsiders. However, the situation has been changing recently and more information is now available to foreign investors at a low cost from an increasing number of state agencies.

However, data obtained from state offices in the country should always be subjected to critical analysis. A precondition for this is knowledge of the calculation methods used. These methods differ considerably from those used in Western Europe although this difference has recently been reducing. A figure such as return on sales says little about the situation of a Hungarian enterprise unless we know the method used to calculate it.

### Evaluation and analysis of data obtained

To be taken into consideration here are, above all, (1) reliability of the figures, (2) reality of the material and (3) trends in what may be rapid changes. This applies especially to the existing rules and legal regulations that may soon become invalid under the pressures of economic restructuring in Hungary.

### Adding the investor's own investigations and more detailed analyses

To be taken into consideration here is the cost-benefit situation in the industry concerned. It is important to know the stage deregulation has reached in the industry, or whether progress is expected. It is usually industrial sectors of relatively high home profitability potential where there is the possibility of intentional delay in deregulation, as a strategic weapon against increasing competition. The case of some West European airlines is an example of such strategic retardation. A competitor subsidized by the state has a number of unfair options, such as using subsidized price wars, to considerably reduce the profitability of an investment by a competitor.

## The Decision To Go

In spite of thorough and detailed analyses, a decision for investment in Hungary involves a considerable risk, firstly because of the uncertainty of much of the data, that cannot be improved by good information management. The reducing marginal benefit of additional information acquisition must be kept in view. After a certain point, little growth in knowledge can be expected from additional data. Thus a significant reduction of the risk of the investment cannot be expected either.

However, well-established sensitivity analysis methods permitted many possible environmental situations to be included in the investment calculations. This anticipation of environmental situations helped us to make the risks of an investment in Hungary more appraisable, and the extent of potential imponderables more predictable.

According to the results of our analysis, the risk of our investment in Hungary was predictable and acceptable.

The decisive question was the availability of competent management that would be able to overcome the probable problems so that the investment would not be put at risk.

# SETTING UP THE VENTURE

## Some Characteristics of Green-Field Investments in Hungary

As has been implied earlier, we decided not to use an existing Hungarian plant or building for Pharmavit Ltd. Instead, a completely new plant has been constructed. Our decision was based on the philosophy that the operation of a new plant with new equipment, organization and products would be simpler than to try to modify existing structures. In this way, we provided a greater freedom for the management of the new enterprise in development of the overall policy for the enterprise, especially decisions in the fields of personnel, product and financial policy, where the management could enjoy absolute independence and freedom. However, we had to face at the same time some additional risk.

### Risk in relation to sites

The infrastructure of the site available was inadequate, considering the magnitude of the industrial plant planned. The costs of bringing the infrastructure to the requirements of production increased the investment considerably.

### Risk in relation to labour market

There was no efficient labour available in the vicinity of the site, which was located at a distance of 25 km from Budapest. The place is difficult to reach by public transport facilities. Therefore, transport of production staff had to be organized for two shifts a day.

## Financial Aspects

An important point in planning for the investment was determining the financial needs of the project as accurately as possible. In doing so, we investigated the financing possibilities in the Hungarian capital market, taking into consideration a reasonable debt acceptable with respect to the risk involved.

### A capital structure to start with

In Hungary, the interests on a risk capital were around 25% per annum in 1988. On the basis of the expected profit on the invested capital and the required ROI over a maximum of four years, we decided to undertake a debt at a rate of 1 to 2 (shareholders to external capital). Thus, on the expected profit of 35% on total invested capital, we expected a positive leverage. The promising expected results and a favourable operating leverage offset high financial risk. (The ratio of fixed to variable costs is 1 to 1.8.)

The shareholders agreed that the overall vulnerability of the investment was controllable.

### Raising domestic funds

Due to the significant capital demands of the investment, the long-term credits offered by Hungarian commercial banks were insufficient to finance the project. The premium for risk required by the banks would have increased the financing costs unfavourably. As a result, the payments of interest and repayment of credits would have imposed a heavy burden on the investment in the critical initial phase.

Therefore, sources more favourable than the long-term credits of Hungarian banks have been used to meet the long-term capital demand of the investment.

*The bond market*. We decided that the best option was a loan of Ft 70 million from the industrial loans market. Cash flows for a zero-coupon loan of an expiration of four years were best suited for the purposes of our green-field investment. No interest payment or repayment of the loan is required in the four-year period before expiration.

The effective interest on the loan amounts to 17% annually. In view of the inflation rate of about 30% per year prevailing in Hungary, the effective value of the interest on the loan lies, however, well below an annual 17% and thus the loan is certainly superior to the long-term bank credit.

*The stock exchange*. Opening of the stock market in Budapest had been planned for the year 1988 but did not take place at that time. Thus no shares could be issued at the time the enterprise was set up. However, shares are planned to be launched through the stock market to increase the capital in the future and to significantly contribute to the formation of domestic capital.

This attractive method of financing has therefore been one of the motives for deciding on a share company as the legal form of the enterprise. While the procedure of setting up a share company is more complicated as compared with a limited liability company, the possibilities of future financing are more favourable in the first case.

*Raising foreign funds*

The necessity of financing in hard currency is a result of the Hungarian exchange control that has not changed yet.

The necessary imported machines are registered as a deposit of movable property within the capital of the joint venture. Options for hard currency financing are:

(1)   Borrowing hard currency as a credit by the parent house
(2)   Borrowing hard currency as a credit by the Hungarian subsidiary
(3)   Cross-border leasing transactions by the Hungarian subsidiary

Within the framework of the Pharmavit project the latter two possibilities were discussed with particular intensity. They will be discussed here in detail although it is only hard currency borrowing by Hungary that has been implemented in the Pharmavit project.

*Foreign loans.* Typically, the construction of credit taken in hard currency by Pharmavit has been for assets to purchase investment goods rather than of export financing.

However, on the basis of the feasibility study, it was not difficult for Pharmavit to find a Swiss bank ready to advance Swiss francs at a favourable interest rate.

Credits of this type are available particularly from Swiss and Austrian banks because there is a wide secondary market for East European needs in Vienna and Zurich.

*Cross-border leasing.* Cross-border leasing was offered by an international commercial bank operated in Hungary. The principle was similar to that of well-known western leasing contracts. A difference lay, however, in that authorization by three different organizations, (1) the Ministry of Trade, (2) the Ministry of Finance and (3) the Hungarian National Bank, was required for the transaction in Hungary. The authorization process is subject to presentation of a feasibility study to show that the project is specifically designed to substitute for imports and to result in export sales in the future.

The feasibility study had to prove that the value of the imported goods could be trebled in hard currency as a result of the investment. However, the investment in question was expected in the first instance to supply the domestic market with new products.

Because of these restrictions and the considerably higher costs, a leasing contract was not concluded.

# Developing the Infrastructure

Another important step towards implementation of the investment was to develop the infrastructure of the site in accordance with the needs of the project. The infrastructural development included:

- fresh water and process water pipes of an appropriate size. Because there was a relatively efficient water supply system on the site, we were spared the expenses of well-boring.
- According to the Hungarian waste water regulations, waste water tanks had to be provided for the plant, and waste water disposal had to be organized.
- The local electrical network was insufficient for the production demands. Electricity supply for the plant was possible only by means of the plant's own transformer substation.
- No telephone lines for trunk dialling service were available on the site. Therefore, two international telephone lines had to be installed, brought out of the neighbouring town.

As a result of close and smooth cooperation with the local authorities and other regional organizations, the infrastructural developments were completed within the specified time.

Our attitude, based on awareness of our responsibilities together with an appropriate information policy, helped us to convince those involved of the advantages promised by an industry like the project for the region. This acceptance facilitated our work considerably.

## Recruiting the Staff

The success of Pharmavit when entering the domestic labour market as a potential employer is very important in respect of the future shape of the industrial personnel policy. Only an efficient personnel policy can be expected to attract labour that had to meet our requirements in respect of integrative behaviour, degree of knowledge and ability to learn.

The first thing foreign investors have to do is to become acquainted with, and take into consideration, the education system in Hungary, as it differs considerably from the system of the western countries, although this difference seems to be reducing. This applies to education for both skilled workers and business people, including managers. Therefore, western personnel demand estimates and the production quality strategies of foreign enterprises based on them are often incompatible with the labour supply.

Another problem is that neither the technologies nor the management techniques to be adopted had been used previously in Hungary. Therefore, the central question of personnel policy was not whether the available labour met the demands of the enterprise completely, but rather whether and how far the necessary staff could be trained at the lowest costs possible. An efficient training concept is therefore an integral part of our industrial personnel policy in Hungary.

Appropriate motivations are required to encourage the Hungarian staff to work and learn. An important factor in this respect can be, in addition to material and other labour incentives, a specific "enterprise philosophy". The identification of Hungarian employees with the personal contribution they are making to the quality and efficiency of the enterprise can be an important motivator.

## Corporate Identity from the Very Beginning

While the "enterprise philosophy" has an internal effect, the corporate identity affects the exterior. One of the first steps taken by Pharmavit was the development of a complete corporate identity concept. A comprehensive corporate identity was worked out with the help of the Budapest office of an international advertising agency. This contributed significantly to a recognition of the enterprise as early as the setting up and construction phase, and allowed of a purposeful information policy long before market entry.

# GENERATING CASH FLOWS

The description of the operating activities of the enterprise in the Hungarian market is restricted here to some selected aspects from the domain of marketing and finance, and which are typical of business in Hungary.

## Innovative Marketing in a Socialist Country

In our opinion, the time of the classic supply market is over in Hungary, at least in the pharmaceutical and food industry, for two reasons.

(1)     Consumers are becoming more and more exacting as the supply of international products increases due to increasing import liberalization.
(2)     In recent years, the domestic industry has successfully and significantly improved the quality of its products and pursues an increasingly demand-oriented policy, with growing success.

    In our opinion, innovative marketing and communication must include a marketing policy and public relations strategies designed specifically for Hungarian consumers. Efficient sales strategies and functioning distribution concepts, including merchandising and rack-jobbing, should be a component of future marketing concepts.

### Renaissance of the travelling salesman

Wholesale practices in Hungary typically result in recurrent shortages in supply, usually followed by excess supply, a significant disadvantage since customers develop an aversion to products advertised but never found in the shop. This experience over years and decades has made customers dislike so-called "phantom goods".

The employment of travelling salesmen has therefore been introduced. The salesman is an agent and at the same time the supplier of retail traders, whose supply by the state wholesale trade is far from perfect. Also, the salesman is a collector of important information.

### Advertising that sells

The Hungarian health market, with consumers taking an interest in health problems, had not developed to any extent, so Pharmavit vitamin products entered virgin land.

Hence, our advertising job was not only to give information about our products but also to make vitamins and health in general part of a modern-living program. Customers in general remembered and welcomed the emotional tone of our testimonial campaigns.

### Uptrading strategies

A moderate uptrading strategy proved successful in our case. Products promising the customers prestige due to their western appearance sell at especially favourable prices. However, beyond a certain limit, no gain in prestige can make the Hungarian customer interested in an expensive, and therefore inaccessible, product.

### "Hard selling"

Important in respect of having a distribution covering the market are first of all the state-owned wholesale organizations because they have stores and transport facilities. However, the operating methods of these organizations are often not adjusted to market demand and they are rather inflexible in placing orders. As a result, the flow of goods between manufacturer and retail trader is far from being optimum and shortages in supply occur again and again, causing considerable loss of sales.

Important elements of a sales organization in Hungary are reliable customer care in combination with an efficient incentive strategy to cope with the problems mentioned above.

## Financing Day-to-Day Operations

The following considerations are relevant to day-to-day financial management in Hungary and differ from what is usually experienced in other countries.

- The rate of inflation in the country lies at about 30%, with an upward tendency, endangering the rate of economic growth.
- Bottlenecks occur in liquidity.
- Only limited risk capital is available.
- The financial practice of banks has been adjusted to the requirements of the new economic system. Credit terms have become hard, compliance with the terms is continuously checked, and non-compliance is severely penalized.

Discussed in detail below are three important short-term financing instruments that have been used by the financial management in the present case.

### Advantages of commercial bills

Commercial bills are used in western trade mostly in emergencies, usually by enterprises that have got into financial trouble. In Hungary, the use of bills is common and at the same time a reasonable instrument considering the slow rate of bank-to-bank payments. Commercial bills guaranteed by the Hungarian National Bank provide an efficient means of protecting against delayed debt, especially in the case of an overall liquidity bottleneck.

### Stretching payables

Supplier's credit against price allowance is not used in Hungary at present. A legal payment target of eight bank days and a prompt collection system leave little freedom for speculation if there is a bottleneck in financing in the growth phase of an enterprise. However, for the sake of good business relations in the future, agreement with suppliers on individual terms of payment is possible in most cases.

On the other hand, this system makes us feel happier about the status of our own outstanding debt. Cash flows can be calculated and planned by this method.

### Raising loans from the founders

There are possibilities of raising short-term loans from the shareholders, especially in the case of corporations where credits to provide working assets are unavailable or available only on unfavourable terms, from banks.

In most cases, the required assets can be easily obtained in this way provided the enterprise is big enough and the shareholders are personally interested in the success of their venture.

# TOWARDS A GROWTH-ORIENTED STRATEGY

Within six months after a successful market entry, the enterprise had moved into profit. Also the planned investment payback of three years seems to be achievable considering our rapidly increasing share and stable position in the market.

An important requirement of the shareholders will be met in this way, namely the reduction of the risk of the investment to not more than four years. Within this period, full amortization of the original investment and a return of the risk capital are expected.

What has been said so far leads to questions of whether, and what, growth strategy resulted in such a successful investment and how could future growth objectives be financed.

## Financing Further Investment

In Hungary, some favourable sources of financing are available for a profitable enterprise with prospects for significant future profits. One of these sources is financing from World Bank credits, especially for investments to increase production in fields which are in the interests of the national economy. In this case, long-term credits can be raised on favourable conditions on the basis of a well-prepared feasibility study.

Issue of shares in the Budapest stock market is mentioned here again, and should not be left out of consideration for future investments in Hungary.

## Dividend Policies Applicable

However, internal financing may also be more or less important depending on the vulnerability of the enterprise and the attitude of the owners.

In the case of an explicit growth strategy, retention of all the profit with a view to financing further investments is worthy of consideration, all the more because a reduced tax is payable on retained profit in Hungary, 36% as compared with 56% on profit used for dividend payments.

However, it is questionable whether the shareholders, especially the Hungarians, would give their agreement to a zero-dividend policy. Although there are good examples of the success of such a strategy, for example DEC and other Silicon Valley enterprises, in our experience it is difficult to arrive at a consensus with the shareholders to carry through such a growth strategy. The value of a share seems to compete with the annual dividend as a basis for decision.

## New Challenges from Growing Market Opportunities

To sum up, the changes in the political and economic environment in Hungary have not come to an end yet. The continuous changes in the course of restructuring require that investors be flexible and economically highly competent. However, the chances of affecting the future environmental conditions of a business are promising, especially on a sectoral scale. What is required can usually be realized. Pioneers in new markets are therefore in the position to create the conditions for their business and competition.

Thus barriers can be erected against newcomers by the pioneers in a new market. This situation is an opportunity for enterprises that are not leaders in the international market. They have still the chance in Hungary and in the other East European countries.

# NOTE

This chapter was originally presented as a paper at a Conference "Strategies for Business Ventures in Central and Eastern Europe: Building Strategic Alliances", Budapest, 12–15 November, 1990. It is included because it provides a detailed case history of the topical issue of a western company establishing a business in Central Europe.

# MAILING ADDRESSES OF CONTRIBUTORS

**Prof. C. D. Combs**  *Medical College of Hampton Roads, Virginia, USA*

**Ms. L. Cornelius**  *Old Dominion University, Graduate School of Business and Public Administration, Norfolk, Virginia 23529–0218, USA*

**Prof. D. G. Dologite**  *City University of New York, Bernard M. Baruch College, New York, USA*

**Ms. K. Donoghue**  *Old Dominion University, Graduate School of Business and Public Administration, Norfolk, Virginia 23529–0218, USA*

**Prof. Kasra Ferdows**  *INSEAD, Boulevard de Constance, F-77305 Fontainebleau, France*

**Dr K. M. Fischer**  *Pharmavit, Budapest, Hungary*

**Mr D. E. Hussey**  *Harbridge Consulting Group Ltd, 3 Hanover Square, London W1R 9RD, UK*

**Mr R. Lewis**  *Harbridge Consulting Group Ltd, 3 Hanover Square, London W1R 9RD, UK*

**Dr J. McGee**  *Templeton College, Kennington, Oxford OX1 5NY, UK*

**Prof. P. McNamee**  *University of Ulster, Shore Road, Newtownabbey, Co Antrim, Northern Ireland BT37 0QB*

**Prof. R. J. Mockler**  *St John's University Graduate School of Business, New York, USA*

**Prof. Gen-Ichi Nakamura**  *SMI 21, 1–27–7 Nako-cho, Meguro-ku, Tokyo 153, Japan*

**Dr W. Pindur**  *Old Dominion University, Graduate School of Business and Public Administration, Norfolk, Virginia 23529–0218, USA*

**Dr I. Somody**  *Pharmavit Ltd, Budapest, Hungary*

**Ms R. Stanat**  *Strategic Intelligence Systems, 404 Park Avenue S, New York, NY 10016, USA*

**Mr. K.-E. Sveiby**  *Ledarskap, Box 70497, S-107 Stockholm, Sweden*

**Prof. Atsuhiko Takeuchi**  *Nippon Institute of Technology, Miyashiro-Machi, Saitama-ken 345, Japan*

**Prof. H. Thomas**  *Dept of Business Administration, University of Illinois at Urbana, 350 Commerce Building West, 1206 South Sixth St, Champaign, IL 61820, USA*

# INDEX

*Index compiled by Geoffrey C. Jones*

# CUMULATIVE CONTENTS LISTS TO THE SERIES*

## CUMULATIVE CONTENTS BY TOPIC

*Numbering scheme indicates **volume** (number): page range, for example **2**(1): 3–69 is Volume 2, Number 1, pages 3 to 69 (i.e. Chapter 1).

# Process

# Methods and Techniques

# CUMULATIVE CONTENTS BY CONTRIBUTOR

# SUBSCRIPTION NOTICE

**T**his Wiley product is updated annually to reflect important developments in the subject field.

If you purchased this copy directly from John Wiley & Sons, we will have already recorded your subscription and will inform you of new volumes.

If, however, you purchased this product from a bookseller and wish to be notified of future volumes, please fill in your details and return to Wiley (address printed overleaf).

*NAME:* _____

*ADDRESS:* _____

_____

_____

*COUNTRY:* _____

*TELEPHONE:* _____

*Bookseller where purchased*

_____

 **WILEY**

*Publishers Since 1807*

**By air mail**
*Par avion*

IBRS/CCRI NUMBER:
PHQ–D/1204/PO

NE PAS AFFRANCHIR

NO STAMP REQUIRED

# REPONSE PAYEE
# GRANDE-BRETAGNE

Sarah Stevens (MARKETING)
John Wiley & Sons Ltd.
Baffins Lane
CHICHESTER
West Sussex
GREAT BRITAIN
PO19 1YN